MW01137176

EXCLUSIVELY
ROSEVILLE

PRICE AND INVENTORY
GUIDE FOR THE
COLLECTOR/DEALER

by
JOHN, MALINDA AND NANCY BOMM

© 2004

Published by
L-W BOOK SALES
PO Box 69
Gas City, IN 46933

ISBN# 0-89538-117-6

Published by: L-W Book Sales
              PO Box 69
              Gas City, IN 46933

Please write for our free catalog.

Printed by IMAGE GRAPHICS, INC., Paducah, Kentucky USA

TABLE OF CONTENTS

TABLE OF CONTENTS CONTINUED

ABOUT THE BOMM FAMILY

John, Malinda and Nancy Bomm have continued in their quest to assist both dealers and collectors in their knowledge of Roseville Pottery. John Jr. was a youngster when his father and mother started collecting Roseville. His parents started collecting Roseville some 25 years ago. Over the years, they acquired and sold over 500 pieces of pottery. They have been classified the experts on The Roseville Pottery Company for the past ten years. In 1991, they formed the Roseville of the Past Pottery Club and in 1994 they ran the first Antique American Art Pottery Show and Auction in Orlando, Florida. Their first book "Roseville In All Its Splendor" was first published September 1998. Since then Jack has gone to the Lord, March 20, 1999. Always there to help, John and Malinda were always available no matter what project was being worked on. When Jack passed away, they moved in with Nancy and have been there again to help out. This past year, 2003, John and Malinda have had their biggest dream come true. They have adopted four wonderful children, all brothers and a sister, Eric (12), Gerard (10), Ramey (7), and Sirjesim (6). Their love of family has enhanced their desire to continue on with the work started so many years ago by their father.

This book is a continuation of Jack's love of Roseville. John Jr. and Malinda along with Nancy have continued carrying on in his name. They feel this book is long in coming. Everyone who collects needs to keep track of his or her collection.

"We, Jack's family, dedicate this book to the one we have lost"

Nancy Bomm
Author

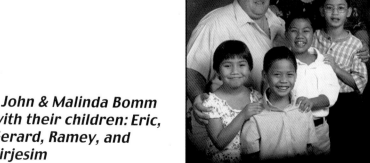

John & Malinda Bomm
with their children: Eric,
Gerard, Ramey, and
Sirjesim

INTRODUCTION

Prices listed in this publication are guidelines only. Pricing is determined by location, condition of item, coloring, and of course, demand. The authors of this book take no responsibility for variations in pricing. Pricing should be used only as a generalization, not an actual.

ACKNOWLEDGMENTS

We wish to thank the Ohio Historical Society who has stored these plates in their vaults for these many years. Without them this book would not have been completed.

A special thanks and heart felt love goes out to the Krauses', Jon and Patty, who had in their possession all of the lost information from 1945 to 1954. Jon has also left this life and is greatly missed. Without these pages the book would have been incomplete.

Special thanks to Mark Bassett for the use of several of his pictures from his Mark Bassett, INTRODUCTING ROSEVILLE POTTERY (Atglen, PA; Schiffer 1999).

Many thanks to our friends who gladly gave us pictures and information we were missing.

And, of course, we need to express our deepest love to our father and my husband, Jack Bomm. Without his love of Roseville none of this would have ever been continued.

NEW INFORMATION

We are still looking for more information on the Roseville Pottery Co. Many plates are still missing. They may be out there somewhere. If you have additional information, please contact the Bomm family either through L-W Books or directly at 6441 Swallow Hill Drive, Orlando, FL 32818; email: rosepast@hotmail.com.

Information regarding specific patterns listed in this book: We have found much more information on the Roseville Pottery Co. patterns. Regretfully, we do not have pictures to go with all the the different mold numbers that were found in the minutes of the factory. We have incorporated these within their respective patterns. Other new patterns we have listed without pictures.

ROSEVILLE COAT OF ARMS

The front cover shows the original Roseville Coat of Arms designed by The F. & R. Lazarus & Co., from Columbus, Ohio. There is no date listed. It lists the motto of Roseville "Facta Non Veva" (Deeds Not Words). The Coat of Arms incorporated a star for achievement, the blue bird that brings happiness into retail skies, the industrious bee, the ermine and coronet of nobility, the strong right arm and sword that fend off re-conversion harzards.

The Roseville Pottery Company 1890-1954

J.F. Weaver and several local potters started the Roseville Pottery Company in late 1890 in Roseville, Ohio. Though the company was moved to Zanesville, Ohio several years later the name remained.

George F. Young was born February 24, 1863 in Lower Salem, Ohio. He joined the Roseville Pottery in 1891 as a salesman. When the company was incorporated in January 4, 1892, he was elected secretary and general manager. The pottery was then named Roseville Pottery Company.

Just after the incorporation it was decided to purchase the old J.B. Owens plant which expanded their production of pottery. In 1895, they also purchased the Midland Pottery and doubled production. At that time, several more kilns were also added. In 1901, they purchased the Mosaic Tile plant as an auxiliary. In 1902, they again purchased from Peters and Reed the Muskingum stoneware plant in Zanesville. Another addition was done in 1903 when they added a two story brick office and sample room.

Young hired Ross C. Purdy in 1900. Purdy introduced the Rozane Royal line. He also hired John J. Herold to take over as art director and designer. He was responsible for winning first place for their Mongol style. Frederick Hurten Rhead was named Art Director from 1904 until 1908. He was responsible for such pieces as Mara, Egypto, Mongol, Woodland, updated Rozane Royal, Olympic, Crystalline, Della Robbia. Frederick was succeeded by his brother Harry in 1908. He was known for the Pauleo line and his most famous Donatello line.

George Young closed the Roseville, Ohio plant in 1910, but continued to maintain the two plants in Zanesville. The Muskingum Plant was burned down in 1917 which left only the plant on Linden Avenue. He handed over leadership of the company to his son, Russell in 1919. Russell stayed in this position until 1932. Anna Young his mother became president of the company and re-incorporated the company under the name of Roseville Pottery, Inc.

In 1919, Frank Ferrel succeeded Hary Rhead as art director and designer. He teamed up with George Krause to produce several new lines. Their most successful line was the Pinecone pattern.

Anna Young died in 1938. She was followed by her son in law, F.S. Clements. He stayed with the company until 1945 when Robert Windish came on board. Windish stayed with the company until it closed its doors on January 2, 1954.

ANTIQUE MATT GREEN   1910-1914

COMPLIMENTS OF THE OHIO HISTORICAL SOCIETY

X	DESCRIPTION	SECONDARY MARKET	PRICE PAID	DATE BOUGHT	CONDITION
	4" JARDINIERE	150-200			
	6" JARDINIERE	200-250			
	7" JARDINIERE	275-325			
	8" JARDINIERE	375-475			
	9" JARDINIERE	500-600			
	10" JARDINIERE	700-900			
	12" JARDINIERE	1000-1500			
	10" x 261/4" JARD. & PED.	1400-1600			
	12" x 331/2" JARD. & PED.	2000-2400			

APPLE BLOSSOM 1948

GEORGE KRAUSE COLLECTION

X	DESCRIPTION	SECONDARY MARKET	PRICE PAID	DATE BOUGHT	CONDITION
	381-6 VASE	100-175			
	382-7 VASE	125-190			
	323-8 CORNUCOPIA	130-240			
	379-7 BUD VASE	100-175			
	321-6 CORNUCOPIA	100-160			
	387-9 VASE	100-175			
	373-7 VASE	130-200			
	316-8 EWER	200-300			
	385-8 VASE	125-190			
	390-12 PILLOW VASE	225-350			
	389-10 VASE	175-300			
	388-10 VASE	175-300			
	391-12 VASE	300-400			
	318-15 EWER	700-1400			
	363-18 VASE	800-1600			
	392-15 VASE	400-650			

APPLE BLOSSOM 1948

GEORGE KRAUSE COLLECTION

X	DESCRIPTION	SECONDARY MARKET	PRICE PAID	DATE BOUGHT	CONDITION
	368-8 WINDOW BOX	150-200			
	371-P TEAPORT	250-350			
	371-C CREAMER	75-150			
	371-S SUGAR	75-150			
	369-12 WINDOW BOX	200-300			
	300-4 JARDINIERE	150-200			
	359-2 BOOKENDS (PR)	200-275			
	342-6 PLANTER	150-275			
	302-8 JARDINIERE	350-500			
	356-5 FLOWER POT & SAUCER	150-250			
	301-6 JARDINIERE	150-250			
	305-8 JARD & PED	1250-2500			
	311-12 BASKET	350-500			

APPLE BLOSSOM 1948

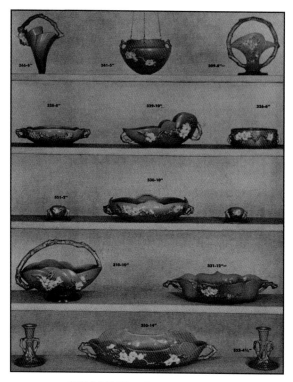

GEORGE KRAUSE COLLECTION

X	DESCRIPTION	SECONDARY MARKET	PRICE PAID	DATE BOUGHT	CONDITION
	366-8 WALL POCKET	275-400			
	361-5 HANGING BASKET	275-325			
	309-8 BASKET	275-400			
	328-8 BOWL	175-250			
	329-10 BOWL	150-250			
	326-6 BOWL	125-200			
	351-2 CANDLESTICKS	100-150			
	330-10 COMPOTE	150-225			
	310-10 BASKET	300-475			
	331-14 COMPOTE	150-275			
	333-14 COMPOTE	200-300			
	352-4 1/2 CANDLESTICKS	200-375			

ART PICTURES NOT SHOWN:

X	DESCRIPTION	SECONDARY MARKET	PRICE PAID	DATE BOUGHT	CONDITION
	438-7 JARDINIERE	250-300			
	438-8 JARDINIERE	300-350			
	438-9 JARDINIERE	350-400			
	438-10 JARDINIERE	400-450			
	438-12 JARDINIERE	450-500			
	438-14 JARDINIERE	600-700			
	438-9 X 22 JARD. & PEDESTAL	1000-1200			
	438-10 X 24 JARD. & PEDESTAL	1000-1200			
	438-12 X 28 JARD. & PEDESTAL	1200-1400			
	438-14 X 32 JARD. & PEDESTAL	1400-1800			
	476-9 X 22 JARD. & PEDESTAL	1000-1200			
	476-10 X 24 JARD. & PEDESTAL	1000-1200			
	476-12 X 28 JARD. & PEDESTAL	1200-1400			
	476-14 X 32 JARD. & PEDESTAL	1400-1800			
	723-9 X 21 UMBRELLA	1500-1750			
	724-9 X 20 UMBRELLA	1750-2000			
	725-10 X23 UMBRELLA	2000-2500			
	728-10 X20 UMBRELLA	1750-2000			

ARTWOOD 1951

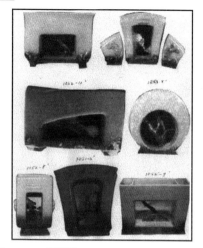

X	DESCRIPTION	SECONDARY MARKET PRICE	DATE PAID	BOUGHT	CONDITION
	1054-8.5 PLANTER	100-150			
	1050-2 PLANTER	75-125			
	1056-10 PLANTER	150-200			
	1053-8 VASE	150-200			
	1052-8 VASE	125-150			
	1051-6 3 PC.SET	125-175			
	1055-9 PLANTER	100-125			

X	DESCRIPTION	SECONDARY MARKET	PRICE PAID	DATE BOUGHT	CONDITION
	1057-8 VASE	150-200			
	1061-10 BOWL	150-200			
	1060-12 VASE	300-500			
	1062-5 BOWL	150-200			
	1058-8 PLANTER	150-200			
	1059-10 VASE	150-200			

AUTUMN CIRCA 1910

COMPLIMENTS OF THE OHIO HISTORICAL SOCIETY

X	DESCRIPTION	SECONDARY MARKET	PRICE PAID	DATE BOUGHT	CONDITION
	480-7 JARDINIERE	250-300			
	498-7 JARDINIERE	250-300			
	498-8 JARDINIERE	300-400			
	498-9 JARDINIERE	400-500			
	498-10 JARD.	450-500			
	480-10 JARD.	450-500			
	480-9 JARDINIERE	400-500			
	480-8 JARDINIERE	300-400			

COMPLIMENTS OF THE OHIO HISTORICAL SOCIETY

X	DESCRIPTION	SECONDARY MARKET	PRICE PAID	DATE BOUGHT	CONDITION
	TOOTHBRUSH HOLDER	100-150			
	CHAMBER POT	400-500			
	PITCHER	275-350			
	COMBINETT	600-800			
	MUG	150-200			
	POWDER JAR	175-225			
	LARGE PITCHER	400-500			
	BASIN	300-350			

AZTEC ART 1904

COMPLIMENTS OF THE OHIO HISTORICAL SOCIETY

X	DESCRIPTION	SECONDARY MARKET	PRICE PAID	DATE BOUGHT	CONDITION
	14 VASE	450-550			
	15 VASE	450-550			
	22 VASE	475-575			
	18 VASE	400-500			
	24 VASE	400-500			
	23 VASE	450-550			
	13 VASE	450-550			
	17 VASE	450-550			
	10 VASE	400-500			
	9 VASE	450-550			
	15 VASE	400-450			
	21 VASE	400-450			
	16 VASE	400-450			
	4 VASE	350-450			
	19 VASE	400-500			
	20 VASE	400-500			
	1 VASE	400-500			
	8 VASE	450-550			
	2 VASE	425-525			
	3 VASE	475-575			
	11 VASE	475-575			
	7 VASE	450-550			
	5 VASE	400-450			
	6 VASE	450-550			

COMPLIMENTS OF THE OHIO HISTORICAL SOCIETY

	DESCRIPTION	SECONDARY MARKET	PRICE PAID	DATE BOUGHT	CONDITION
	1 PITCHER	350-450			
	2 PITCHER	650-750			
	3 PITCHER	400-450			

AZUREAN 1902

COMPLIMENTS OF THE OHIO HISTORICAL SOCIETY

X	DESCRIPTION	SECONDARY MARKET	PRICE PAID	DATE BOUGHT	CONDITION
	814-9 1/4 VASE	1800-2000			
	958-11 VASE	1300-1600			
	892-8 1/2 VASE	1200-1500			
	935-5 1/4 CHOCOLATE POT	1500-2000			
	937-8 PITCHER	1500-1800			
	936-8 COFFEE POT	2000-2500			
	882-9 PILLOW VASE	4000-5000			
	813-7 3/4 VASE	1500-1800			
	845-11 1/2 VASE	3500-4500			
	812-12 VASE	3000-4000			
	865-17 1/4 VASE	4500-5500			
	955-17 VASE	4500-5500			
	933-15 1/4 VASE	4500-5500			
	832-15 1/2 VASE	4500-5500			
	931-14 1/4 VASE	3000-4000			
	891-14 VASE	4500-5500			

AZUREAN 1902

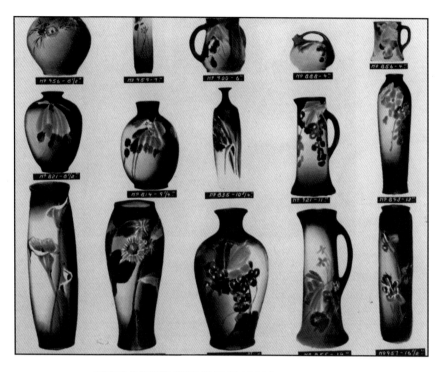

COMPLIMENTS OF THE OHIO HISTORICAL SOCIETY

X	DESCRIPTION	SECONDARY MARKET	PRICE PAID	DATE BOUGHT	CONDITION
	956-8 1/2 VASE	1000-1500			
	959-7 VASE	500-750			
	900-6 VASE	500-750			
	888-4 VASE	500-700			
	856-4 MUG	300-350			
	821-8 1/2 VASE	750-1000			
	814-9 1/4 VASE	1800-2200			
	835-10 3/4 VASE	1500-2500			
	921-11 TANKER	1000-1500			
	893-13 VASE	1200-1500			
	955-17 VASE	5000-6000			
	933-15 1/4 VASE	2000-2500			
	931-14 3/4 VASE	3000-3500			
	855-14 TANKER	2000-2500			
	957-16 1/2 VASE	1500-1800			

COMPLIMENTS OF THE OHIO HISTORICAL SOCIETY

X	DESCRIPTION	SECONDARY MARKET	PRICE PAID	DATE BOUGHT	CONDITION
	95-7 BOWL	125-150			
	66-4 BOWL	125-150			
	93-10 BOWL	125-150			
	598-5 PLANTER	200-225			
	598-6 PLANTER	225-250			
	93-8 BOWL	125-150			
	96-6 BOWL	125-150			
	1029-3 3/4 CANDLESTICK	125-150			
	1034-15 CANDLESTICK	400-500			
	1033-12 CANDLESTICK	300-350			
	1031-6 CANDLESTICK	175-225			
	94-5 BOWL	125-150			
	93-12 COMPOTE	150-175			
	315-11 BASKET	350-400			
	316-9 1/2 BASKET	325-375			
	1032-8 CANDLESTICK	175-225			
	1030-4 CANDLESTICK	125-150			
	313-11 BASKET	350-400			
	317-13 1/2 BASKET	400-500			
	181-12 VASE	250-300			
	183-14 VASE	325-375			
	314-11 1/2 BASKET	350-400			
	318-13 BASKET	400-500			
	182-12 VASE	250-300			
	180-10 VASE	200-250			

BANEDA 1933

GEORGE KRAUSE COLLECTION

X	DESCRIPTION	SECONDARY MARKET	PRICE PAID	DATE BOUGHT	CONDITION
	600-15 VASE	1800-3200			
	594-9 VASE	700-1200			
	596-9 VASE	900-1500			
	598-12 VASE	1000-1900			
	605-6 VASE	400-500			
	233-8 WINDOW BOX	325-500			
	603-4 VASE	325-400			
	604-7 VASE	450-550			
	590-7 VASE	450-550			
	626-4 VASE	1800-2200			
	588-6 VASE	350-450			
	592-7 VASE	450-550			

GEORGE KRAUSE COLLECTION

X	DESCRIPTION	SECONDARY MARKET	PRICE PAID	DATE BOUGHT	CONDITION
	626-5 VASE	400-500			
	610-7 VASE	550-650			
	1269-8 WALL POCKET	1500-2000			
	237-12 WINDOW BOX	450-550			
	1088-4 CANDLESTICK	300-400			
	626-7 JARDINIERE	1000-1200			
	626-6 JARDINIERE	750-1000			
	626-9 JARDINIERE	1500-1700			
	626-8 JARD. & PED.	3000-3500			
	626-10 JARD. & PED.	4000-5000			

BANEDA 1933

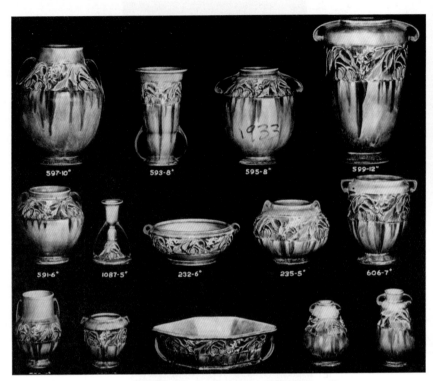

GEORGE KRAUSE COLLECTION

X	DESCRIPTION	SECONDARY MARKET	PRICE PAID	DATE BOUGHT	CONDITION
	597-10 VASE	900-1500			
	593-8 VASE	400-550			
	595-8 VASE	750-1000			
	599-12 VASE	1500-2000			
	591-6 VASE	450-600			
	1087-5 CANDLESTICK	300-350			
	232-6 BOWL	350-450			
	235-5 VASE	500-600			
	606-7 VASE	550-700			
	589-6 VASE	400-600			
	587-4 VASE	375-475			
	234-10 WINDOW BOX	450-550			
	601-5 VASE	350-400			
	602-6 VASE	325-425			

BANKS & NOVELITIES EARLY 1900s

COMPLIMENTS OF THE OHIO HISTORICAL SOCIETY

X	DESCRIPTION	SECONDARY MARKET	PRICE PAID	DATE BOUGHT	CONDITION
	CAT HEAD	300-350			
	UNCLE SAM	300-350			
	LARGE BEE HIVE	350-450			
	SMALL BEE HIVE	200-300			
	LARGE LAYING PIG	250-300			
	STANDING PIG	200-250			
	SMALL LAYING PIG	200-250			
	SM. PARROT HEAD	200-250			
	LARGE DOG HEAD	300-350			
	BUFFALO	300-350			
	LG. EAGLE HEAD	350-400			
	SMALL DOG HEAD	250-300			

X	DESCRIPTION	SECONDARY MARKET	PRICE PAID	DATE BOUGHT	CONDITION
	SM. MONKEY BOTTLE	250-300			
	LG. MONKEY BOTTLE	300-400			
	SMALL YE OLD TIME JUG	200-250			
	LARGE YE OLD TIME JUG	300-350			

BITTERSWEET 1951

GEORGE KRAUSE COLLECTION

X	DESCRIPTION	SECONDARY MARKET	PRICE PAID	DATE BOUGHT	CONDITION
	809-8 BASKET	250-300			
	868-8 WINDOW BOX	150-200			
	808-6 BASKET	200-250			
	841-5 VASE	125-175			
	829-12 PLANTER	150-175			
	863-4 VASE	100-125			
	810-10 BASKET	200-300			
	842-7 VASE	150-225			
	811-10 BASKET	225-325			
	827-8 PLANTER	125-175			
	828-10 WINDOW BOX	200-250			
	826-6 BOWL	100-150			
	851-3 CANDLESTICK	100-150			
	830-14 COMPOTE	225-275			

BITTERSWEET 1951

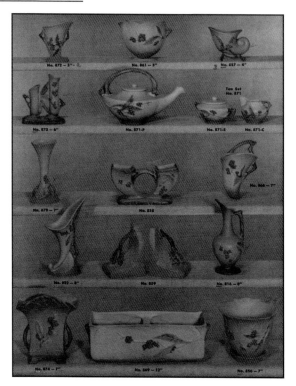

GEORGE KRAUSE COLLECTION

X	DESCRIPTION	SECONDARY MARKET	PRICE PAID	DATE BOUGHT	CONDITION
	872-5 VASE	100-125			
	861-5 VASE	100-150			
	857-4 VASE	100-150			
	873-6 DOUBLE VASE	125-175			
	871-P TEAPOT	250-300			
	871-S SUGAR	75-100			
	871-C CREAMER	75-100			
	879-7 VASE	100-125			
	858 BRIDGE	150-200			
	866-7 WALL POCKET	250-350			
	822-8 VASE	125-175			
	859 BOOKENDS	300-400			
	816-8 EWER	175-250			
	874-7 VASE	100-125			
	869-12 WINDOW BOX	150-225			
	856-7 PLANTER	125-150			

BITTERSWEET 1951

GEORGE KRAUSE COLLECTION

X	DESCRIPTION	SECONDARY MARKET	PRICE PAID	DATE BOUGHT	CONDITION
	881-6 VASE	100-125			
	886-12 VASE	150-250			
	883-8 VASE	125-150			
	882-6 VASE	100-125			
	801-6 JARDINIERE	125-175			
	800-4 JARDINIERE	100-150			
	884-8 VASE	100-125			
	885-10 VASE	150-175			
	888-16 VASE	350-400			
	887-14 VASE	250-350			
	805-8 JARD. & PEDESTAL	1200-1600			

BLACKBERRY 1932

COMPLIMENTS OF THE OHIO HISTORICAL SOCIETY

X	DESCRIPTION	SECONDARY MARKET	PRICE PAID	DATE BOUGHT	CONDITION
	623-10 JARD. & PED.	3000-3500			
	623-7 JARDINIERE	625-725			
	624-12 VASE	1400-1500			
	623-12 JARDINIERE	2000-2500			
	623-6 JARDINIERE	475-600			
	623-5 JARDINIERE	425-525			
	623-4 JARDINIERE	350-450			
	623-9 JARDINIERE	1200-1600			
	577-10 VASE	1000-1200			
	623-8 VASE	700-1000			

BLACKBERRY 1932

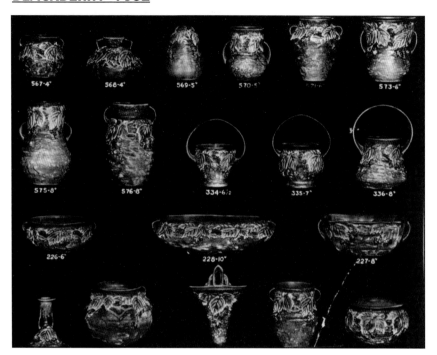

COMPLIMENTS OF THE OHIO HISTORICAL SOCIETY

X	DESCRIPTION	SECONDARY MARKET	PRICE PAID	DATE BOUGHT	CONDITION
	567-4 JARDINIERE	425-525			
	568-4 VASE	500-550			
	569-5 VASE	500-600			
	570-5 VASE	450-550			
	571-6 VASE	525-625			
	573-6 VASE	525-650			
	575-8 VASE	725-825			
	576-8 VASE	625-825			
	334-6 1/2 BASKET	725-925			
	335-7 BASKET	825-925			
	336-8 BASKET	750-850			
	226-6 BOWL	450-550			
	228-10 WINDOW BOX	1000-2000			
	227-8 WINDOW BOX	425-475			
	1086-4 1/2 CANDLESTICK	550-650			
	574-6 JARDINIERE	550-650			
	1267-8 WALL POCKET	1100-1300			
	572-6 VASE	550-650			
	348-5 JARDINIERE	1000-1300			

BLEEDING HEART 1940

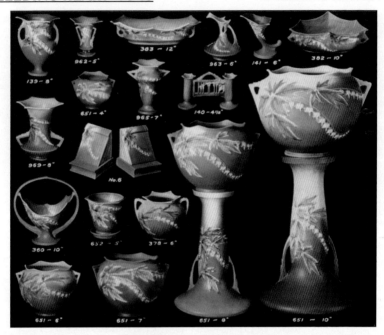

GEORGE KRAUSE COLLECTION

X	DESCRIPTION	SECONDARY MARKET	PRICE PAID	DATE BOUGHT	CONDITION
	139-8 VASE	200-250			
	962-5 VASE	150-200			
	383-12 COMPOTE	250-300			
	963-6 EWER	175-250			
	141-8 CORNUCOPIA	150-175			
	382-10 COMPOTE	150-225			
	651-6 JARDINIERE	225-275			
	965-7 VASE	150-200			
	140-4 1/2 BRIDGE	150-200			
	969-8 VASE	225-275			
	6 BOOKENDS	350-400			
	360-10 BASKET	325-400			
	652-5 PLANTER	125-175			
	378-6 JARDINIERE	200-250			
	651-6 JARDINIERE	225-275			
	651-7 JARDINIERE	275-325			
	651-8 JARD. & PEDESTAL	1500-2000			
	651-10 JARD. & PEDESTAL	1800-3200			

BLEEDING HEART 1940

GEORGE KRAUSE COLLECTION

X	DESCRIPTION	SECONDARY MARKET	PRICE PAID	DATE BOUGHT	CONDITION
	954-6 VASE	150-200			
	380-8 BOWL	200-275			
	1287-8 WALL POCKET	425-600			
	1140 CANDLESTICK	100-125			
	1139-4 1/2 CANDLESTICK	175-250			
	362-5 HANGING BASKET	350-400			
	359-8 BASKET	250-375			
	966-7 VASE	175-250			
	968-8 VASE	200-250			
	970-9 VASE	275-325			
	377-4 JARDINIERE	175-225			
	379-6 BOWL	200-275			
	1232 PITCHER	375-425			
	651-5 JARDINIERE	175-225			
	971-9 VASE	250-300			
	361-12 BASKET	350-425			
	40 FROG	100-125			
	138-14 VASE	100-150			
	384-14 COMPOTE	275-325			
	967-7 VASE	175-225			
	961-4 VASE	125-175			
	651-3 JARDINIERE	100-125			
	142-8 CORNUCOPIA	175-200			
	381-10 DISH	175-225			
	976-15 VASE	600-800			
	974-12 VASE	400-450			
	973-10 VASE	300-350			
	972-10 EWER	275-325			
	975-15 EWER	600-800			
	977-18 VASE	1100-1800			

BLENDED CIRCA EARLY 1900s

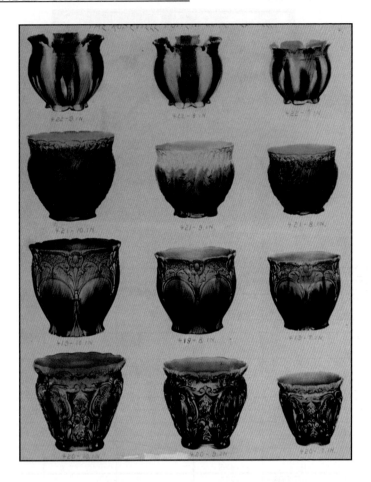

COMPLIMENTS OF THE OHIO HISTORICAL SOCIETY

X	DESCRIPTION	SECONDARY MARKET	PRICE PAID	DATE BOUGHT	CONDITION
	422-9 JARDINIERE	275-325			
	422-8 JARDINIERE	250-300			
	422-7 JARDINIERE	200-225			
	421-10 JARDINIERE	300-350			
	421-9 JARDINIERE	275-300			
	421-8 JARDINIERE	225-250			
	419-10 JARDINIERE	275-325			
	419-8 JARDINIERE	250-300			
	419-7 JARDINIERE	200-225			
	420-10 JARDINIERE	300-350			
	420-9 JARDINIERE	275-300			
	420-7 JARDINIERE	200-225			

BLENDED CIRCA EARLY 1900s

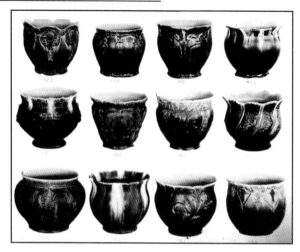

COMPLIMENTS OF THE OHIO HISTORICAL SOCIETY

X	DESCRIPTION	SECONDARY MARKET	PRICE PAID	DATE BOUGHT	CONDITION
	423-6 JARDINIERE	125-150			
	423-7 JARDINIERE	150-200			
	423-8 JARDINIERE	225-250			
	423-9 JARDINIERE	250-275			
	423-10 JARDINIERE	300-350			
	403-6 JARDINIERE	125-150			
	403-7 JARDINIERE	150-200			
	403-8 JARDINIERE	225-250			
	403-9 JARDINIERE	250-275			
	403-10 JARDINIERE	300-350			
	419-6 JARDINIERE	125-150			
	419-7 JARDINIERE	200-225			
	419-8 JARDINIERE	225-250			
	419-9 JARDINIERE	250-275			
	419-10 JARDINIERE	300-350			
	422-6 JARDINIERE	125-150			
	422-7 JARDINIERE	150-200			
	422-8 JARDINIERE	225-250			
	422-9 JARDINIERE	250-275			
	422-10 JARDINIERE	300-350			
	410-6 JARDINIERE	125-150			
	410-7 JARDINIERE	150-200			
	410-8 JARDINIERE	225-250			
	410-9 JARDINIERE	250-275			
	410-10 JARDINIERE	300-350			
	420-6 JARDINIERE	125-150			
	420-7 JARDINIERE	150-200			
	420-8 JARDINIERE	225-250			
	420-9 JARDINIERE	250-275			
	420-10 JARDINIERE	300-350			

BLENDED CIRCA EARLY 1900s

X	DESCRIPTION	SECONDARY MARKET	PRICE PAID	DATE BOUGHT	CONDITION
	421-6 JARDINIERE	125-150			
	421-7 JARDINIERE	150-200			
	421-8 JARDINIERE	225-250			
	421-9 JARDINIERE	250-275			
	421-10 JARDINIERE	300-350			
	407-6 JARDINIERE	125-150			
	407-7 JARDINIERE	150-200			
	407-8 JARDINIERE	225-250			
	407-9 JARDINIERE	250-275			
	407-10 JARDINIERE	300-350			
	404-6 JARDINIERE	125-150			
	404-7 JARDINIERE	150-200			
	404-8 JARDINIERE	225-250			
	404-9 JARDINIERE	250-275			
	404-10 JARDINIERE	300-350			
	430-6 JARDINIERE	125-150			
	430-7 JARDINIERE	150-200			
	430-8 JARDINIERE	225-250			
	430-9 JARDINIERE	250-275			
	430-10 JARDINIERE	300-350			
	421-6 JARDINIERE	125-150			
	421-7 JARDINIERE	150-200			
	421-8 JARDINIERE	225-250			
	421-9 JARDINIERE	250-275			
	421-10 JARDINIERE	300-350			
	426-6 JARDINIERE	125-150			
	426-7 JARDINIERE	150-200			
	426-8 JARDINIERE	225-250			
	426-9 JARDINIERE	250-275			
	426-10 JARDINIERE	300-350			

BLENDED JARDINIERE

BLENDED CIRCA EARLY 1900s

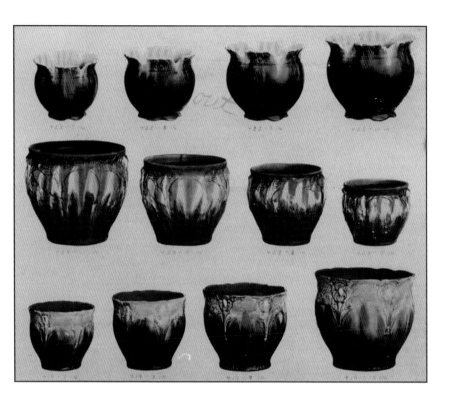

COMPLIMENTS OF THE OHIO HISTORICAL SOCIETY

X	DESCRIPTION	SECONDARY MARKET	PRICE PAID	DATE BOUGHT	CONDITION
	422-7 JARDINIERE	200-225			
	422-8 JARDINIERE	250-300			
	422-9 JARDINIERE	275-325			
	422-10 JARDINIERE	300-350			
	458-10 JARDINIERE	300-350			
	458-9 JARDINIERE	275-325			
	458-8 JARDINIERE	250-300			
	458-9 JARDINIERE	275-325			
	458-8 JARDINIERE	250-300			
	458-7 JARDINIERE	200-225			
	419-7 JARDINIERE	200-225			
	419-8 JARDINIERE	250-300			
	419-9 JARDINIERE	275-325			
	419-10 JARDINIERE	300-350			

BLENDED CIRCA EARLY 1900s

COMPLIMENTS OF THE OHIO HISTORICAL SOCIETY

X	DESCRIPTION	SECONDARY MARKET	PRICE PAID	DATE BOUGHT	CONDITION
	409 JARDINIERE	275-325			
	417 JARDINIERE	150-175			
	418 JARDINIERE	125-150			
	407 JARDINIERE	275-325			
	413 JARDINIERE	300-350			
	411 JARDINIERE	300-350			

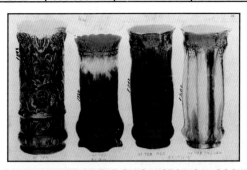

COMPLIMENTS OF THE OHIO HISTORICAL SOCIETY

X	DESCRIPTION	SECONDARY MARKET	PRICE PAID	DATE BOUGHT	CONDITION
	706 8X21 UMBRELLA	500-600			
	705 8 X 18 UMBRELLA	450-550			
	708R 8 X 19½ UMBRELLA	550-650			
	708Y 8 X 19½ UMBRELLA	550-650			

BLENDED CIRCA EARLY 1900s

COMPLIMENTS OF THE OHIO HISTORICAL SOCIETY

X	DESCRIPTION	SECONDARY MARKET	PRICE PAID	DATE BOUGHT	CONDITION
	508-7 JARDINIERE	250-300			
	508-8 JARDINIERE	300-400			
	508-10 JARDINIERE	500-600			
	506-8 JARDINIERE	350-450			
	506-9 JARDINIERE	450-550			
	506-10 JARDINIERE	500-600			
	506-12 JARDINIERE	600-700			

	701 10 X 21 UMBRELLA	600-700			
	706 8 X 21 UMBRELLA	700-750			
	719 8 1/2 X 21 UMBRELLA	700-750			

BLENDED CIRCA EARLY 1900s

COMPLIMENTS OF THE OHIO HISTORICAL SOCIETY

X	DESCRIPTION	SECONDARY MARKET	PRICE PAID	DATE BOUGHT	CONDITION
	405-35 JARD & PED	1200-1500			
	406-30 JARD & PED	700-900			
	407-30 JARD & PED	700-900			

	404-27 1/2 JARD. & PEDESTAL	800-1000			
	1201-25 JARD & PEDESTAL	500-600			
	120-325 JARD & PEDESTAL	600-700			

BLENDED CIRCA EARLY 1900s

COMPLIMENTS OF THE OHIO HISTORICAL SOCIETY

X	DESCRIPTION	SECONDARY MARKET	PRICE PAID	DATE BOUGHT	CONDITION
	1203 10 X 25 JARD. & PED.	700-800			
	431 10 X 25 JARD. & PED.	400-500			
	430 15 X 25 JARD. & PED.	400-500			

COMPLIMENTS OF THE OHIO HISTORICAL SOCIETY

X	DESCRIPTION	SECONDARY MARKET	PRICE PAID	DATE BOUGHT	CONDITION
	454-4 JARDINIERE	75-100			
	454-5 JARDINIERE	100-125			
	454-6 JARDINIERE	125-150			
	465 10 X 25 JARD. & PED.	500-600			
	458 10 X 25 JARD. & PED.	600-800			
	460 10 X 25 JARD. & PED.	800-900			
	459 10 X 25 JARD. & PED.	800-900			

BLENDED CIRCA EARLY 1900s

COMPLIMENTS OF THE OHIO HISTORICAL SOCIETY

X	DESCRIPTION	SECONDARY MARKET	PRICE PAID	DATE BOUGHT	CONDITION
	431 10 X 23 JARD. & PED.	600-700			
	448 12x23 JARD. & PEDESTAL	700-900			
	479 10x30 JARD. & PEDESTAL	800-1000			
	452 14x33 JARD. & PEDESTAL	1600-2000			

COMPLIMENTS OF THE OHIO HISTORICAL SOCIETY

X	DESCRIPTION	SECONDARY MARKET	PRICE PAID	DATE BOUGHT	CONDITION
	425 44" JARD & PED	2000-2500			
	410 37" JARD & PED	1500-1700			
	414 33" JARD & PED	1700-2000			

BLENDED CIRCA EARLY 1900s

COMPLIMENTS OF THE OHIO HISTORICAL SOCIETY

X	DESCRIPTION	SECONDARY MARKET	PRICE PAID	DATE BOUGHT	CONDITION
	422-7 JARDINIERE	100-125			
	422-8 JARDINIERE	125-150			
	422-9 JARDINIERE	150-175			
	422-10 JARDINIERE	175-200			
	422-11 JARDINIERE	200-225			
	422-12 JARDINIERE	225-250			
	422 10X24 JAR & PED	500-600			
	422 10X29 JAR & PED	1000-1300			
	404-8 JARDINIERE	100-125			
	404-10 JARDINIERE	150-175			
	404-12 JARDINIERE	200-225			
	404 12 X 27 1/2 JARD & PED	600-700			
	457-12 JARDINIERE	200-225			
	457-13 JARDINIERE	250-275			
	457 13X27 JAR & PED	800-900			

BLENDED CIRCA EARLY 1900s

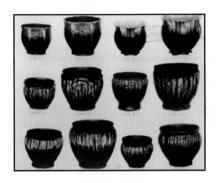

COMPLIMENTS OF THE OHIO HISTORICAL SOCIETY

X	DESCRIPTION	SECONDARY MARKET	PRICE PAID	DATE BOUGHT	CONDITION
	419-7 JARDINIERE	200-225			
	419-9 JARDINIERE	250-275			
	422-8 JARDINIERE	225-275			
	422-10 JARDINIERE	300-350			
	458-7 JARDINIERE	200-225			
	458-9 JARDINIERE	250-275			
	458-8 JARDINIERE	225-250			
	459-10 JARDINIERE	300-325			
	460-8 JARDINIERE	225-250			
	460-10 JARDINIERE	300-325			
	464-7 JARDINIERE	200-225			
	464-9 JARDINIERE	250-275			

COMPLIMENTS OF THE OHIO HISTORICAL SOCIETY

X	DESCRIPTION	SECONDARY MARKET	PRICE PAID	DATE BOUGHT	CONDITION
	405 JARDINIERE	250-300			
	410 JARDINIERE	300-325			
	404 JARDINIERE	250-300			
	423 JARDINIERE	300-350			
	406 JARDINIERE	250-300			

BLENDED CIRCA EARLY 1900s

PICTURES NOT SHOWN

X	DESCRIPTION	SECONDARY MARKET	PRICE PAID	DATE BOUGHT	CONDITION
	531-7 JARDINIERE	200-225			
	531-8 JARDINIERE	225-250			
	531-9 JARDINIERE	250-275			
	531-10 JARDINIERE	275-300			
	547-6 JARDINIERE	175-200			
	547-8 JARDINIERE	225-250			
	547-9 JARDINIERE	250-275			
	547-10 JARDINIERE	275-300			
	571-7 JARDINIERE	200-225			
	571-8 JARDINIERE	225-250			
	571-9 JARDINIERE	250-275			
	571-10 JARDINIERE	275-300			
	508 10X27 JAR & PED	1000-1500			
	531 10X28 JAR & PED	1000-1500			
	533 10X28 JAR & PED	1000-1500			
	534 10X29 JAR & PED	1200-1500			
	537 10X28 JAR & PED	1000-1500			
	547 10X28 JAR & PED	1000-1500			
	550 10X28 JAR & PED	1000-1500			
	550 12X33 JAR & PED	1500-1750			
	720 10X24 UMBRELLA	750-1250			
	727 10X21 UMBRELLA	750-1000			
	739 10X19 UMBRELLA	750-1000			
	734 10X21 UMBRELLA	750-1000			
	743 10X20 UMBRELLA	1000-1200			
	744 10X21 UMBRELLA	1000-1200			
	745 10X19 UMBRELLA	1000-1200			
	746 9X20 UMBRELLA	1000-1200			
	747 10X19 UMBRELLA	1000-1200			
	748 10X20 UMBRELLA	1000-1200			
	749 10X20 UMBRELLA	1000-1200			

BLUE/BLACK TEAPOTS 1920s

COMPLIMENTS OF THE OHIO HISTORICAL SOCIETY

X	DESCRIPTION	SECONDARY MARKET	PRICE PAID	DATE BOUGHT	CONDITION
	1	400-450			
	2	300-400			
	3	250-300			
	4	250-300			
	5	300-350			
	6	400-500			

	241	50-75			
	242	75-100			
	243	100-125			
	244	125-150			

BLUE/GREEN/RED & GOLD   EARLY 1900s

COMPLIMENTS OF THE OHIO HISTORICAL SOCIETY

X	DESCRIPTION	SECONDARY MARKET	PRICE PAID	DATE BOUGHT	CONDITION
	ALL 3 JARD & PED	1000-1300			

ITEMS BELOW NOT PICTURED

	615 SPITTOON	150-200			
	607 SPITTOON	150-200			
	BASIN	200-250			
	TOOTHBRUSH HOLDER	100-125			
	DRINKING MUG	100-125			
	LARGE PITCHER	200-250			

BROWN CUSPIDOR   EARLY 1900s

X	DESCRIPTION	SECONDARY MARKET	PRICE PAID	DATE BOUGHT	CONDITION
	GREEN/BROWN CUSPIDOR	200-250			

BURMESE CIRCA 1950

GEORGE KRAUSE COLLECTION

X	DESCRIPTION	SECONDARY MARKET	PRICE PAID	DATE BOUGHT	CONDITION
	70B MALE CANDLE	250-350			
	71B MALE BOOKEND	250-350			
	72B MALE WALLPOCKET	275-375			
	75B CANDLEHOLDER	125-150			
	80B FEMALE CANDLE	250-350			
	81B FEMALE BOOKEND	250-350			
	82B FEMALE WALLPOCKET	275-375			
	90B-10 ORIENTAL BOWL	100-175			

GEORGE KRAUSE COLLECTION

X	DESCRIPTION	SECONDARY MARKET	PRICE PAID	DATE BOUGHT	CONDITION
	384-8 WINDOW PLANTER	125-200			
	2-S SUGAR	100-125			
	2-C CREAMER	100-125			
	28-4 VASE	100-125			
	383-6 PLANTER	100-200			
	657-4 VASE	100-175			
	30-6 VASE	100-175			
	2-T TEAPOT	250-350			
	9 BOOKEND	200-350			
	155-8 DOUBLE VASE	150-225			
	658-5 PLANTER	325-400			
	34-8 VASE	175-225			
	1-3 1/2 MUG	100-150			
	657-3 VASE	100-150			
	369- 6 1/2 BASKET	200-350			
	29-6 VASE	150-200			
	1191-8 WALL POCKET	300-350			
	31-7 VASE	150-225			
	2-10 EWER	200-300			
	1325 PITCHER	400-600			
	3 PLANTER	600-1000			
	32-7 VASE	200-275			
	370-8 BASKET	200-300			
	1-10 COMPOTE	225-300			
	414-10 COMPOTE	150-225			
	415-10 COMPOTE	150-250			

BUSHBERRY 1941

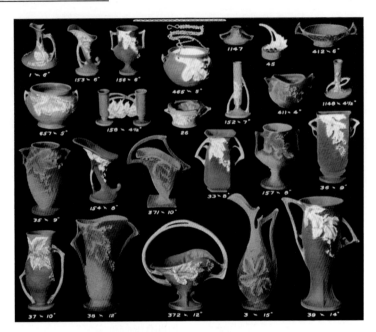

GEORGE KRAUSE COLLECTION

X	DESCRIPTION	SECONDARY MARKET	PRICE PAID	DATE BOUGHT	CONDITION
	1-6 EWER	150-225			
	153-6 CORNUCOPIA	100-150			
	156-6 VASE	125-175			
	465-5 HANGING BASKET	350-450			
	1147 CANDLESTICK	100-150			
	45 FROG	150-225			
	412-6 COMPOTE	150-200			
	657-5 JARDINIERE	150-200			
	158-4 1/2 BRIDGE	125-175			
	26 ASHTRAY	125-200			
	152-7 BUD VASE	100-150			
	411-4 JARDINIERE	100-150			
	1148-4 1/2 BUD VASE	150-225			
	35-9 VASE	200-300			
	154-8 CORNUCOPIA	150-250			
	371-10 BASKET	225-300			
	33-8 VASE	175-300			
	157-8 VASE	200-350			
	36-7 VASE	225-325			
	37-10 VASE	250-350			
	38-12 VASE	325-425			
	372-12 BASKET	350-400			
	3-15 FLOOR VASE	600-1000			
	39-14 FLOOR VASE	500-600			

BUSHBERRY 1941

GEORGE KRAUSE COLLECTION

X	DESCRIPTION	SECONDARY MARKET	PRICE PAID	DATE BOUGHT	CONDITION
	411-6 JARDINIERE	200-300			
	657-6 JARDINIERE	175-250			
	417-14 PLANTER	250-300			
	416-12 WINDOW BOX	200-225			
	40-15 FLOOR VASE	750-1200			
	411-8 VASE	300-350			
	385-10 PLANTER	150-250			
	778-14 SAND JAR	1500-2200			
	779-20 FLOOR VASE	1000-1500			
	657-8 JARD & PED	2000-2500			
	657-10 JARD & PED	2500-3000			

CANVASSER'S OUTFIT 1896

X	DESCRIPTION	SECONDARY MARKET	PRICE PAID	DATE BOUGHT	CONDITION
	120 ORANGE BANK	100-150			
	21 APPLE BANK	100-150			

CAL ART 1950

X	DESCRIPTION	SECONDARY MARKET	PRICE PAID	DATE BOUGHT	CONDITION
	1507 PIN TRAY	100-150			

CAMEO 1910

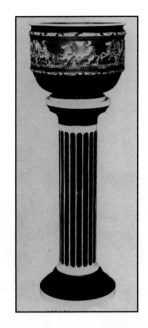

COMPLIMENTS OF THE OHIO HISTORICAL SOCIETY

X	DESCRIPTION	SECONDARY MARKET	PRICE PAID	DATE BOUGHT	CONDITION
	497 18 X 25 JARD. & PED.	3500-4500			

CAMEO 1910

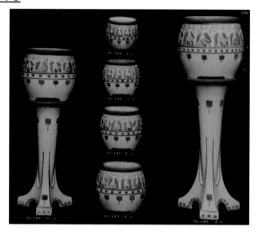

COMPLIMENTS OF THE OHIO HISTORICAL SOCIETY

X	DESCRIPTION	SECONDARY MARKET	PRICE PAID	DATE BOUGHT	CONDITION
	489-6 JARDINIERE	250-350			
	489-7 JARDINIERE	300-375			
	489-8 JARDINIERE	375-425			
	489-9 JARDINIERE	400-475			
	489-10 JARD & PED	2000-2500			
	489-12 JARD & PED	2500-3000			

COMPLIMENTS OF THE OHIO HISTORICAL SOCIETY

X	DESCRIPTION	SECONDARY MARKET	PRICE PAID	DATE BOUGHT	CONDITION
	488 10 X 42 JARD. & PED.	1800-2200			
	488 13 x 42 JARD. & PED.	2000-2600			

CAPRI 1950

GEORGE KRAUSE COLLECTION

X	DESCRIPTION	SECONDARY MARKET	PRICE PAID	DATE BOUGHT	CONDITION
	583-9 VASE	125-175			
	586-12 VASE	150-200			
	593-12 VASE	150-200			
	570-13 WINDOW BOX	100-150			
	581-9 VASE	125-150			
	522-13 PIN TRAY	125-150			
	580-6 VASE	100-150			
	597-7 ASHTRAY	75-100			
	563-10 SEASHELL	100-150			
	531-14 PIN TRAY	125-150			
	599-13 ASHTRAY	100-150			
	534-16 PIN TRAY	125-175			
	598-9 ASHTRAY	100-150			

CAPRI 1950

GEORGE KRAUSE COLLECTION

X	DESCRIPTION	SECONDARY MARKET	PRICE PAID	DATE BOUGHT	CONDITION
	528-9 VASE	100-150			
	552-4 VASE	100-150			
	556-6 SHELL	100-150			
	569-10 WINDOW BOX	100-150			
	529-9 BOWL	100-150			
	532-15 BOWL	125-150			
	530-12 WINDOW BOX	100-150			
	555-7 PLANTER	100-125			
	527-7 BOWL	100-125			
	526-7 PLANTER	100-125			
	583-4 PLANTER	100-125			
	C1009-8 PLANTER	100-150			
	C1010-10 PLANTER	100-125			
	525-5 BOWL	100-125			
	578-8 VASE	100-125			
	357-6 PLANTER	100-125			
	554-6 WINDOW BOX	100-125			
	510-10 WINDOW BOX W/FROG	150-200			
	508-7 PLANTER	100-150			
	557-7 VASE	100-125			

CAPRI 1950

X	DESCRIPTION	SECONDARY MARKET	PRICE PAID	DATE BOUGHT	CONDITION
	508-7 BASKET	100-150			
	599-8 BASKET	100-125			
	510-10 BASKET	150-200			
	C1012-10 BASKET	150-200			
	527-7 BOWL	100-125			
	526-7 BOWL	100-125			
	529-9 BOWL	100-125			
	531-14 BOWL	125-150			
	532-15 BOWL	125-150			
	C1009-8 BOWL	100-125			
	C1010-10 BOWL	100-125			
	555-7 PLANTER	75-100			
	556-6 PLANTER	100-125			
	557-7 PLANTER	100-125			
	558 PLANTER	100-125			
	559-10 WINDOW BOX	100-150			
	572-8 PLANTER VASE	100-150			
	580-6 VASE	100-125			
	582-9 VASE	125-150			
	586-12 VASE	150-200			
	C1003-8 VASE	100-150			
	C1004-9 VASE	125-175			
	C1016-10 VASE	175-250			
	C1017-12 VASE	200-250			
	597-7 ASHTRAY	75-100			
	59-9 ASHTRAY	100-125			
	599-13 ASHTRAY	125-150			
	C1119 SHELL	125-150			
	C1118 SHELL	100-125			
	C1120 SHELL	150-200			
	C1151 CANDLESTICK	100-125			

GEORGE KRAUSE COLLECTION

X	DESCRIPTION	SECONDARY MARKET	PRICE PAID	DATE BOUGHT	CONDITION
	61 X 21/2 X 6 WINDOW BOX	150-200			
	1063-3 CANDLESTICK	150-200			
	1064-3 CANDLESTICK	225-325			
	58-31/2 FROG	100-150			
	1065-4 CANDLESTICK	225-300			
	59-31/2 FROG	100-150			
	57-3 FROG	100-150			
	63-31/2 FROG	100-150			
	65-2-6 PLANTER	150-200			
	64-2-5 PLANTER	150-200			
	1313-12 PITCHER	325-400			
	1312-10 PITCHER	325-400			
	1311-10 PITCHER	300-375			
	1315-15 PITCHER	450-550			
	63-51/2 FROG	100-150			
	1314-8 PITCHER	450-500			
	60-6 FROG	150-200			
	1316-18 PITCHER	600-900			

CARNELIAN I 1915-1927

GEORGE KRAUSE COLLECTION

X	DESCRIPTION	SECONDARY MARKET	PRICE PAID	DATE BOUGHT	CONDITION
	159-6 PLANTER	150-200			
	164-9 PLANTER	200-250			
	165-9 PLANTER	200-250			
	17-3-4½ FROG	100-125			
	161-7 PLANTER	125-150			
	17-2-3½ FROG	100-125			
	167-12 PLANTER	200-250			
	166-10 PLANTER	175-200			
	160-7 PLANTER	125-150			
	162-8 PLANTER	150-175			
	163-8 PLANTER	150-175			
	168-10 PLANTER	175-200			
	170-14 WINDOW BOX	225-275			
	169-12 PLANTER	200-250			

CARNELIAN I 1915-1927

GEORGE KRAUSE COLLECTION

X	DESCRIPTION	SECONDARY MARKET	PRICE PAID	DATE BOUGHT	CONDITION
	336-9 VASE	225-275			
	331-7 VASE	150-200			
	1251-8 WALL POCKET	225-275			
	1253-8 WALL POCKET	250-325			
	1252-8 WALL POCKET	250-325			
	335-9 VASE	225-300			
	333-6 VASE	200-275			
	332-8 VASE	150-200			
	334-8 VASE	250-300			
	339-15 VASE	450-500			
	337-10 VASE	300-350			
	338-12 VASE	350-400			
	340-18 VASE	450-550			

CARNELIAN I 1915-1927

X	DESCRIPTION	GEORGE KRAUSE COLLECTION SECONDARY MARKET	PRICE PAID	DATE BOUGHT	CONDITION
	50-4 FROG	150-225			
	1058-2 CANDLESTICK	150-200			
	15-31/2 FROG	75-100			
	1059-21/2 CANDLESTICK	150-200			
	15-41/2 FROG	100-125			
	1246-7 WALL POCK.	250-300			
	1060-3 CANDLESTICK	200-300			
	56-5 BRIDGE	250-300			
	154-6 CONSOLE	150-200			
	152-4 BOWL	100-150			
	152-5 BOWL	100-150			
	152-6 BOWL	125-175			
	155-8 CONSOLE	150-200			
	154-6 VASE	150-200			
	1247-8 WALL POCK.	300-400			
	306-6 VASE	150-175			
	51-5 VASE	150-200			
	157-14 CONSOLE	300-350			
	153-5 CHALICE	125-175			
	152-5 BOWL	100-150			
	149-9 WALL POCK.	300-350			
	158-12 CONSOLE	275-325			
	315-8 FROG	75-100			
	308-6 WINDOW BOX	200-225			

CARNELIAN I 1915-1927

GEORGE KRAUSE COLLECTION

X	DESCRIPTION	SECONDARY MARKET	PRICE PAID	DATE BOUGHT	CONDITION
	319-9 VASE	275-300			
	311-7 VASE	200-250			
	310-6 VASE	175-200			
	308-7 VASE	200-250			
	310-7 VASE	200-250			
	318-8 VASE	250-350			
	314-9 VASE	275-300			
	313-9 VASE	275-300			
	311-6 VASE	150-175			
	317-8 VASE	200-250			
	316-8 VASE	200-250			
	921-15 FLOOR VASE	400-450			
	324-10 VASE	300-325			
	515-10 VASE	225-275			
	323-10 VASE	225-275			
	325-12 VASE	275-300			
	327-18 FLOOR VASE	400-450			

CARNELIAN II 1915–1931

X	DESCRIPTION	GEORGE KRAUSE COLLECTION			
		SECONDARY MARKET	PRICE PAID	DATE BOUGHT	CONDITION
	440-8 VASE	600-700			
	439-9 VASE	500-600			
	444-12 VASE	800-1200			
	443-13 VASE	1000-1500			
	441-8 VASE	600-700			
	446-12 VASE	1500-2000			
	442-12 VASE	1000-1800			
	445-12 VASE	1200-1600			
	450-14 FLOOR VASE	2800-3500			

X	DESCRIPTION	GEORGE KRAUSE COLLECTION			
		SECONDARY MARKET	PRICE PAID	DATE BOUGHT	CONDITION
	460-28 FLOOR VASE	3500-5000			
	461-28 FLOOR VASE	3500-5000			
	459-28 FLOOR VASE	3000-4000			

CARNELIAN II 1915-1931

		GEORGE KRAUSE COLLECTION			
		SECONDARY	PRICE	DATE	
X	DESCRIPTION	MARKET	PAID	BOUGHT	CONDITION
	456-20 FLOOR VASE	3200-4200			
	458-24 FLOOR VASE	2800-3800			
	457-24 FLOOR VASE	2800-3800			

Anna M. Young

George F. Young

COMPLIMENTS OF THE OHIO HISTORICAL SOCIETY

X	DESCRIPTION	SECONDARY MARKET	PRICE PAID	DATE BOUGHT	CONDITION
	516-4 JARDINIERE	175-200			
	516-4 JARDINIERE	200-225			
	516-7 JARDINIERE	275-300			
	516-8 JARDINIERE	300-325			
	515-4 (MATT) JARD.	175-200			
	515-6 (MATT) JARD.	225-250			
	515-8 (MATT) JARD.	300-325			
	515-10 (MATT) JARD.	400-425			
	514-4 JARDINIERE	175-200			
	514-7 JARDINIERE	275-300			
	514-8 JARDINIERE	300-325			
	514-10 JARDINIERE	400-425			
	516-4 (MATT) JARD.	175-200			
	516-5 (MATT) JARD.	200-225			
	516-7 (MATT) JARD.	275-300			
	516-8 (MATT) JARD.	300-325			
	515-4 JARDINIERE	175-200			
	515-6 JARDINIERE	225-250			
	515-8 JARDINIERE	300-325			
	515-10 JARDINIERE	400-425			
	514-4 (MATT) JARD.	175-200			
	514-7 (MATT) JARD.	275-300			
	514-8 (MATT) JARD.	300-325			
	514-10 (MATT) JARD.	400-425			

CERAMIC DESIGN EARLY 1900

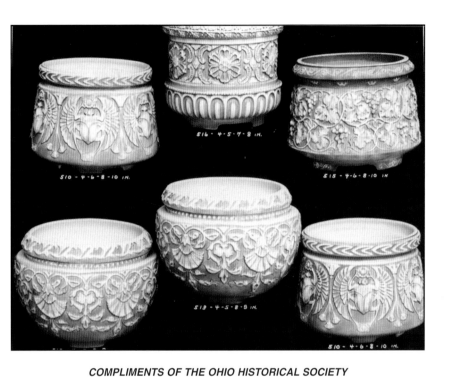

X	DESCRIPTION	SECONDARY MARKET	PRICE PAID	DATE BOUGHT	CONDITION
	510-4 JARDINIERE	200-250			
	510-6 JARDINIERE	275-300			
	510-8 JARDINIERE	325-350			
	510-10 JARDINIERE	400-425			
	516-4 JARDINIERE	175-200			
	516-5 JARDINIERE	200-225			
	516-7 JARDINIERE	300-325			
	516-8 JARDINIERE	350-400			
	515-4 JARDINIERE	175-200			
	515-6 JARDINIERE	250-275			
	515-8 JARDINIERE	300-325			
	515-10 JARDINIERE	400-450			
	513-4 JARDINIERE	175-200			
	513-5 JARDINIERE	200-225			
	513-8 JARDINIERE	300-325			
	513-9 JARDINIERE	350-400			

JARDINIERES NUMBER WITH 510 AND 513 ARE A TWO PIECE JAR

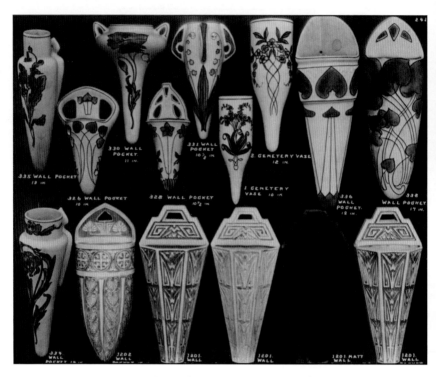

COMPLIMENTS OF THE OHIO HISTORICAL SOCIETY

X	DESCRIPTION	SECONDARY MARKET	PRICE PAID	DATE BOUGHT	CONDITION
	335-12 WALL POCKET	700-800			
	330-11 WALL POCKET	600-700			
	331-10 1/2 WALL POCKET	600-700			
	2-12 CEMETARY VASE	500-600			
	326-10 WALL POCKET	500-600			
	328-10 1/2 WALL POCKET	500-600			
	1-10 CEMETARY VASE	500-600			
	336-18 WALL POCKET	800-1000			
	338-17 WALL POCKET	800-1000			
	334-14 WALL POCKET	750-850			
	1202-15 WALL POCKET	500-600			
	1201-14 1/2 WALL POCKET (ALL 4 DESIGNS)	500-600			

CERAMIC DESIGN EARLY 1900

COMPLIMENTS OF THE OHIO HISTORICAL SOCIETY

X	DESCRIPTION	SECONDARY MARKET	PRICE PAID	DATE BOUGHT	CONDITION
	462-5 JARDINIERE	200-250			
	462-6 JARDINIERE	225-250			
	462-7 JARDINIERE	200-225			
	462-8 JARDINIERE	250-275			
	462-9 JARDINIERE	300-325			
	462-10 JARDINIERE	350-400			
	523-4 JARDINIERE	125-150			
	523-5 JARDINIERE	150-175			
	523-6 JARDINIERE	175-200			
	523-7 JARDINIERE	200-225			
	523-8 JARDINIERE	250-275			
	523-9 JARDINIERE	300-325			
	523-10 JARDINIERE	350-400			
	532-8 JARDINIERE	250-275			
	532-9 JARDINIERE	275-325			
	532-10 JARDINIERE	350-400			
	532-12 JARDINIERE	450-500			
	532-14 JARDINIERE	550-600			
	532-16 JARDINIERE	600-650			
	489-4$^{1/2}$ JARDINIERE	175-250			
	489-7 JARDINIERE	200-225			
	489-8 JARDINIERE	250-275			
	489-9 JARDINIERE	300-325			
	489-10 JARDINIERE	350-400			
	489-12 JARDINIERE	450-500			
	531-7 JARDINIERE	200-225			
	531-8 JARDINIERE	250-275			
	531-9 JARDINIERE	300-325			
	531-10 JARDINIERE	350-400			
	510-4 JARDINIERE	125-150			
	510-6 JARDINIERE	175-200			
	510-8 JARDINIERE	250-275			
	510-10 JARDINIERE	350-400			
	513-4 JARDINIERE	125-150			
	513-5 JARDINIERE	200-225			
	513-8 JARDINIERE	250-275			

CERAMIC DESIGN EARLY 1900

CONTINUED FROM PAGE 62

X	DESCRIPTION	SECONDARY MARKET	PRICE PAID	DATE BOUGHT	CONDITION
	513-9 JARDINIERE	300-325			
	514-4 JARDINIERE	125-150			
	514-7 JARDINIERE	200-225			
	514-8 JARDINIERE	250-275			
	514-10 JARDINIERE	350-400			
	515-4 JARDINIERE	125-150			
	515-6 JARDINIERE	175-200			
	515-8 JARDINIERE	250-275			
	515-9 JARDINIERE	300-325			
	516-4 JARDINIERE	125-150			
	516-5 JARDINIERE	150-175			
	516-7 JARDINIERE	200-275			
	516-8 JARDINIERE	250-275			
	507-4 JARDINIERE	125-150			
	507-6 JARDINIERE	175-200			
	507-8 JARDINIERE	250-275			

PICTURES NOT SHOWN:

	1203-10 WALLPOCKET	300-400			
	1203-12 WALLPOCKET	400-500			
	1204-10 WALLPOCKET	300-400			
	1204-12 WALLPOCKET	400-500			

COMPLIMENTS OF THE OHIO HISTORICAL SOCEITY

X	DESCRIPTION	SECONDARY MARKET	PRICE PAID	DATE BOUGHT	CONDITION
	527-8 PLANTER	400-500			
	532-8 PLANTER	400-500			
	532-9 PLANTER	500-600			
	532-10 PLANTER	600-700			
	532-12 PLANTER	700-800			

ALL PLANTERS ARE WITH LINERS AND BRASS HOLDERS

CERAMIC DESIGN EARLY 1900

COMPLIMENTS OF THE OHIO HISTORICAL SOCIETY

X	DESCRIPTION	SECONDARY MARKET	PRICE PAID	DATE BOUGHT	CONDITION
	205-3 PLANTER	125-150			
	205-5 PLANTER	175-200			
	204-3 PLANTER	125-150			
	204-4 PLANTER	150-175			
	204-5 PLANTER	175-200			
	202-4 PLANTER	150-175			
	202-5 PLANTER	175-200			
	202-6 PLANTER	200-225			
	203-4 (MATT) PLANTER	150-175			
	203-5 (MATT) PLANTER	175-200			
	203-6 (MATT) PLANTER	200-225			
	201-4 Yellow Planter	150-175			
	201-5 Yellow Planter	175-200			
	201-6 Yellow Planter	200-225			
	201-7 Yellow Planter	225-250			
	201-4 (MATT) PLANTER	150-175			
	201-5 (MATT) PLANTER	175-200			
	201-6 (MATT) PLANTER	200-225			
	201-7 (MATT) PLANTER	225-250			
	201-4 (GREEN) PLANTER	150-175			
	201-5 (GREEN) PLANTER	175-200			
	201-6 (GREEN) PLANTER	200-225			
	201-7 (GREEN) PLANTER	225-250			
	203-4 (LAND/S) PLANTER	150-175			
	203-5 LAND/S) PLANTER	175-200			
	203-6 (LAND/S) PLANTER	200-225			
	206-4 PLANTER	150-175			
	206-5 PLANTER	175-200			
	206-6 PLANTER	200-225			
	206-7 PLANTER	225-250			

CERAMIC DESIGN EARLY 1900

COMPLIMENTS OF THE OHIO HISTORICAL SOCIETY

X	DESCRIPTION	SECONDARY MARKET	PRICE PAID	DATE BOUGHT	CONDITION
	216-4 PLANTER	175-200			
	204-3 PLANTER	50-75			
	204-4 PLANTER	75-100			
	204-5 PLANTER	100-125			
	215-4 (MATT) PLANTER	175-200			
	215-5 (MATT) PLANTER	200-225			
	215-4 (PERSIAN) PLANTER	175-200			
	215-5 (PERSIAN) PLANTER	200-225			
	217-5 PLANTER	200-225			
	218-3 1/2 (PERSIAN) PLANTER	100-125			
	218-4 (PERSIAN) PLANTER	125-150			
	218-5 (PERSIAN) PLANTER	150-175			
	218-3 1/2 (MATT) PLANTER	100-125			
	218-4 (MATT) PLANTER	125-150			
	218-5 (MATT) PLANTER	150-175			
	214-4 (PERSIAN) PLANTER	125-150			
	214-5 (PERSIAN) PLANTER	150-175			
	214-4 (MATT) PLANTER	125-150			
	214-5 (MATT) PLANTER	150-175			
	213-3 1/2 (MATT) PLANTER	100-125			
	213-4 1/4 (MATT) PLANTER	125-150			
	213-5 1/4 (MATT)	150-175			
	213-3 1/2 (PERSIAN) PLANTER	100-125			
	213-4 1/4 (PERSIAN) PLANTER	125-150			
	213-5 1/4 (PERSIAN) PLANTER	150-175			
	210-4X8 PLANTER	350-400			
	211-3 1/2 X6 PLANTER	300-350			
	209-6 PLANTER	250-300			
	208-7 PLANTER	325-350			
	212-10 1/2 PLANTER	600-700			

CHERRY BLOSSOM 1932

X	DESCRIPTION	SECONDARY MARKET	PRICE PAID	DATE BOUGHT	CONDITION
	627-5 JARDINIERE	325-375			
	350-5 JARDINIERE	400-450			
	627-4 JARDINIERE	275-325			
	627-7 JARDINIERE	475-525			
	627-6 JARDINIERE	375-450			
	627-8 JARD. & PED.	2500-3500			
	627-10 JARDINIERE	1000-1200			
	627-9 JARDINIERE	900-1000			
	627-10 JARD. & PED.	3500-4500			

CHERRY BLOSSOM 1932

627-12" 620-7" 625-8" 623-7" 624-8" 626-10"
627-4" 621-6" 1090-4" 240-8"
239-5" 1270-8" 617-3½" 628-15" 622-7" 618-5" 619-5"

COMPLIMENTS OF THE OHIO HISTORICAL SOCEITY

X	DESCRIPTION	SECONDARY MARKET	PRICE PAID	DATE BOUGHT	CONDITION
	627-12 VASE	1600-2100			
	620-7 VASE	350-400			
	625-8 VASE	850-950			
	623-7 VASE	550-600			
	624-8 VASE	550-600			
	626-10 VASE	850-950			
	627-4 JARDINIERE	275-325			
	621-6 VASE	500-575			
	1090-4 CANDLESTICK	350-400			
	240-8 WINDOW BOX	400-450			
	239-5 PLANTER	350-400			
	1270-8 WALL POCKET	1000-1500			
	617-31/2 VASE	350-400			
	628-15 FLOOR VASE	2500-3000			
	622-7 VASE	475-525			
	618-5 VASE	400-425			
	619-5 VASE	350-400			

CHERRY JUBILEE   EARLY 1900

X	DESCRIPTION	SECONDARY MARKET	PRICE PAID	DATE BOUGHT	CONDITION
	MUG	150-200			
	81/2" TEAPOT	200-250			
	6" TRIVET	100-175			
	111/2" CHOCOLATE POT	350-450			

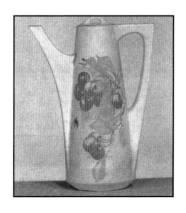

CHLORON 1907

COMPLIMENTS OF THE OHIO HISTORICAL SOCEITY

X	DESCRIPTION	SECONDARY MARKET	PRICE PAID	DATE BOUGHT	CONDITION
	7-16 VASE	700-900			
	3-16 VASE	800-1000			
	344-12 WALL CANDLESTICK	1100-1200			
	338-17½ WALL POCKET	1500-1600			
	336-18 WALL POCKET	1200-1400			
	330-11½ CEMETARY VASE	400-450			
	342-2½ X 9 GOOD NIGHT CANDLESTICK	275-325			
	341-7 CANDLESTICK	500-600			
	358-8½ WALL POCKET	1200-1500			
	337-15¾ WALL POCKET	1200-1500			
	339-12½ WALL CANDLESTICK	2000-2500			
	346-9½ WALL POCKET	1500-1800			
	345-9¼ WALL POCKET	1500-1800			

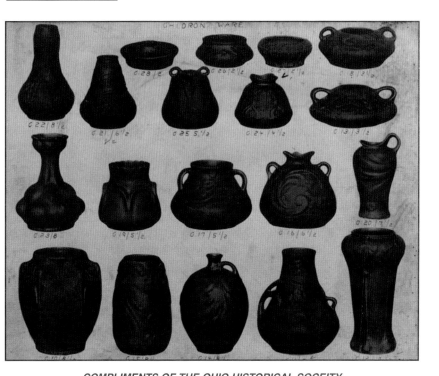

COMPLIMENTS OF THE OHIO HISTORICAL SOCEITY

X	DESCRIPTION	SECONDARY MARKET	PRICE PAID	DATE BOUGHT	CONDITION
	C22-8$^{1/2}$ VASE	350-400			
	C21-6$^{1/2}$ VASE	300-350			
	C28-2 CANDLESTICK	100-150			
	C25-5$^{1/2}$ VASE	275-325			
	C26-2$^{1/2}$ BOWL	100-125			
	C24-4$^{1/2}$ VASE	250-300			
	C27-2$^{1/2}$ BOWL	100-125			
	C18-3$^{1/2}$ BOWL	200-250			
	C13-3$^{1/2}$ BOWL	225-250			
	C23-8 VASE	375-425			
	C19-5$^{1/2}$ VASE	325-375			
	C17-5$^{1/2}$ VASE	350-400			
	C16-6$^{1/2}$ VASE	375-425			
	C20-7$^{1/2}$ VASE	225-275			
	C10-8$^{1/2}$ VASE	600-700			
	C15-8$^{1/2}$ VASE	400-450			
	C14-8$^{1/2}$ VASE	400-500			
	C11-9$^{1/2}$ VASE	450-500			
	C12-10$^{1/2}$ VASE	500-600			

CHLORON 1907

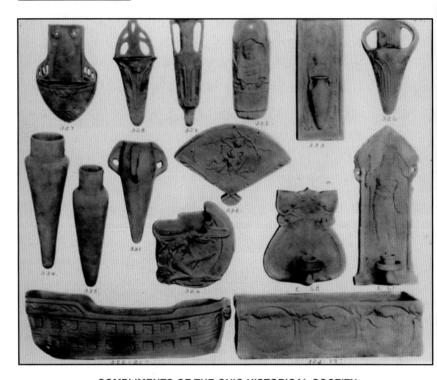

X	DESCRIPTION	SECONDARY MARKET	PRICE PAID	DATE BOUGHT	CONDITION
	327 WALL POCKET	750-850			
	328 WALL POCKET	600-700			
	329 WALL POCKET	675-750			
	325 WALL POCKET	650-750			
	333 WALL POCKET	1000-1200			
	326 WALL POCKET	400-500			
	334 CEMETARY VASE	550-600			
	335 CEMETARY VASE	500-600			
	331 WALL POCKET	400-500			
	332 WALL POCKET	1000-1200			
	324 PLANTER	1000-1200			
	E62 WALL CANDLESTICK	900-1100			
	E61 WALL CANDLESTICK	1100-1300			
	322-21 WINDOW BOX	1300-1500			
	323-19 WINDOW BOX	1200-1400			

CHOCOLATE/COFFEE/TEAPOTS OR SETS 1910

X	DESCRIPTION	SECONDARY MARKET	PRICE PAID	DATE BOUGHT	CONDITION
	BLUE CHOC. POT	300-350			
	BLUE TEAPOT	300-350			
	BLUE COFFEE POT	300-350			
	UNIQUE COFFEE POT	300-350			
	UNIQUE TEAPOT	300-350			
	UNIQUE CHOC. POT	300-350			
	DECOR. CHOC. POT	400-450			
	DECOR. PITCHER	325-375			
	DECOR. TEAPOT	375-425			
	DECOR. CREAMER	100-125			
	DECORATED SUGAR	125-150			

CLEMENA 1934

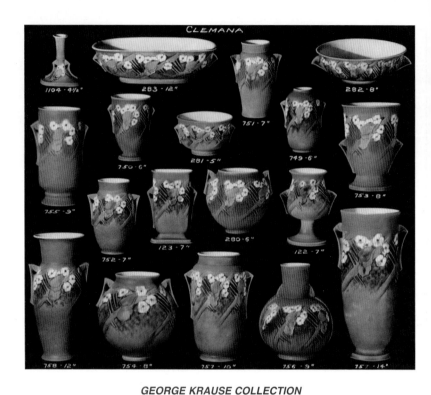

GEORGE KRAUSE COLLECTION

X	DESCRIPTION	SECONDARY MARKET	PRICE PAID	DATE BOUGHT	CONDITION
	1104-4 1/2 CANDLESTICK	275-325			
	283-12 WINDOW BOX	350-400			
	751-7 VASE	275-300			
	282-8 WINDOW BOX	300-350			
	755-9 VASE	325-425			
	750-6 VASE	250-300			
	281-5 PLANTER	175-225			
	749-6 VASE	250-300			
	753-8 VASE	350-400			
	752-7 VASE	275-300			
	123-7 VASE	250-275			
	280-6 VASE	250-300			
	122-7 VASE	275-325			
	758-12 VASE	500-550			
	754-8 VASE	350-400			
	757-10 VASE	400-450			
	756-9 VASE	375-425			
	757-14 FLOOR VASE	400-450			

CLEMATIS 1944

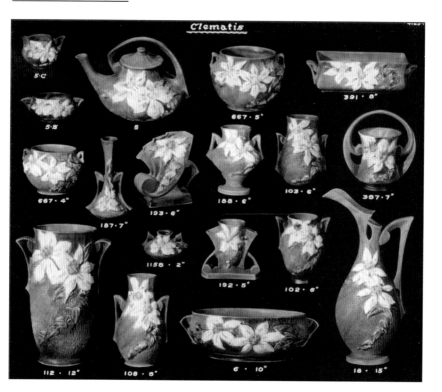

GEORGE KRAUSE COLLECTION

X	DESCRIPTION	SECONDARY MARKET	PRICE PAID	DATE BOUGHT	CONDITION
	5C CREAMER	100-125			
	5S SUGAR	100-125			
	5 TEAPOT	250-275			
	667-5 JARDINIERE	150-200			
	391-8 WINDOW BOX	125-175			
	667-4 JARDINIERE	100-150			
	187-7 VASE	100-125			
	193-6 CORNUCOPIA VASE	100-125			
	188-6 VASE	100-125			
	103-6 VASE	100-150			
	387-7 BASKET	200-250			
	1158-2 CANDLESTICK	100-125			
	192-5 TRIPLE VASE	125-150			
	102-6 VASE	100-125			
	112-12 VASE	250-325			
	108-8 VASE	100-175			
	6-10 WINDOW BOX	200-250			
	18-15 EWER	300-350			

CLEMATIS 1944

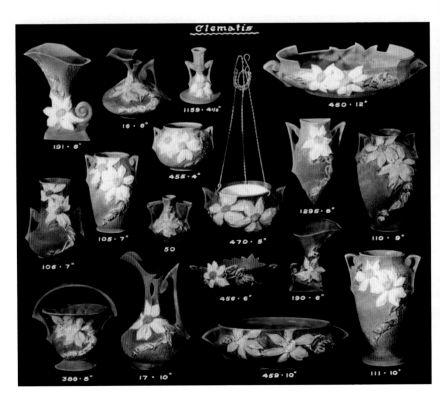

CLEMATIS 1944

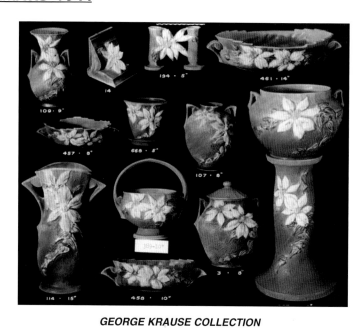

GEORGE KRAUSE COLLECTION

X	DESCRIPTION	SECONDARY MARKET	PRICE PAID	DATE BOUGHT	CONDITION
	109-9 VASE	150-200			
	14 BOOKENDS	250-300			
	194-5 BRIDGE	100-150			
	461-14 COMPOTE	275-325			
	457-8 COMPOTE	150-175			
	668-5 PLANTER	175-225			
	107-8 VASE	175-200			
	114-15 FLOOR VASE	400-500			
	389-10 BASKET	250-325			
	458-10 COMPOTE	200-275			
	3-8 COOKIE JAR	400-500			
	667-8 JARD. & PED.	800-1200			

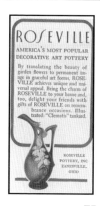

MAY 1945 AD
FOR THE
CLEMATIS LINE

COLONIAL TURN OF THE CENTURY

COMPLIMENTS OF THE OHIO HISTORICAL SOCIETY

X	DESCRIPTION	SECONDARY MARKET	PRICE PAID	DATE BOUGHT	CONDITION
	SOAP DISH	125-150			
	SHAVING MUG	100-125			
	TOOTHBRUSH HOLDER	125-150			
	SMALL PITCHER	150-200			
	BASIN	200-225			
	TALL PITCHER	225-275			
	CHAMBER POT	275-350			
	COMBINETTE POT	375-425			

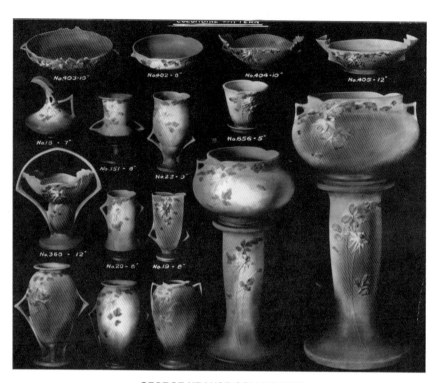

GEORGE KRAUSE COLLECTION

X	DESCRIPTION	SECONDARY MARKET	PRICE PAID	DATE BOUGHT	CONDITION
	403-10 COMPOTE	150-175			
	402-8 COMPOTE	100-125			
	404-10 PLANTER	150-175			
	405-12 PLANTER	200-225			
	18-7 EWER	175-225			
	151-8 VASE	150-200			
	22-9 VASE	175-225			
	656-5 PLANTER	175-200			
	368-12 BASKET	325-375			
	20-8 VASE	150-175			
	19-8 VASE	150-175			
	25-12 VASE	450-500			
	24-10 VASE	200-225			
	23-10 VASE	275-325			
	655-8 JARD. & PED.	1000-1500			
	655-10 JARD. & PED.	1600-2000			

COLUMBINE 1941

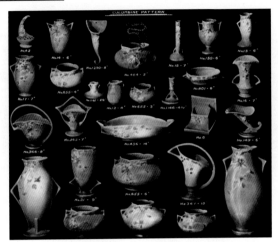

X	DESCRIPTION	GEORGE KRAUSE COLLECTION SECONDARY MARKET	PRICE PAID	DATE BOUGHT	CONDITION
	42 FROG	125-175			
	14-6 VASE	125-150			
	290-8 WALL POCKET	250-300			
	464-5 HANGING BASKET	275-300			
	15-7 VASE	100-150			
	150-6 VASE	125-150			
	13-6 VASE	75-100			
	17-7 VASE	175-225			
	655-4 JARDINIERE	125-150			
	1145-2$1/2$ CANDLESTICK	150-175			
	12-4 VASE	100-125			
	655-3 JARDINIERE	100-125			
	1146-4$1/2$ CANDLESTICK	150-175			
	401-6 COMPOTE	100-125			
	16-7 VASE	150-175			
	366-8 BASKET	300-350			
	365-7 BASKET	225-300			
	406-14 COMPOTE	225-275			
	8 BOOKENDS	300-350			
	149-6 CORNUCOPIA	125-175			
	21-9 VASE	175-225			
	655-6 JARDINIERE	225-250			
	367-10 BASKET	300-350			
	26-14 FLOOR VASE	500-600			
	655-5 JARDINIERE	175-200			
	400-6 JARDINIERE	150-175			
	399-4 JARDINIERE	100-125			
	27-16 FLOOR VASE	550-650			

COMPLIMENTS OF THE OHIO HISTORICAL SOCIETY

X	DESCRIPTION	SECONDARY MARKET	PRICE PAID	DATE BOUGHT	CONDITION
	218-8 VASE	175-200			
	215-7 VASE	150-175			
	235-6 VASE	125-150			
	213-6 VASE	125-175			
	1048-8 CANDLESTICK	325-425			
	1232-8 WALL POCKETS	300-350			
	214-6 VASE	125-175			
	1229-12 WALL POCK.	350-450			
	1228-10 WALL POCK.	250-300			
	216-7 VASE	150-175			
	212-6 VASE	125-150			
	235-8 VASE	175-200			
	217-8 VASE	150-200			
	219-10 VASE	200-250			
	220-12 VASE	250-300			
	235-10 VASE	250-300			

CORINTHIAN 1923

COMPLIMENTS OF THE OHIO HISTORICAL SOCIETY

X	DESCRIPTION	SECONDARY MARKET	PRICE PAID	DATE BOUGHT	CONDITION
	601-6 JARDINIERE	150-200			
	601-8 JARDINIERE	250-350			
	601-9 JARDINIERE	300-400			
	235-12 VASE	200-275			
	235-15 FLOOR VASE	300-400			
	601-12 JARD. & PED.	2500-3500			
	60-101 JARD. & PED.	1500-2000			

WORKERS FROM THE ROSEVILLE PLANT

COMPLIMENTS OF THE OHIO HISTORICAL SOCIETY

X	DESCRIPTION	SECONDARY MARKET	PRICE PAID	DATE BOUGHT	CONDITION
	14-21/2 FROG	75-100			
	14-31/2 FROG	75-100			
	256-5 JARDINIERE	150-175			
	336-6 HANG. BASK.	250-300			
	336-8 HANG. BASK.	300-400			
	601-5 JARDINIERE	150-175			
	603-5 PLANTERW/DISH	175-225			
	42 BRIDGE	175-225			
	37 BRIDGE	250-300			
	121-5 JARDINIERE	125-150			
	235-8 JARD. W/LINER	150-200			
	235-6 JARDINIERE	125-150			
	235-7 JARD. W/LINER	150-175			
	256-6 JARD. W/LINER	125-150			
	15-8 COMPOTE	200-250			
	601-7 JARDINIERE	200-250			
	121-7 JARDINIERE	125-150			
	603-6 PLANTER W/DISH	225-275			

CORNELIAN COOKING WARE 1900

COMPLIMENTS OF THE OHIO HISTORICAL SOCIETY

X	DESCRIPTION	SECONDARY MARKET	PRICE PAID	DATE BOUGHT	CONDITION
	SOAP DISH	125-150			
	SHAVING MUG	125-150			
	BRUSH HOLDER	150-175			
	MOUTH EWER	200-250			
	EWER & BASIN	500-750			
	CHAMBER	350-400			
	COMBINETTE	450-550			

ARIEL VIEW OF THE ROSEVILLE PLANT, ZANESVILLE, OHIO

CORNELIAN COOKING WARE 1900

X	DESCRIPTION	SECONDARY MARKET	PRICE PAID	DATE BOUGHT	CONDITION
	6 PT. PITCHER	200-225			
	3 PT. PITCHER	150-175			
	2 PT. PITCHER	125-150			
	1 PT. PITCHER	100-125			
	CRACKER JAR	250-275			
	OATMEAL JAR	100-150			
	CUSTARD SET	50-75			
	4" SHERRED EGG CUP	50-75			
	5" SHERRED EGG CUP	75-100			
	BUTTER	200-225			
	FRUIT DISH	200-225			
	7" MIXING BOWL	100-125			
	8" MIXING BOWL	125-150			
	9" MIXING BOWL	150-175			
	10" MIXING BOWL	175-200			
	12" MIXING BOWL	200-225			
	14" MIXING BOWL	250-300			
	4" PUDDING DISH	50-75			
	5" PUDDING DISH	75-100			
	6" PUDDING DISH	100-125			
	7" PUDDING DISH	125-150			
	8" PUDDING DISH	150-175			
	9" PUDDING DISH	175-200			
	10" PUDDING DISH	200-225			
	12" PUDDING DISH	225-250			
	PUNCH BOWL	350-400			

CORNELIAN COOKING WARE 1900

COMPLIMENTS OF THE OHIO HISTORICAL SOCIETY

X	DESCRIPTION	SECONDARY MARKET	PRICE PAID	DATE BOUGHT	CONDITION
	E1 PITCHER	100-125			
	E2 PITCHER	125-150			
	E3 PITCHER	150-175			
	E4 PITCHER	175-200			
	E5 PITCHER	200-225			
	TOBACCO JAR	350-400			
	D2 PITCHER	150-175			
	D3 PITCHER	175-200			
	BERRY SET	550-650			
	BREAD & MILK SET	250-350			

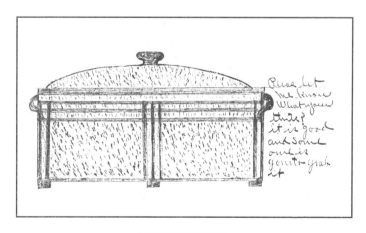

ARTIST DRAWING

COSMOS 1929

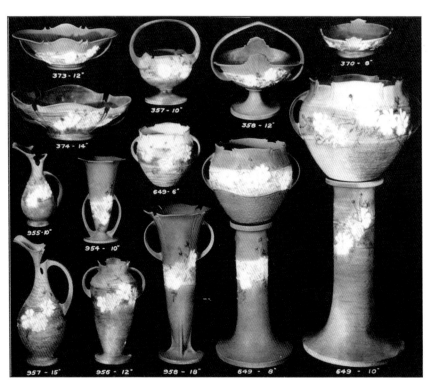

GEORGE KRAUSE COLLECTION

X	DESCRIPTION	SECONDARY MARKET	PRICE PAID	DATE BOUGHT	CONDITION
	373-12 BOWL	300-350			
	357-10 BASKET	300-350			
	358-12 BASKET	450-500			
	370-8 BOWL	200-225			
	374-14 BOWL	275-325			
	649-6 JARDINIERE	250-300			
	955-10 EWER	275-375			
	954-10 VASE	250-350			
	957-15 EWER	600-800			
	956-12 VASE	400-500			
	958-18 FLOOR VASE	800-1200			
	649-8 JARD. & PED.	1200-1500			
	649-10 JARD. & PED.	2000-2200			

COSMOS 1929

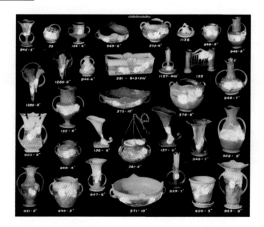

COMPLIMENTS OF THE OHIO HISTORICAL SOCIETY

X	DESCRIPTION	SECONDARY MARKET	PRICE PAID	DATE BOUGHT	CONDITION
	945-5 VASE	100-150			
	39 FROG	100-175			
	134-4 VASE	100-175			
	369-4 VASE	125-150			
	375-4 JARDINIERE	175-225			
	1136 CANDLESTICK	150-200			
	649-3 JARDINIERE	100-150			
	946-6 VASE	125-150			
	1286-8 WALL POCKET	450-550			
	1285-6 WALL POCKET	400-500			
	944-4 VASE	100-125			
	381-9X3X3 1/2 WINDOW BOX	250-350			
	1137-4 1/2 CANDLESTICK	150-200			
	131 BRIDGE	150-200			
	135-8 VASE	200-275			
	372-10 COMPOTE	200-250			
	376-6 JARDINIERE	225-325			
	948-7 VASE	175-200			
	950-8 VASE	275-325			
	649-4 JARDINIERE	100-150			
	136-6 CORNUCOPIA	150-175			
	361-5 HANGING BASKET	300-375			
	137-8 CORNUCOPIA	150-225			
	949-7 VASE	150-225			
	952-9 VASE	225-300			
	951-8 VASE	225-300			
	649-5 JARDINIERE	175-200			
	947-6 VASE	150-200			
	371-10 COMPOTE	300-350			
	959-7 VASE	150-175			
	650-5 PLANTER	275-325			
	953-9 VASE	275-300			

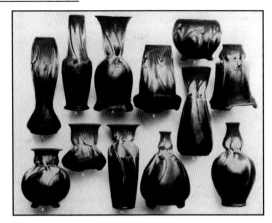

COMPLIMENTS OF THE OHIO HISTORICAL SOCIETY

X	DESCRIPTION	SECONDARY MARKET	PRICE PAID	DATE BOUGHT	CONDITION
	1 VASE	900-1100			
	2 VASE	900-1100			
	3 VASE	1200-1400			
	4 VASE	900-1100			
	5 JARDINIERE	800-1000			
	6 VASE	1000-1200			
	7 VASE	1000-1200			
	8 VASE	1000-1200			
	9 VASE	800-1000			
	10 VASE	1100-1300			
	11 VASE	1200-1400			
	12 VASE	1100-1300			

MAY 1928 AD FOR
THE CREMONA LINE

CREMONA 1927

GEORGE KRAUSE COLLECTION

X	DESCRIPTION	SECONDARY MARKET	PRICE PAID	DATE BOUGHT	CONDITION
	353-5 PLANTER	150-200			
	72-4 PLANTER	100-175			
	351-4 VASE	150-200			
	176-6 PLANTER	150-175			
	74-6 VASE	175-225			
	75 FROG	150-175			
	352-5 VASE	150-200			
	177-8 BOWL	150-200			
	73-5 VASE	125-175			
	357-8 VASE	250-300			
	355-8 VASE	200-275			
	1068-4 CANDLESTICK	175-275			
	178-8 BOWL	175-225			
	354-7 VASE	175-225			
	356-8 VASE	200-275			
	360-10 VASE	300-350			
	361-12 VASE	350-400			
	362-12 VASE	350-400			
	358-10 VASE	275-325			
	359-10 VASE	300-375			

PICTURES NOT SHOWN:

	DESCRIPTION	SECONDARY MARKET	PRICE PAID	DATE BOUGHT	CONDITION
	TANKARD	200-250			
	STEINS	100-125			
	SMOKER SET	1200-1500			
	TRAY	200-300			
	ASHTRAY	150-200			
	CIGAR JAR	350-450			
	MATCH HOLDER	300-400			
	DRESSER SET #1	1000-1500			
	TRAY	200-300			
	POWDER BOX	250-350			
	HAIR RECEIVER	300-400			
	RING STAND	200-300			
	TOBACCO JAR	350-450			
	CANDLESTICK	300-400			
	TEASET #2	400-500			
	SUGAR	150-200			
	CREAMER	150-200			
	TEASET #3	300-350			

CROCUS 1910-1914

X	DESCRIPTION	SECONDARY MARKET	PRICE PAID	DATE BOUGHT	CONDITION
	VASE	500-600			
	JARDINIERE (Bottom)	800-900			

CUSPIDORS 1892 TO 1920s

X	DESCRIPTION	SECONDARY MARKET	PRICE PAID	DATE BOUGHT	CONDITION
	606 BLENDED	175-225			
	602 BLENDED	175-225			
	607 BLENDED	175-225			
	608 BLENDED	175-225			
	603 BLENDED	250-300			
	601 BLENDED	175-225			
	608 BLENDED	175-225			
	604 BLENDED	175-225			

COMPLIMENTS OF THE OHIO HISTORICAL SOCIETY

	909 MATT GREEN	350-400			
	909 TOURIST	1500-2000			
	909 ROZANE ROYAL	1500-2000			

CUSPIDORS 1892 TO 1920s

COMPLIMENTS OF THE OHIO HISTORICAL SOCIETY

X	DESCRIPTION	SECONDARY MARKET	PRICE PAID	DATE BOUGHT	CONDITION
	612 BLENDED	175-225			
	608 BLENDED	175-225			
	611 BLENDED	150-175			
	614 BLENDED	175-225			
	608 BLENDED	175-225			
	612 BLENDED	175-225			
	614 BLENDED	175-225			
	613 BLENDED	150-175			
	612 BLENDED	150-175			
	613 BLENDED	150-175			
	611 BLENDED	150-175			
	611 BLENDED	150-175			

COMPLIMENTS OF THE OHIO HISTORICAL SOCIETY

X	DESCRIPTION	SECONDARY MARKET	PRICE PAID	DATE BOUGHT	CONDITION
	615 COBALT BLUE W/GOLD	175-225			
	626 MATT GREEN	175-225			
	627 MATT GREEN	175-225			

CUSPIDORS 1892 TO 1920s

COMPLIMENTS OF THE OHIO HISTORICAL SOCIETY

X	DESCRIPTION	SECONDARY MARKET	PRICE PAID	DATE BOUGHT	CONDITION
	610 COLONIAL BLUE	150-175			
	610 COLONIAL YELLOW	150-175			
	610 COLONIAL GREEN	150-175			
	607 COLONIAL YELLOW	175-225			
	607 COLONIAL GREEN	175-225			
	607 COLONIAL BLUE	175-225			
	609 COLONIAL GREEN	200-250			
	609 COLONIAL BLUE	200-250			
	609 COL. LAVENDER	200-250			

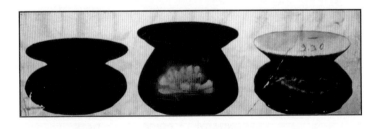

	629 COBALT BLUE	175-225			
	626 ROZANE ROYAL	1000-1250			
	907 BLENDED	175-225			

COMPLIMENTS OF THE OHIO HISTORICAL SOCIETY

X	DESCRIPTION	SECONDARY MARKET	PRICE PAID	DATE BOUGHT	CONDITION
	76-6 TRIPLE BUD VASE	200-250			
	78-8 TRIPLE BUD VASE	200-250			
	77-7 BUD VASE	200-250			
	363-6 VASE	125-175			
	79-6 BRIDGE	150-200			
	343-6 JARDINIERE	300-350			
	1069-3 CANDLESTICK	175-225			
	179-8 COMPOTE	125-175			
	1258-8 WALL POCKET	300-400			
	1259-10 WALL POCKET	400-500			
	365-8 VASE	250-300			
	180-8 COMPOTE	175-225			
	364-6 VASE	175-225			
	366-8 VASE	175-250			
	367-8 VASE	200-275			
	368-10 VASE	275-375			
	369-10 VASE	300-400			
	370-12 VASE	400-500			

DAHLROSE MIDDLE 1920s

X	DESCRIPTION	SECONDARY MARKET	PRICE PAID	DATE BOUGHT	CONDITION
	614-9 JARDINIERE	300-400			
	375-14 WINDOW BOX	350-450			
	375-10 WINDOW BOX	300-400			
	614-8 JARD. & PED.	1200-1600			
	614-6 JARDINIERE	200-225			
	614-7 JARDINIERE	225-275			
	614-12 JARDINIERE	500-700			
	614-10 JARD. & PED.	2000-2500			

UNGLAZED POTTERY WAITING TO BE PAINTED.

DAWN 1937

X	DESCRIPTION	SECONDARY MARKET	PRICE PAID	DATE BOUGHT	CONDITION
	830-8 VASE	200-250			
	4-5 BOOKENDS	300-350			
	1121-2 CANDLESTICK	150-175			
	31 - 3X4 FROG	125-175			
	345-8 BASKET	275-325			
	319-6 VASE W/ATTACHED CANDLESTICKS	400-450			
	315-4 JARDINIERE	125-150			
	828-8 VASE	125-175			
	829-8 VASE	150-200			
	318-14 WINDOW BOX	200-250			
	317-10 WINDOW BOX	175-225			
	827-6 VASE	150-200			
	826-6 VASE	150-200			
	831-9 VASE	275-325			
	834-15 FLOOR VASE	500-700			
	316-6 JARDINIERE	150-175			
	832-10 VASE	300-400			
	833-12 VASE	400-500			

DECORATED ART TURN OF THE CENTURY

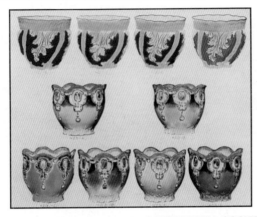

COMPLIMENTS OF THE OHIO HISTORICAL SOCIETY

X	DESCRIPTION	SECONDARY MARKET	PRICE PAID	DATE BOUGHT	CONDITION
	421-A JARDINIERE	275-325			
	421-B JARDINIERE	275-325			
	421-C JARDINIERE	275-325			
	421-D JARDINIERE	275-325			
	423-A JARDINIERE	275-325			
	423-B JARDINIERE	275-325			
	423-C JARDINIERE	275-325			
	423-D JARDINIERE	275-325			
	423-E JARDINIERE	275-325			
	423-F JARDINIERE	275-325			

COMPLIMENTS OF THE OHIO HISTORICAL SOCIETY

X	DESCRIPTION	SECONDARY MARKET	PRICE PAID	DATE BOUGHT	CONDITION
	405-35 JARD. & PED.	2000-2500			
	414-33 JARD. & PED.	2000-2500			

DECORATED ART TURN OF THE CENTURY

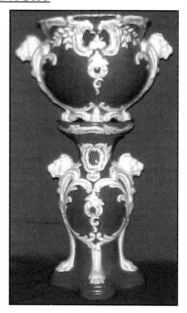

GORDON HOPPE COLLECTION

COMPLIMENTS OF THE OHIO HISTORICAL SOCIETY

X	DESCRIPTION	SECONDARY MARKET	PRICE PAID	DATE BOUGHT	CONDITION
	414-14 X 33 JARD.$ PED.	2000-2500			

COMPLIMENTS OF THE OHIO HISTORICAL SOCIETY

X	DESCRIPTION	SECONDARY MARKET	PRICE PAID	DATE BOUGHT	CONDITION
	441- 9X12X37A JARD. & PED.	2000-2500			
	411- 9X12X37B JARD. & PED.	2000-2500			

DECORATED ART TURN OF THE CENTURY

COMPLIMENTS OF THE OHIO HISTORICAL SOCIETY

X	DESCRIPTION	SECONDARY MARKET	PRICE PAID	DATE BOUGHT	CONDITION
	438- 14X 32$1/2$ JARD. & PED.	2000-2500			

COMPLIMENTS OF THE OHIO HISTORICAL SOCIETY

X	DESCRIPTION	SECONDARY MARKET	PRICE PAID	DATE BOUGHT	CONDITION
	414- 14X23 JARD. & PED.	1800-2200			
	440- 15X12X45 JARD. & PED.	2800-3300			

DECORATED ART TURN OF THE CENTURY

X	DESCRIPTION	SECONDARY MARKET	PRICE PAID	DATE BOUGHT	CONDITION
	439-12X34 JARD. & PED.	2000-2500			

DECORATED ART TURN OF THE CENTURY

X	DESCRIPTION	SECONDARY MARKET	PRICE PAID	DATE BOUGHT	CONDITION
	526-6 JARDINIERE	225-275			
	526-8 1/2 JARDINIERE	275-325			
	527-4 JARDINIERE	175-225			
	527-6 JARDINIERE	225-275			
	527-8 JARDINIERE	275-325			
	511-8 JARDINIERE	275-325			
	462-10X27 JARD. & PED.	2500-3000			
	462- 12x33 JARD. & PED.	4000-5000			
	316-6 FERN DISH	75-100			
	316-7 FERN DISH	100-125			
	316-8 FERN DISH	125-150			
	217-5 SQUARE FERN DISH	75-100			
	315-4 HANGING BASKET	250-300			
	315-5 HANGING BASKET	300-350			
	315-6 HANGING BASKET	350-400			
	315-7 HANGING BASKET	400-450			
	315-8 HANGING BASKET	450-500			
	326-10 WALL POCKET	300-350			
	328-10 WALL POCKET	300-350			
	#1-3X3 FROG	75-100			
	#1-3X4 FROG	75-100			
	#1-3X6 FROG	75-100			
	#1-4X3 FROG	75-100			
	#1-4X4 FROG	75-100			
	#1-4X6 FROG	100-125			
	#1-6X3 FROG	100-125			
	#1-6X4 FROG	100-125			
	#1-6X6 FROG	125-150			
	#2-3X3 FROG	75-100			
	#2-4X3 FROG	75-100			
	#2-3X4 FROG	75-100			
	#2-4X4 FROG	75-100			
	#2-3X6 FROG	75-100			
	#2-4X6 FROG	100-125			
	#4- 3 FROG	50-75			
	#5- 6 FROG	50-75			
	#6- 4 FROG	50-75			
	362 CANDLESTICK	100-175			
	1007 CANDLESTICK	100-175			
	1004 CANDLESTICK	100-175			

DECORATED LANDSCAPE 1900

COMPLIMENTS OF THE OHIO HISTORICAL SOCIETY

X	DESCRIPTION	SECONDARY MARKET	PRICE PAID	DATE BOUGHT	CONDITION
	456-5 JARDINIERE	200-300			
	456-6 JARDINIERE	300-400			
	456-7 JARDINIERE	400-500			
	456-8 JARDINIERE	500-600			
	456-9 JARDINIERE	600-700			
	456-10 JARDINIERE	700-800			
	456-10X27 JARD. & PEDESTAL	2500-3000			
	456-12X31 JARD. & PEDESTAL	3000-3500			

DECORATED MATT 1900

COMPLIMENTS OF THE OHIO HISTORICAL SOCIETY

X	DESCRIPTION	SECONDARY MARKET	PRICE PAID	DATE BOUGHT	CONDITION
	724 UMBRELLA STAND	2250-3000			
	723 UMBRELLA STAND	2000-2750			

DECORATED BOWLS & PITCHERS LATE TEENS & 1940s

COMPLIMENTS OF THE OHIO HISTORICAL SOCIETY

X	DESCRIPTION	SECONDARY MARKET	PRICE PAID	DATE BOUGHT	CONDITION
	3-10" BOWL	175-200			
	3-8" BOWL	150-175			
	3-6" BOWL	125-150			
	4-9 BOWL & PLATE	175-200			
	1318 PITCHER	100-125			
	1319 PITCHER	100-125			
	1320 PITCHER	125-150			
	2-10" BOWL	150-175			
	2-8" BOWL	125-150			
	2-6" BOWL	100-125			
	1-4" BOWL	100-125			
	1-6" BOWL	100-125			
	1-8" BOWL	125-150			
	1-10" BOWL	150-175			
	1-8" BOWL	125-150			
	1-6" BOWL	100-125			
	1309 PITCHER	100-125			
	1310 PITCHER	125-150			
	1317 PITCHER	150-175			

PICTURES NOT SHOWN

	1303 PITCHER	200-300			
	1304 PITCHER	200-300			
	1305 PITCHER	200-300			
	226 PITCHER	200-300			

DOG DISH EARLY 1900s

X	DESCRIPTION	SECONDARY MARKET	PRICE PAID	DATE BOUGHT	CONDITION
	LARGE DISH	150-200			
	SMALL DISH	100-150			

DOGWOOD I 1916–1919

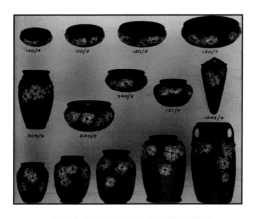

GEORGE KRAUSE COLLECTION

X	DESCRIPTION	SECONDARY MARKET	PRICE PAID	DATE BOUGHT	CONDITION
	150-4 BOWL	100-150			
	150-5 BOWL	100-150			
	150-6 BOWL	150-175			
	150-7 BOWL	175-200			
	303-9 VASE	250-325			
	340-6 HANGING BASKET	275-325			
	340-5 HANGING BASKET	250-300			
	151-4 JARDINIERE	125-175			
	1245-9 WALL POCKET	250-350			
	300-6 VASE	150-175			
	301-7 VASE	175-200			
	302-8 VASE	200-225			
	304-10 VASE	250-300			
	305-12 VASE	300-350			

DOGWOOD I 1916-1919

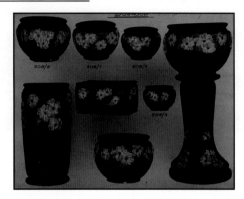

COMPLIMENTS OF THE OHIO HISTORICAL SOCIETY

X	DESCRIPTION	SECONDARY MARKET	PRICE PAID	DATE BOUGHT	CONDITION
	608-8 JARDINIERE	250-300			
	608-7 JARDINIERE	225-250			
	608-6 JARDINIERE	200-225			
	374-10 WINDOW BOX	250-300			
	608-5 JARDINIERE	125-175			
	766-20-8 JARD.& PED.	650-850			
	608-9 JARDINIERE	300-350			
	608-10 JARD.& PED.	1000-1250			

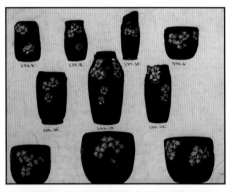

COMPLIMENTS OF THE OHIO HISTORICAL SOCIETY

X	DESCRIPTION	SECONDARY MARKET	PRICE PAID	DATE BOUGHT	CONDITION
	136-8 VASE	200-250			
	135-8 VASE	250-300			
	137-10 VASE	225-275			
	139-10 VASE	300-325			
	140-15 FLOOR VASE	500-700			
	139-12 VASE	325-375			
	590-7 JARDINERE	200-225			
	590-9 JARDINIERE	400-500			
	590-8 JARDINIERE	300-400			

DOGWOOD II 1916-1919

X	DESCRIPTION	SECONDARY MARKET	PRICE PAID	DATE BOUGHT	CONDITION
	590-12 JARD. & PED.	1800-2400			
	758-21 UMBRELLA STAND	700-900			
	590-10 JARD. & PED.	1100-1500			

ARTIST DRAWING

DONATELLA TEA SETS 1912

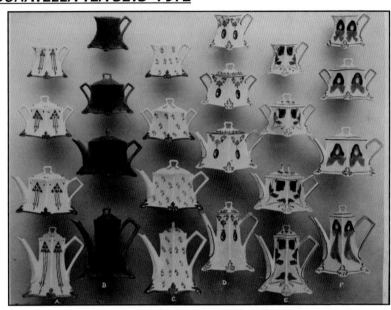

COMPLIMENTS OF THE OHIO HISTORICAL SOCIETY

X	DESCRIPTION	SECONDARY MARKET	PRICE PAID	DATE BOUGHT	CONDITION
	A CREAMER	100-125			
	A SUGAR	100-125			
	A TEAPOT	200-300			
	A COFFEE POT	250-350			
	B CREAMER	100-125			
	B SUGAR	100-125			
	B TEAPOT	200-300			
	B COFFEE POT	250-350			
	C CREAMER	100-125			
	C SUGAR	100-125			
	C TEAPOT	200-300			
	D CREAMER	100-125			
	D SUGAR	100-125			
	D TEAPOT	200-300			
	D COFFEE POT	250-350			
	E CREAMER	100-125			
	E SUGAR	100-125			
	E TEAPOT	200-300			
	E COFFEE POT	250-350			
	F CREAMER	100-125			
	F SUGAR	100-125			
	F TEAPOT	200-300			
	F COFFEE POT	250-350			

DONATELLO 1915

COMPLIMENTS OF THE OHIO HISTORICAL SOCIETY

X	DESCRIPTION	SECONDARY MARKET	PRICE PAID	DATE BOUGHT	CONDITION
	103-8 VASE	150-200			
	101-8 VASE	150-200			
	102-8 VASE	150-200			
	104-8 VASE	150-200			
	105-10 VASE	175-225			
	107-10 VASE	175-225			
	106-10 VASE	175-225			
	108-10 VASE	175-225			
	111-12 VASE	250-300			
	109-12 VASE	250-300			
	112-12 VASE	250-300			
	110-12 VASE	250-300			

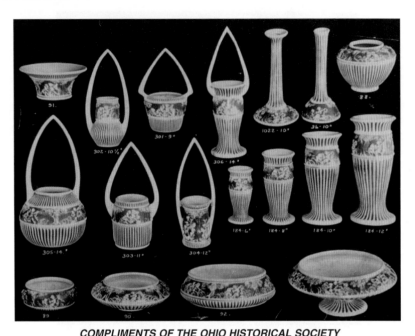

COMPLIMENTS OF THE OHIO HISTORICAL SOCIETY

X	DESCRIPTION	SECONDARY MARKET	PRICE PAID	DATE BOUGHT	CONDITION
	91 BOWL	100-150			
	302-10½ BASKET	450-550			
	301-9 BASKET	400-500			
	306-14 BASKET	450-550			
	1022-10 CANDLESTICK	225-300			
	36-10 CANDLESTICK	150-200			
	88 BOWL	125-150			
	305-14 BASKET	450-550			
	303-11 BASKET	400-500			
	304-12 BASKET	400-500			
	184-6 VASE	100-125			
	184-8 VASE	125-150			
	184-10 VASE	150-175			
	184-12 VASE	175-200			
	89 BOWL	100-150			
	90 BOWL	100-125			
	92 BOWL	125-150			
	9-9 COMPOTE	150-175			

DONATELLO 1915

COMPLIMENTS OF THE OHIO HISTORICAL SOCIETY

X	DESCRIPTION	SECONDARY MARKET	PRICE PAID	DATE BOUGHT	CONDITION
	1009-6 GOOD NIGHT CANDLESTICK	100-150			
	118-8 VASE	125-150			
	118-6 VASE	100-125			
	1006 CANDLESTICK	100-125			
	327-6 HANGING BASKET	225-275			
	327-8 HANGING BASKET	275-325			
	8 BRIDGE	100-125			
	231-5 PED. BOWL	100-125			
	1202-10 WALL POCK.	200-225			
	9 BRIDGE	100-125			
	227-4 BOWL	75-100			
	119-7 VASE	125-150			
	15 ASHTRAY	175-200			
	53-6 PEDESTAL BOWL	100-125			
	238-6 BOWL W/ LINER	125-150			
	227-5 BOWL W/ LINER	125-150			
	1307 PITCHER	200-250			
	53-7 BOWL W/FROG	100-125			
	1212-12 WALL POCKET	250-300			
	113-10 VASE	175-225			
	238-5 BOWL W/ LINER	100-125			
	227-6 BOWL W/ LINER	125-150			
	238-7 BOWL W/ LINER	150-175			
	54-8 BOWL W/ FROG	100-150			

PICTURES NOT SHOWN

	575-6 JARDINIERE	150-175			
	575-7 JARDINIERE	175-200			
	575-8 JARDINIERE	175-200			
	575-9 JARDINIERE	200-225			
	575-10 JARDINIERE	225-250			
	575-6X18 JARD. & PED.	600-900			
	229-4X9 FERN DISH W/LINER	225-250			
	236-6 BASKET	300-350			
	233-7 BASKET	400-450			
	53-6 BOWL W/ FROG	75-100			
	58-10 BOWL W/FROG	100-125			
	60-6 OVAL BOWL	100-125			
	60-8 OVAL BOWL	125-150			
	61-10 ROUND BOWL	400-450			
	41/2X101/2 WINDOW BOX	300-400			
	#1 HAIR RECEIVER	300-350			

DONATELLO 1915

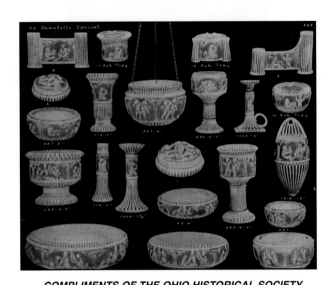

COMPLIMENTS OF THE OHIO HISTORICAL SOCIETY

X	DESCRIPTION	SECONDARY MARKET	PRICE PAID	DATE BOUGHT	CONDITION
	8 BRIDGE	100-125			
	17 ASHTRAY	150-175			
	15 ASHTRAY	175-200			
	9 BRIDGE	100-125			
	2 HAIR SAVER	300-350			
	113-7 VASE	125-150			
	327-6 HANG. BASKET	225-250			
	230-3X7 CHALICE	175-200			
	1009-6 GOOD NIGHT CANDLESTICK	100-125			
	16 ASHTRAY	150-175			
	227-6 BOWL	100-125			
	228-6 PEDESTAL PLANTER	200-225			
	114-7 VASE	125-150			
	1008-7 1/2 CANDLESTICK	200-225			
	1 HAIR SAVER	300-400			
	53-6 BOWL	100-125			
	223-4X3 CHALICE	175-200			
	1212-10 WALL POCK.	225-250			
	227 BOWL	100-125			
	55-10 BOWL	150-200			
	54-8 BOWL	125-150			
	227-4 BOWL W/LINER	100-125			
	227-5 BOWL W/LINER	125-150			
	227-6 BOWL W/LINER	150-175			

COMPLIMENTS OF THE OHIO HISTORICAL SOCIETY

X	DESCRIPTION	SECONDARY MARKET	PRICE PAID	DATE BOUGHT	CONDITION
	233 BASKET	275-300			
	115-10 VASE	200-225			
	116-6 CHALICE	150-200			
	14-3 1/2 FROG	75-100			
	14-2 1/2 FROG	75-100			
	60-6 OVAL BOWL	100-125			
	575-4 JARDINIERE	75-100			
	60-8 OVAL BOWL	125-150			
	1212-12 WALL POCK.	250-300			
	1011 CANDLESTICK	150-175			
	575-5 JARDINIERE	100-125			
	60-10 PVAL BOWL	150-200			
	61-6 DISH	300-350			
	61-8 DISH	350-400			
	60-12 OVAL BOWL	200-250			

DONATELLO 1915

COMPLIMENTS OF THE OHIO HISTORICAL SOCIETY

X	DESCRIPTION	SECONDARY MARKET	PRICE PAID	DATE BOUGHT	CONDITION
	580-4 PLANTER W/ TRAY	125-150			
	580-5 PLANTER W/ TRAY	150-175			
	580-6 PLANTER W/ TRAY	175-200			
	327-8 HANG. BASKET	225-250			
	232 CHALICE	200-250			
	1307 PITCHER	200-250			
	231-4 PEDESTAL BOWL W/LINER	100-125			
	231-5 PEDESTAL BOWL W/LINER	125-150			
	231-6 PEDESTAL BOWL W/LINER	150-175			
	113-8 VASE	125-150			
	113-10 VASE	150-175			
	113-12 VASE	175-200			
	113-15 FLOOR VASE	225-250			
	579-6 JARDINIERE	150-175			
	579-8 JARDINIERE	175-200			
	579-10 JARDINIERE	200-225			
	579-12 JARDINIERE	225-250			

DONATELLO 1915

X	DESCRIPTION	SECONDARY MARKET	PRICE PAID	DATE BOUGHT	CONDITION
	8¹/₂" VASE	200-250			
	6¹/₄" VASE	150-225			
	6" VASE	300-400			
	7" DOUBLE BUD VASE	300-400			
	3¹/₂" INSENSE BURNER	500-600			
	5x14 WINDOW BOX	400-500			
	626 CUSPIDOR	200-300			
	7" PEDESTAL BOWL	300-400			
	5" VASE	175-225			
	4" PEDESTAL BOWL	200-250			

DONATELLO 1915

X	DESCRIPTION	SECONDARY MARKET	PRICE PAID	DATE BOUGHT	CONDITION
	2¹/₂" PEDESTAL BOWL	75-100			
	#16 ASHTRAY	200-250			
	6³/₄" PEDESTAL VASE W/FROG	175-225			
	5" CHALICE	150-200			
	575-10X28 JARD. & PEDESTAL	1200-1500			
	579-10X28 JARD. & PEDESTAL	1200-1500			

DONATELLO 1915

X	DESCRIPTION	SECONDARY MARKET	PRICE PAID	DATE BOUGHT	CONDITION
	579-8X24 JARD. & PEDESTAL	1000-1200			
	753-10X21 UMBRELLA	800-1200			
	575-8X24 JARD. & PEDESTAL	1000-1200			
	579-12X34 JARD. & PEDESTAL	1500-1800			
	526-6X18 JARD. & PEDESTAL	700-1000			
	526-10X24 JARD. & PEDESTAL	1000-1250			

IVORY DONATELLO 1915

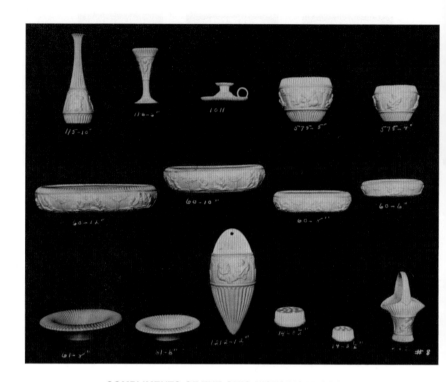

COMPLIMENTS OF THE OHIO HISTORICAL SOCIETY

X	DESCRIPTION	SECONDARY MARKET	PRICE PAID	DATE BOUGHT	CONDITION
	115-10 VASE	125-150			
	116-6 CHALICE	100-125			
	1011 CANDLESTICK	100-125			
	575-5 JARDINIERE	125-150			
	575-4 JARDINIERE	100-125			
	60-12 OVAL BOWL	175-200			
	60-10 OVAL BOWL	150-175			
	60-8 OVAL BOWL	125-150			
	60-4 OVAL BOWL	100-125			
	61-8 DISH	200-225			
	61-6 DISH	175-200			
	1212-12 WALL POCKET	200-250			
	14-3$^{1/2}$ FROG	75-100			
	14-3-2$^{1/2}$ FROG	75-100			
	233 BASKET	200-225			

IVORY DONATELLO 1915

COMPLIMENTS OF THE OHIO HISTORICAL SOCIETY

X	DESCRIPTION	SECONDARY MARKET	PRICE PAID	DATE BOUGHT	CONDITION
	580-6 PLANTER W/TRAY	125-150			
	580-5 PLANTER W/TRAY	100-125			
	580-4 PLANTER W/TRAY	75-100			
	527-8 HANGING BASKET	200-250			
	113-15 FLOOR VASE	250-275			
	113-12 VASE	175-200			
	113-10 VASE	150-175			
	113-8 VASE	125-150			
	282-8 CHALICE	150-175			
	1307 PITCHER	100-125			
	579-6 JARDINIERE	100-125			
	579-8 JARDINIERE	100-125			
	579-10 JARDINIERE	125-150			
	579-12 JARDINIERE	150-175			

DRESSER SETS EARLY TEENS

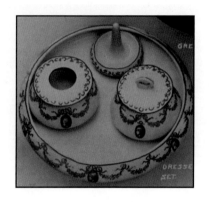

X	DESCRIPTION	SECONDARY MARKET	PRICE PAID	DATE BOUGHT	CONDITION
	MEDALLION TRAY	100-125			
	MEDALLION HAIR SAVER	100-150			
	MEDALLION PIN HOLDER	100-150			
	MEDALLION RING HOLDER	100-150			

PATTERNS NOT SHOWN ARE:
DUTCH, GIBSON GIRL, IVORY TINT, LANDSCAPE & PERSIAN

THANKS TO MARK BASSETT

DUTCH BEFORE 1916

COMPLIMENTS OF THE OHIO HISTORICAL SOCIETY

X	DESCRIPTION	SECONDARY MARKET	PRICE PAID	DATE BOUGHT	CONDITION
	DRINKING CUP	100-125			
	CHAMBER POT	300-325			
	SMALL PITCHER	200-225			
	COMBINETTE	450-550			
	CHILD MUG	100-125			
	SOAP W/LID	125-150			

X	DESCRIPTION	SECONDARY MARKET	PRICE PAID	DATE BOUGHT	CONDITION
	TOOTHBRUSH HOLDER	150-175			
	CHAMBER POT	400-450			
	SOAP W/LID	125-150			
	COMBINETTE	600-700			
	LARGE PITCHER	350-400			
	BASIN	250-300			

COMPLIMENTS OF THE OHIO HISTORICAL SOCIETY

X	DESCRIPTION	SECONDARY MARKET	PRICE PAID	DATE BOUGHT	CONDITION
	#5 TEAPOT	200-225			
	#3 TEAPOT	200-225			
	#2 TEAPOT	200-225			
	#1 TEAPOT	250-300			
	#15 TEAPOT	300-350			
	#17 TEAPOT	300-350			
	#6 TEAPOT	225-250			
	#13 CONVENTIONAL TEAPOT	350-400			
	#13 DUTCH TEAPOT	350-400			
	#14 TEAPOT	250-275			
	#4 TEAPOT	200-225			

EARLAM 1930

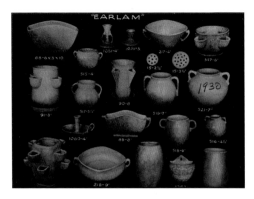

COMPLIMENTS OF THE OHIO HISTORICAL SOCIETY

X	DESCRIPTION	SECONDARY MARKET	PRICE PAID	DATE BOUGHT	CONDITION
	88-6X3X10 WINDOW BOX	300-400			
	515-4 JARDINIERE	125-150			
	1081-4 CANDLESTICK	200-225			
	1059-3 CANDLESTICK	175-200			
	217-4 BOWL	200-250			
	15-2 1/2 FROG	75-100			
	15-3 1/2 FROG	75-100			
	347-6 STRAWBERRY POT	300-400			
	91-8 STRAWBERRTY POT	500-600			
	517-5 1/2 JARDINIERE	200-250			
	90-8 STRAWBERRTY POT	500-600			
	519-7 JARDINIERE	200-250			
	521-7 JARDINIERE	200-250			
	1080-4 CANDLESTICK	150-200			
	89-8 PLANTER	225-275			
	518-6 VASE	200-250			
	516-4 1/2 JARDINIERE	175-200			
	92-9 STRAWBERRTY POT	600-700			
	218-9 COMPOTE	225-275			
	522-9 VASE	300-350			
	1263 WALL POCKET	400-500			

PLAQUE FROM THE FACTORY

EARLY PITCHERS EARLY 1916

COMPLIMENTS OF THE OHIO HISTORICAL SOCIETY

X	DESCRIPTION	SECONDARY MARKET	PRICE PAID	DATE BOUGHT	CONDITION
	WILD ROSE 2 QT.	200-225			
	IRIS 2 QT.	250-300			
	IRIS 3 QT.	300-350			
	WILD ROSE 2 QT.	200-225			
	BULL 2 QT.	275-325			
	TOURIST 1 PT.	100-150			
	TOURIST 2 PT.	125-175			
	TOURIST 3 PT.	150-200			
	TOURIST 4 PT.	175-325			
	ORISIS 1 PT.	100-125			
	ORISIS 2 PT.	125-150			
	ORISIS 3 PT.	150-175			

	#1 HOLLAND	200-250			
	IRIS (GREEN)	250-300			
	TULIP	175-200			
	LANDSCAPE	125-150			
	#2 HOLLAND	225-250			
	TEDDY BEAR	500-600			
	IRIS (YELLOW)	250-300			
	OWL	400-500			

EARLY PITCHERS EARLY 1916

X	DESCRIPTION	SECONDARY MARKET	PRICE PAID	DATE BOUGHT	CONDITION
	C-1 SPONGE BLUE	125-150			
	C-2 SPONGE BLUE	125-150			
	B-1 ORISIS	100-125			
	B-2 ORISIS	125-150			
	B-3 ORISIS	150-175			
	C-3 WILD ROSE	200-225			
	C-4 WILD ROSE	200-225			
	C-5 SPONGE YELLOW	125-150			
	C-6 SPONGE YELLOW	125-150			

	THE BRIDGE	150-175			
	THE COW	275-325			
	THE BOY	400-500			
	THE GOLDEN ROD	250-300			
	THE WILD ROSE	200-225			
	THE MILL	300-350			
	THE GRAPE	150-175			

ELSIE, THE COW AFTER WORLD WAR II

		HARDY HUDSON COLLECTION			
		SECONDARY	PRICE	DATE	
X	DESCRIPTION	MARKET	PAID	BOUGHT	CONDITION
	COMPLETE SET IN BOX	1000-1400			
	PLATE	200-225			
	DISH	200-225			
	CUP	150-200			

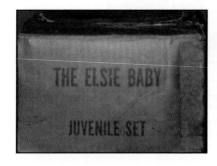

FALLINE 1933

CONTINUED FROM PATE 115

COMPLIMENTS OF THE OHIO HISTORICAL SOCIETY

X	DESCRIPTION	SECONDARY MARKET	PRICE PAID	DATE BOUGHT	CONDITION
	649-8 VASE	700-1100			
	648-7 VASE	600-800			
	1092-3 1/2 CANDLESTICK	400-600			
	643-6 VASE	350-450			
	647-7 VASE	700-800			
	645-6 1/2 VASE	700-800			
	244-8 COMPOTE	350-450			
	646-8 VASE	600-700			
	650-6 VASE	500-600			
	644-6 VASE	450-500			
	642-6 VASE	375-475			
	655-15 FLOOR VASE	2000-3000			
	653-12 VASE	1200-1500			
	651-8 VASE	600-800			
	652-9 VASE	800-1000			
	654-13 1/2 FLOOR VASE	1500-2000			

FATIMA/RAYMAN CLUB WHISKEY *(PROMOTIONAL LINE)* TEENS

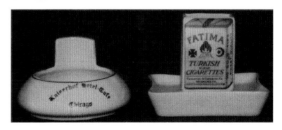

X	DESCRIPTION	SECONDARY MARKET	PRICE PAID	DATE BOUGHT	CONDITION
	PROMOTIONAL ASHTRAYS	100-125			
	FATIMA TURKISH CIGARETTE	100-150			

FEELLA 1931

X	DESCRIPTION	SECONDARY MARKET	PRICE PAID	DATE BOUGHT	CONDITION
	504-5 1/2 VASE	500-700			
	502-6 VASE	400-600			
	620-4 PLANTER W/ DISH	500-600			
	506-8 VASE	600-700			
	507-9 VASE	700-800			
	503-5 PLANTER	500-600			
	509-8 VASE	750-900			
	87-8 DISH W/FROG	500-700			
	498-4 VASE	300-400			
	500-5 VASE	400-500			
	499-6 VASE	600-700			
	510-8 VASE	500-700			
	497-4 FROG	350-400			
	15-3 1/2 FROG	125-175			
	15-2 1/2 FROG	100-150			
	210-4 BOWL	400-500			
	211-8 BOWL	600-800			
	1266-6 1/2 WALL POCKET	900-1000			
	505-6 VASE	500-600			
	501-6 VASE	500-600			
	511-10 VASE	900-1100			
	212-12X7 COMPOTE	750-1000			
	1078-4 CANDLESTICK	400-600			
	508-8 VASE	600-700			

FERN DISH 1900

X	DESCRIPTION	SECONDARY MARKET	PRICE PAID	DATE BOUGHT	CONDITION
	6" DISH W/LINER (ALL)	300-400			
	E-11 FOOTED DISH W/LINER (ALL)	350-450			
	8" DISH W/LINER	150-200			
	7" DISH W/LINER	125-175			
	6" DISH W/LINER	100-150			
	7" BLUE SPONGE	125-150			
	8" BLENDED	150-175			
	9" BLENDED	175-200			
	7" BLENDED	125-150			
	8" BLUE SPONGE	150-175			
	9" BLENDED	175-200			

FERN TRAIL CUSPIDORS EARLY 1900s

X	DESCRIPTION	SECONDARY MARKET	PRICE PAID	DATE BOUGHT	CONDITION
	621 YELLOW CUSPIDOR (TOP)	175-200			
	621 GREEN CUSPIDOR (BOTTOM)	175-200			

FLEUR DELIS EARLY 1900s

X	DESCRIPTION	SECONDARY MARKET	PRICE PAID	DATE BOUGHT	CONDITION
	412-20 JARDINIERE & PEDESTAL	1000-1250			

FLORANE 1920

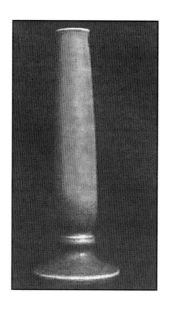

X	DESCRIPTION	SECONDARY MARKET	PRICE PAID	DATE BOUGHT	CONDITION
	VASE	100-125			
	DISH	100-125			

FLORANE II 1949

GEORGE KRAUSE COLLECTION

X	DESCRIPTION	SECONDARY MARKET	PRICE PAID	DATE BOUGHT	CONDITION
	71-4 PLANTER	50-75			
	72-5 PLANTER	75-100			
	73-6 PLANTER	100-125			
	95-10 DISH	75-100			
	52-12 LG. PLANTER	150-175			
	51-10 LG. PLANTER	125-150			
	50-8 LG. PLANTER	100-125			

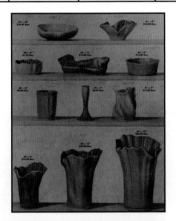

GEORGE KRAUSE COLLECTION

X	DESCRIPTION	SECONDARY MARKET	PRICE PAID	DATE BOUGHT	CONDITION
	63-10 DISH	75-100			
	61-9 DISH	75-100			
	60-6 DISH	50-75			
	64-12 WINDOW BOX	100-125			
	62-8 DISH	75-100			
	80-6 VASE	75-100			
	79-7 VASE	75-100			
	81-7 VASE	75-100			
	82-9 VASE	100-125			
	83-11 VASE	125-150			
	84-4 FLOOR VASE	150-175			

FLOOR VASES TURN OF THE CENTURY

COMPLIMENTS OF THE OHIO HISTORICAL SOCIETY

X	DESCRIPTION	SECONDARY MARKET	PRICE PAID	DATE BOUGHT	CONDITION
	910 DECORATED A 10 X 22	1000-1800			
	910 DECORATED B 10 X 22	1000-1800			
	910 DECORATED C 10 X 22	1000-1800			
	910 DECORATED A 22"	1000-1800			
	910 DECORATED B 22"	1000-1800			

COMPLIMENTS OF THE OHIO HISTORICAL SOCIETY

X	DESCRIPTION	SECONDARY MARKET	PRICE PAID	DATE BOUGHT	CONDITION
	826 22" VASE	3250-3750			
	832 22" VASE	3500-3750			
	863 21" VASE	3000-3500			
	832 20" VASE	2750-3000			
	826 21" VASE	3000-3500			
	863 21" VASE	3000-3500			

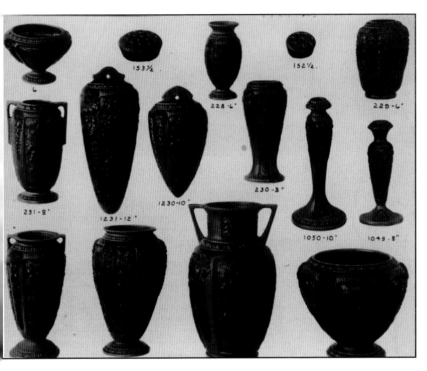

COMPLIMENTS OF THE OHIO HISTORICAL SOCIETY

X	DESCRIPTION	SECONDARY MARKET	PRICE PAID	DATE BOUGHT	CONDITION
	6 PEDESTAL DISH	100-125			
	15-3 1/2 FROG	75-100			
	228-6 VASE	100-150			
	15-2 1/2 FROG	75-100			
	229-6 VASE	100-150			
	231-8 VASE	150-175			
	1231-12 WALL POCKET	350-400			
	1230-10 WALL POCKET	300-400			
	230-8 VASE	150-175			
	1050-10 CANDLESTICK	275-375			
	1049-8 CANDLESTICK	175-225			
	233-10 VASE	200-225			
	232-10 VASE	175-225			
	234-12 VASE	250-300			
	9 PEDESTAL DISH	200-250			

FLORENTINE I 1924

COMPLIMENTS OF THE OHIO HISTORICAL SOCIETY

X	DESCRIPTION	SECONDARY MARKET	PRICE PAID	DATE BOUGHT	CONDITION
	41-6 BRIDGE	175-225			
	125-5 BOWL	100-125			
	126-5 BOWL	100-125			
	40-41½ BRIDGE	150-200			
	126-6 BOWL	150-175			
	257-6 BOWL W/LINER	150-200			
	238-6 BOWL W/LINER	125-150			
	125-6 BOWL	100-125			
	257-6 BOWL W/LINER	150-200			
	258-7 BOWL	100-150			
	125-7 BOWL	100-150			
	17-8 COMPOTE	200-250			
	126-7 BOWL	125-150			

COMPLIMENTS OF THE OHIO HISTORICAL SOCIETY

X	DESCRIPTION	SECONDARY MARKET	PRICE PAID	DATE BOUGHT	CONDITION
	337-6 HANGING BASKET W/LINER	300-350			
	602-100 JARD. & PED.	1000-1500			
	337-7 HANGING BASKET W/LINER	400-450			
	602-6 JARDINIERE	150-175			
	602-6 JARDINIERE	175-200			
	602-7 JARDINIERE	200-225			
	602-8 JARDINIERE	225-250			
	602-9 JARDINIERE	250-275			

FLORENTINE I 1924

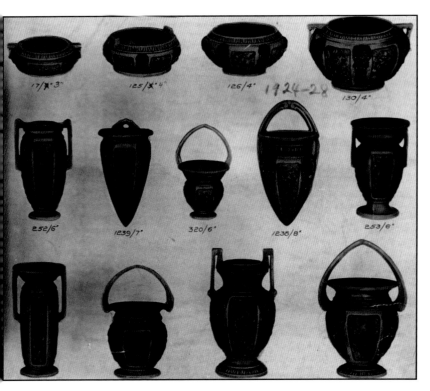

X	DESCRIPTION	SECONDARY MARKET	PRICE PAID	DATE BOUGHT	CONDITION
	17-3 BOWL	150-200			
	125-4 BOWL	150-200			
	126-4 BOWL	150-200			
	130-4 BOWL	150-200			
	252-6 VASE	175-225			
	1239-7 WALL POCKET	300-400			
	320-6 BASKET	300-350			
	1238-8 WALL POCKET	300-400			
	253-6 VASE	175-225			
	254-7 VASE	200-250			
	321-7 BASKET	250-300			
	255-8 VASE	225-275			
	322-8 BASKET	300-350			

FLORENTINE II 1940

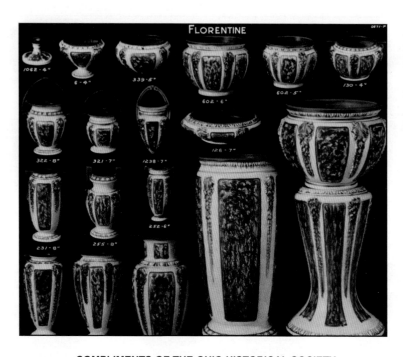

FLORENTINE

X	DESCRIPTION	SECONDARY MARKET	PRICE PAID	DATE BOUGHT	CONDITION
	1062-4 CANDLESTICK	100-150			
	6-4 PEDESTAL BOWL	125-150			
	339-5 HANGING BASKET	200-250			
	602-6 JARDINIERE	200-250			
	602-5 JARDINIERE	175-225			
	130-4 BOWL	100-150			
	322-8 BASKET	300-350			
	321-7 BASKET	250-300			
	1238-7 WALL POCKET	250-275			
	126-7 COMPOTE	125-175			
	231-8 VASE	150-175			
	255-8 VASE	125-175			
	252-6 VASE	100-125			
	233-10 VASE	200-250			
	232-10 VASE	175-225			
	234-12 VASE	225-300			
	763-20 UMBRELLA	550-600			
	602-9 JARD. & PED.	1000-1200			

FOREST 1920

LEN & TERRY CENIOR COLLECTION

X	DESCRIPTION	SECONDARY MARKET	PRICE PAID	DATE BOUGHT	CONDITION
	18" VASE	2000-2500			
	10" VASE	650-1000			
	12" VASE	750-1250			
	15" VASE	1400-2000			
	12X5X5 WINDOW BOX	1200-2200			
	16" VASE	1200-1800			
	31/2X7 BOWL	300-400			
	12" VASE	1200-2000			

FOREST 1920

COMPLIMENTS OF THE OHIO HISTORICAL SOCIETY

X	DESCRIPTION	SECONDARY MARKET	PRICE PAID	DATE BOUGHT	CONDITION
	18" VASE	800-1200			
	7 1/2" BASKET	700-900			
	15" VASE	1400-2000			
	6 1/2" BASKET	500-1000			
	18" VASE	1800-2200			
	12" VASE	800-1200			
	20" UMBRELLA	2500-3500			
	9 1/2" WALL POCKET	1200-1800			

FOREST 1920

X	DESCRIPTION	SECONDARY MARKET	PRICE PAID	DATE BOUGHT	CONDITION
	9½" BASKET	400-500			
	9" HANGING BASKET	500-600			
	10" VASE	450-550			
	18" VASE	1200-1500			
	14" VASE	800-1200			

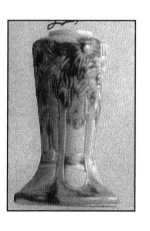 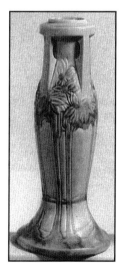 

FOXGLOVE 1942

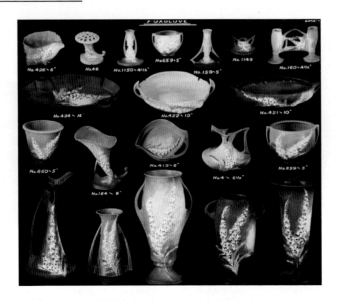

GEORGE KRAUSE COLLECTION

X	DESCRIPTION	SECONDARY MARKET	PRICE PAID	DATE BOUGHT	CONDITION
	426-6 SHELL	200-250			
	46 FROG	150-200			
	1150-4½ CANDLESTICK	175-225			
	659-5 JARDINIERE	125-175			
	159-5 VASE	150-175			
	1149 CANDLESTICK	100-150			
	160-4½ BRIDGE	125-150			
	424-14 PIN TRAY	275-325			
	422-10 BOWL	175-225			
	421-10 BOWL	175-225			
	660-5 PLANTER W/DISH	175-250			
	164-8 CORNUCOPIA	150-225			
	419-6 PIN TRAY	125-150			
	4-6½ EWER	175-225			
	659-5 JARDINIERE	125-175			
	6-15 EWER	600-800			
	51-10 VASE	250-350			
	54-15 FLOOR VASE	650-850			
	52-12 VASE	300-400			
	53-14 FLOOR VASE	500-700			

FOXGLOVE 1942

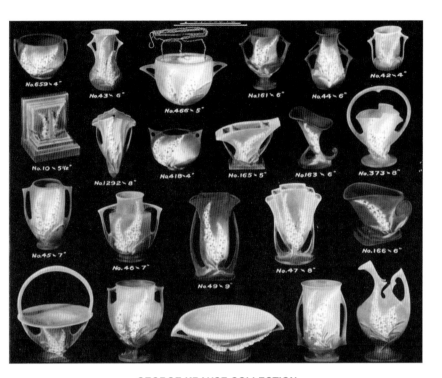

GEORGE KRAUSE COLLECTION

X	DESCRIPTION	SECONDARY MARKET	PRICE PAID	DATE BOUGHT	CONDITION
	659-4 JARDINIERE	100-150			
	46-6 VASE	175-225			
	466-5 HANGING BASKET	250-350			
	161-6 VASE	150-200			
	44-6 VASE	150-200			
	42-4 VASE	100-150			
	10-5 1/2 BOOKENDS	275-325			
	1292-8 WALL POCKET	400-500			
	418-4 BOWL	150-200			
	165-5 VASE	175-225			
	162-6 CORNUCOPIA	125-200			
	373-8 BASKET	225-325			
	45-7 VASE	175-200			
	46-7 VASE	175-200			
	49-8 VASE	200-225			
	47-8 VASE	200-250			
	166-6 VASE	175-225			
	374-10 BASKET	300-350			
	2-10 COMPOTE	225-250			
	48-8 VASE	200-300			
	5-10 EWER	300-400			

FOXGLOVE 1942

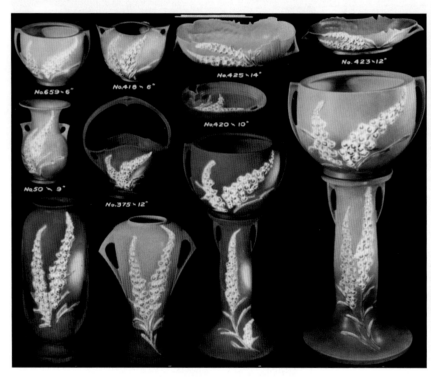

GEORGE KRAUSE COLLECTION

X	DESCRIPTION	SECONDARY MARKET	PRICE PAID	DATE BOUGHT	CONDITION
	659-6 JARDINIERE	175-225			
	418-6 BOWL	175-250			
	425-14 DISH	300-400			
	425-12 DISH	200-300			
	50-9 VASE	200-300			
	375-12 BASKET	450-550			
	420-10 PIN TRAY	200-250			
	56-18 FLOOR VASE	800-1000			
	55-15 FLOOR VASE	600-900			
	659-8 JARD. & PED.	900-1200			
	659-10 JARD. & PED.	1400-1800			

FREESIA 1945

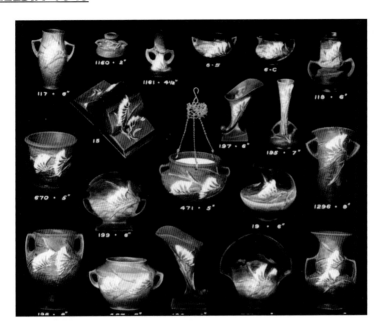

X	DESCRIPTION	SECONDARY MARKET	PRICE PAID	DATE BOUGHT	CONDITION
	117-6 VASE	150-200			
	1160-2 CANDLESTICK	100-125			
	1161-4½ CANDLESTICK	125-150			
	6-S SUGAR	75-100			
	6-C CREAMER	75-100			
	118-6 VASE	125-175			
	670-5 PLANTER	175-225			
	15 BOOKENDS	275-350			
	197-6 CORNUCOPIA	100-150			
	195-7 VASE	125-150			
	199-6 PLANTER	175-200			
	471-5 HANGING BASKET W/LINER	225-300			
	19-6 EWER	175-225			
	1296-8 WALL POCKET	225-325			
	196-8 VASE	200-250			
	463-5 JARDINIERE	175-200			
	198-8 CORNUCOPIA	150-175			
	463-5 JARDINIERE	175-200			
	198-8 CORNUCOPIA	150-175			
	391-8 BASKET	200-300			
	122-8 VASE	175-225			

FREESIA 1945

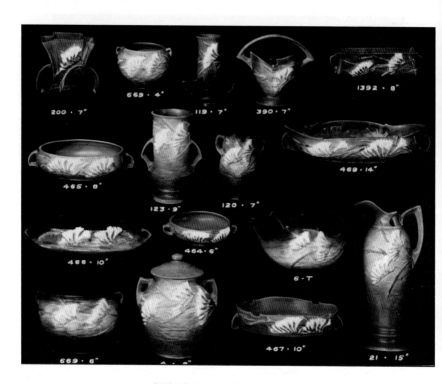

GEORGE KRAUSE COLLECTION

X	DESCRIPTION	SECONDARY MARKET	PRICE PAID	DATE BOUGHT	CONDITION
	200-7 VASE	150-200			
	669-4 BOWL	100-125			
	119-7 VASE	125-150			
	390-7 BASKET	200-250			
	1392-8 WINDOW BOX	175-250			
	465-8 BOWL	150-200			
	123-9 VASE	175-225			
	120-7 VASE	125-175			
	469-14 BOWL	200-300			
	466-10 BOWL	150-200			
	464-6 BOWL	100-150			
	6-T TEAPOT	250-325			
	669-6 JARDINIERE	175-225			
	4-8 COOKIE JAR	400-500			
	467-10 BOWL	450-500			
	21-15 FLOOR VASE	500-700			

FREESIA 1945

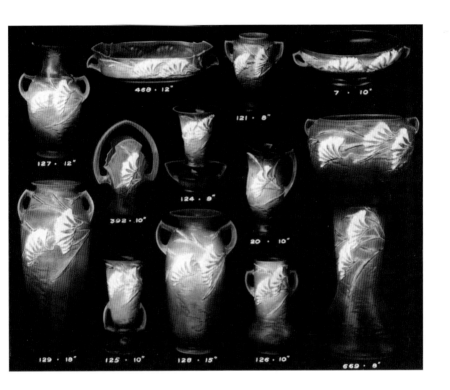

GEORGE KRAUSE COLLECTION

X	DESCRIPTION	SECONDARY MARKET	PRICE PAID	DATE BOUGHT	CONDITION
	127-12 VASE	250-300			
	468-12 BOWL	175-225			
	121-8 VASE	150-200			
	7-10 COMPOTE	175-225			
	392-10 BASKET	350-450			
	124-9 VASE	200-275			
	20-10 EWER	250-350			
	129-18 FLOOR VASE	700-900			
	125-10 VASE	200-300			
	128-15 FLOOR VASE	400-600			
	126-10 VASE	200-300			
	669-8 JARD. & PED.	1000-1500			

FUCHSIA 1938

X	DESCRIPTION	SECONDARY MARKET	PRICE PAID	DATE BOUGHT	CONDITION
	645-6 JARDINIERE	200-300			
	347-6 BOWL	200-300			
	351-10 DISH	275-375			
	353-14 DISH	350-400			
	352-12 DISH	275-350			
	903-12 VASE	600-800			
	901-10 VASE	375-475			
	904-15 FLOOR VASE	800-1200			
	905-18 FLOOR VASE	1200-1500			
	645-8 JARD. & PED.	1000-1200			
	645-10 JARD. & PED.	1500-1800			

FUCHSIA 1938

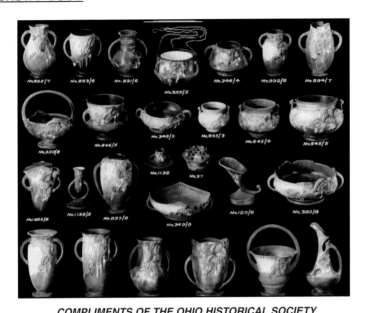

COMPLIMENTS OF THE OHIO HISTORICAL SOCIETY

X	DESCRIPTION	SECONDARY MARKET	PRICE PAID	DATE BOUGHT	CONDITION
	895-7 VASE	225-250			
	893-6 VASE	200-300			
	891-6 VASE	175-225			
	359-5 HANGING BASKET	450-600			
	346-4 BOWL	150-175			
	892-6 VASE	200-250			
	894-7 VASE	175-225			
	350-8 BASKET	275-350			
	646-5 VASE	300-350			
	348-5 BOWL	175-225			
	645-3 BOWL	125-175			
	645-4 BOWL	150-200			
	645-5 BOWL	175-225			
	1282-8 WALL POCKET	250-325			
	1133-5 CANDLESTICK	275-325			
	897-8 VASE	225-275			
	1132 CANDLESTICK	150-200			
	37 FROG	125-150			
	349-9 DISH	150-175			
	129-6 CORUCOPIA	150-200			
	350-8 DISH	225-300			
	899-9 VASE	300-400			
	900-9 VASE	325-425			
	898-8 VASE	300-400			
	896-8 VASE	275-350			
	351-10 BASKET	275-375			
	902-10 EWER	325-425			

FUTURA 1924

X	DESCRIPTION	SECONDARY MARKET	PRICE PAID	DATE BOUGHT	CONDITION
	408-10 VASE	1000-1600			
	398-6½ VASE	325-425			
	405-7½ VASE	900-1100			
	396-5½ VASE	1200-1500			
	406-8 VASE	700-900			
	189-4X6 DISH	550-650			
	376-15X4X6 WINDOW BOX	1200-1500			
	190-3½X6 DISH	350-450			
	409-9 VASE	800-1200			
	400-7 VASE	1000-1500			
	399-7 VASE	425-525			
	412-9 VASE	2500-3500			

X	DESCRIPTION	SECONDARY MARKET	PRICE PAID	DATE BOUGHT	CONDITION
	390-100 VASE	600-800			
	388-9 VASE	500-600			
	15-2½ FROG	150-200			
	15-3½ FROG	175-225			
	188-8 PLANTER	450-600			
	392-10 VASE	750-1000			
	391-10 VASE	900-1200			
	380-6 VASE	400-550			
	381-8 VASE	400-550			
	382-7 VASE	500-750			
	395-10 VASE	800-1200			

FUTURA 1924

X	DESCRIPTION	SECONDARY MARKET	PRICE PAID	DATE BOUGHT	CONDITION
	407-9 VASE	900-1200			
	403-7 VASE	800-1200			
	401-8 VASE	500-800			
	402-8 VASE	600-900			
	404-8 VASE	1100-1300			
	81-5X11/2X5 PLANTER	325-475			
	82-6 VASE	300-400			
	410-12 VASE	1100-1500			
	397-6 VASE	375-475			
	191-8 PLANTER	475-575			
	1073-4 CANDLESTICK	450-650			
	411-14 FLOOR VASE	1800-2200			

X	DESCRIPTION	SECONDARY MARKET	PRICE PAID	DATE BOUGHT	CONDITION
	385-8 VASE	400-600			
	389-9 VASE	1000-1500			
	384-8 VASE	500-700			
	383-8 VASE	500-700			
	381-6 VASE	400-550			
	387-7 VASE	800-1000			
	393-12 VASE	1000-1400			
	189-8 BOWL	450-600			
	1072-4 CANDLESTICK	600-800			
	397-12 VASE	1100-1400			

FUTURA 1924

COMPLIMENTS OF THE OHIO HISTORICAL SOCIETY

X	DESCRIPTION	SECONDARY MARKET	PRICE PAID	DATE BOUGHT	CONDITION
	427-8 VASE	800-1000			
	424-7 VASE	500-700			
	85-4 PLANTER	300-400			
	194-5 DISH	700-1000			
	422-6 VASE	300-500			
	197-6 BOWL	475-675			
	428-8 VASE	400-600			
	198-5 PLANTER	500-700			
	1075-4 CANDLESTICK	700-900			
	195-10 DISH	800-1000			
	425-8 VASE	450-600			
	426-8 VASE	800-1200			
	421-5 VASE	300-500			
	15-3$1/2$ FROG	175-225			
	196-12X5X3$1/2$ COMPOTE	475-625			
	196 FROG	125-175			
	423-6 VASE	300-500			

FUTURA 1924

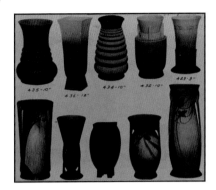

X	DESCRIPTION	SECONDARY MARKET	PRICE PAID	DATE BOUGHT	CONDITION
	435-10 VASE	1200-1500			
	436-12 VASE	2500-3000			
	434-10 VASE	2000-2500			
	432-10 VASE	700-1000			
	429-9 VASE	900-1200			
	437-12 VASE	1200-1700			
	431-10 VASE	700-1000			
	430-9 VASE	900-1200			
	433-10 VASE	800-1200			
	438-15 FLOOR VASE	3000-3500			

X	DESCRIPTION	SECONDARY MARKET	PRICE PAID	DATE BOUGHT	CONDITION
	616-6 JARDINIREE	400-600			
	616-7 JARDINIERE	700-1000			
	616-8 JARDINIERE	700-1000			
	616-9 JARDINIERE	1000-1200			
	616-10 JARD. & PED.	3500-5000			
	1261-8 WALL POCKET	600-900			
	344-5 HANG. BASKET	500-800			
	344-6 HANG. BASKET	600-900			

GARDEN LINE TURN OF THE CENTURY

COMPLIMENTS OF THE OHIO HISTORICAL SOCIETY

X	DESCRIPTION	SECONDARY MARKET	PRICE PAID	DATE BOUGHT	CONDITION
	610-14 PLANTER	300-350			
	610-12 PLANTER	200-250			
	610-10 PLANTER	150-175			
	610-8 PLANTER	100-125			
	611-14 PLANTER	300-350			
	611-12 PLANTER	200-250			
	611-10 PLANTER	150-175			
	611-8 PLANTER	100-125			
	612-14 PLANTER	300-350			
	612-12 PLANTER	200-250			
	612-10 PLANTER	150-175			
	612-8 PLANTER	100-125			

COMPLIMENTS OF THE OHIO HISTORICAL SOCIETY

X	DESCRIPTION	SECONDARY MARKET	PRICE PAID	DATE BOUGHT	CONDITION
	11-12X18 GARDEN PLANTER	350-400			
	10-12X14 GARDEN PLANTER	250-300			
	1-23 BIRD BATH	400-500			
	2-26 BIRD BATH	500-600			
	3-31 BIRD BATH	600-700			

GARDEN LINE TURN OF THE CENTURY

COMPLIMENTS OF THE OHIO HISTORICAL SOCIETY

X	DESCRIPTION	SECONDARY MARKET	PRICE PAID	DATE BOUGHT	CONDITION
	88-8 PLANTER W/DISH	150-175			
	87-7 PLANTER W/DISH	125-150			
	88-6 PLANTER W/DISH	100-125			
	87-5 PLANTER W/DISH	75-100			
	88-4PLANTER W/DISH	75-100			
	71-8 PLANTER W/DISH	150-175			
	71-7 PLANTER W/DISH	125-150			
	71-6 PLANTER W/DISH	100-125			
	71-5 PLANTER W/DISH	75-100			
	71-4 PLANTER W/DISH	75-100			
	70-8 PLANTER W/DISH	150-175			
	70-7 PLANTER W/DISH	125-150			
	70-6 PLANTER W/DISH	100-125			
	70-5 PLANTER W/DISH	75-100			
	70-4 PLANTER W/DISH	75-100			

GARDENIA 1950

GEORGE KRAUSE COLLECTION

X	DESCRIPTION	SECONDARY MARKET	PRICE PAID	DATE BOUGHT	CONDITION
	656-3 PLANTER	100-150			
	682-6 VASE	200-300			
	622-8 DOUBLE VASE	150-200			
	681-6 VASE	100-125			
	657-3 1/2 JARDINIERE	100-150			
	684-8 VASE	150-200			
	683-8 VASE	150-200			
	686-10 VASE	150-200			
	688-12 VASE	200-275			
	685-10 VASE	175-225			
	689-14 FLOOR VASE	450-550			
	690-16 FLOOR VASE	800-900			
	687-12 VASE	275-325			

GARDENIA 1950

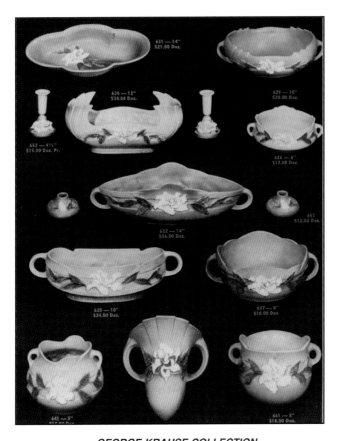

GEORGE KRAUSE COLLECTION

X	DESCRIPTION	SECONDARY MARKET	PRICE PAID	DATE BOUGHT	CONDITION
	631-14 PIN TRAY	200-225			
	629-10 BOWL	150-175			
	652-4 1/2 CANDLESTICK	125-175			
	626-6 BOWL	125-150			
	630-12 COMPOTE	175-200			
	629-10 BOWL	150-175			
	632-14 COMPOTE	175-200			
	651 CANDLESTICK	100-125			
	628-10 OVAL DISH	125-150			
	627-8 BOWL	125-175			
	641-5 BOWL	125-150			
	666-8 WALL POCKET	250-325			
	661-5 HANG. BASKET	300-350			

GARDENIA 1950

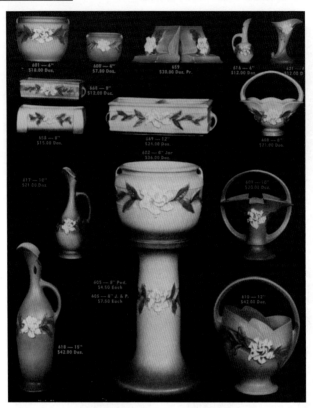

GEORGE KRAUSE COLLECTION

X	DESCRIPTION	SECONDARY MARKET	PRICE PAID	DATE BOUGHT	CONDITION
	601-6 BOWL	100-150			
	600-6 BOWL	200-225			
	659 BOOKENDS	250-325			
	616-6 EWER	175-200			
	621-6 CORNUCOPIA	100-150			
	668-8 WINDOW BOX	125-175			
	658-8 WINDOW BOX	125-175			
	669-12 WINDOW BOX	175-225			
	608-8 BASKET	225-275			
	617-10 EWER	175-225			
	609-10 BASKET	250-325			
	618-15 EWER	275-325			
	610-12 BASKET	275-375			
	605-8 JARD. & PED.	1500-2500			
	(NOT SHOWN) 603-10 JARDINIERE	450-550			
	602-8 JARDINIERE	400-500			
	606-10 JARD. & PED.	1750-2275			

GERMAN COOKING WARE 1902

COMPLIMENTS OF THE OHIO HISTORICAL SOCIETY

X	DESCRIPTION	SECONDARY MARKET	PRICE PAID	DATE BOUGHT	CONDITION
	COFFEE POT	325-350			
	TEAPOT	300-350			
	PITCHER	100-125			
	CREAM PITCHER	50-75			
	CUSTARD OR IND. BEAN POT	50-75			
	EGG COCORTES	50-75			
	LARGE DEEP BAKERS	175-225			
	SMALL DEEPT BAKERS	150-200			
	HAND. COVER CASSEROLE	150-200			
	OPEN CASSEROLE	100-125			
	PIE PAN	75-100			
	SHERRED EGG	50-75			
	PUDDING DISH	50-75			
	BOWL	50-75			

GERMAN COOKING WARE 1902

X	DESCRIPTION	SECONDARY MARKET	PRICE PAID	DATE BOUGHT	CONDITION
	3" COCORTES	50-75			
	3½" COCORTES	50-75			
	5" BOWL	75-85			
	6" BOWL	85-95			
	6½ PUDDING	75-100			
	5½ PUDDING	75-100			
	4½ PUDDING	50-75			
	3½ PUDDING	50-75			

GERMAN FARM WARE 1892–1898

X	DESCRIPTION	SECONDARY MARKET	PRICE PAID	DATE BOUGHT	CONDITION
	CANNING JAR	100-125			
	COFFEE POT	250-300			
	CANNING JAR	100-125			

GIBSON GIRL 1906

COMPLIMENTS OF MARK BASSETT

X	DESCRIPTION	SECONDARY MARKET	PRICE PAID	DATE BOUGHT	CONDITION
	810-8 3/4 VASE	1500-2000			

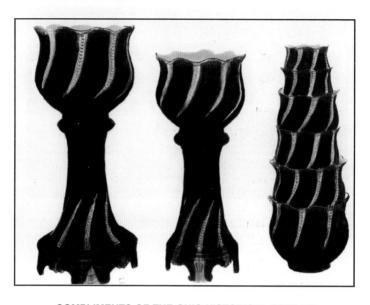

COMPLIMENTS OF THE OHIO HISTORICAL SOCIETY

X	DESCRIPTION	SECONDARY MARKET	PRICE PAID	DATE BOUGHT	CONDITION
	407-14X33 JARD. & PEDESTAL	1000-1500			
	407-12X29 JARD. & PEDESTAL	800-1000			
	407-6 JARDINIERE	150-175			
	407-7 JARDINIERE	175-200			
	407-8 JARDINIERE	200-225			
	407-9 JARDINIERE	225-250			
	407-10 JARDINIERE	250-275			
	407-11 JARDINIERE	275-300			

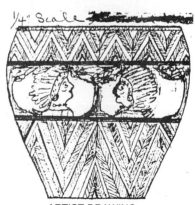

¼" Scale

ARTIST DRAWING

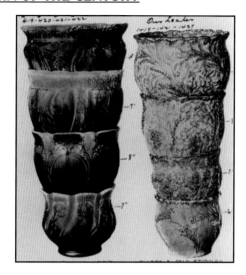

COMPLIMENTS OF THE OHIO HISTORICAL SOCIETY

X	DESCRIPTION	SECONDARY MARKET	PRICE PAID	DATE BOUGHT	CONDITION
	414-10 JARDINIERE	250-275			
	414-9 JARDINIERE	225-250			
	414-8 JARDINIERE	200-225			
	414-7 JARDINIERE	175-200			
	420-10 JARDINIERE	250-275			
	420-9 JARDINIERE	225-250			
	420-8 JARDINIERE	200-225			
	420-7 JARDINIERE	175-200			
	421-10 JARDINIERE	250-275			
	421-9 JARDINIERE	225-250			
	421-8 JARDINIERE	200-225			
	421-7 JARDINIERE	175-200			
	422-10 JARDINIERE	250-275			
	422-9 JARDINIERE	225-250			
	422-8 JARDINIERE	200-225			
	422-7 JARDINIERE	175-200			
	1414-9 JARDINIERE	225-250			
	1414-8 JARDINIERE	200-225			
	1414-7 JARDINIERE	175-200			
	1414-6 JARDINIERE	150-175			
	1421-9 JARDINIERE	225-250			
	1421-8 JARDINIERE	200-225			
	1421-7 JARDINIERE	175-200			
	1421-6 JARDINIERE	150-175			
	1427-9 JARDINIERE	225-250			
	1427-8 JARDINIERE	200-225			
	1427-7 JARDINIERE	175-200			
	1427-6 JARDINIERE	150-175			

GLAZE   TURN OF THE CENTURY

COMPLIMENTS OF THE OHIO HISTORICAL SOCIETY

X	DESCRIPTION	SECONDARY MARKET	PRICE PAID	DATE BOUGHT	CONDITION
	407-12X30 JARD. & PEDESTAL	800-1000			
	407-6 JARDINIERE	150-175			
	407-7 JARDINIERE	175-200			
	407-8 JARDINIERE	200-225			
	407-9 JARDINIERE	225-250			
	407-10 JARDINIERE	250-275			
	407-11 JARDINIERE	275-300			
	407-12 JARDINIERE	300-325			
	403-10X26 JARD. & PEDESTAL	500-750			
	403-7 JARDINIERE	150-175			
	407-8 JARDINIERE	175-200			
	407-9 JARDINIERE	200-225			
	407-10 JARDINIERE	225-250			
	410-12X22 JARD. & PEDESTAL	500-600			
	410-7 JARDINIERE	150-175			
	410-10 JARDINIERE	225-250			
	410-11 JARDINIERE	250-275			
	410-12 JARDINIERE	275-300			

COMPLIMENTS OF THE OHIO HISTORICAL SOCIETY

X	DESCRIPTION	SECONDARY MARKET	PRICE PAID	DATE BOUGHT	CONDITION
	407-19X48 JARD. & PEDESTAL	2000-2500			

PICTURES NOT SHOWN:

X	DESCRIPTION	SECONDARY MARKET	PRICE PAID	DATE BOUGHT	CONDITION
	542-14 JARDINIERE	450-500			
	564-7 JARDINIERE	225-250			
	564-8 JARDINIERE	250-275			
	564-9 JARDINIERE	275-300			
	564-10 JARDINIERE	300-350			
	576-7 JARDINIERE	225-250			
	576-8 JARDINIERE	250-275			
	576-9 JARDINIERE	275-300			
	576-10 JARDINIERE	300-350			
	576-12 JARDINIERE	350-400			
	582-4 POT & SAUCER	125-150			
	452-14X33 JARD. & PEDESTAL	1000-1500			
	564-10X28 JARD. & PEDESTAL	800-1000			
	571-10X28 JARD. & PEDESTAL	800-1000			
	576-10X29 JARD. & PEDESTAL	800-1000			

COMPLIMENTS OF THE OHIO HISTORICAL SOCIETY

X	DESCRIPTION	SECONDARY MARKET	PRICE PAID	DATE BOUGHT	CONDITION
	353-9 CANDLESTICK	150-200			
	356-9 CANDLESTICK	150-200			
	355-9 CANDLESTICK	150-200			
	357-9 CANDLESTICK	150-200			
	354-9 CANDLESTICK	150-200			
	361-9 CANDLESTICK	150-200			
	353-9 CANDLESTICK	150-200			
	356-9 CANDLESTICK	150-200			
	355-9 CANDLESTICK	150-200			
	357-9 CANDLESTICK	150-200			
	354-9 CANDLESTICK	150-200			
	361-9 CANDLESTICK	150-200			

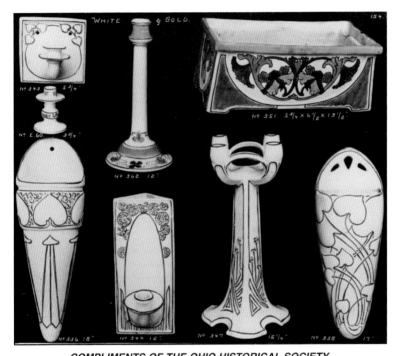

COMPLIMENTS OF THE OHIO HISTORICAL SOCIETY

X	DESCRIPTION	SECONDARY MARKET	PRICE PAID	DATE BOUGHT	CONDITION
	343-5³/4 WALL CANDLESTICK	300-350			
	60-3³/4 CANDLESTICK	200-250			
	362-12 CANDLESTICK	300-350			
	351-5³/4X6¹/4X13¹/2 WINDOW BOX	400-500			
	336-18 WALL POCKET	800-1000			
	344-12 WALL POCKET	700-800			
	347-15¹/4 FOUR CANDLESTICK	400-500			
	338-17 WALL POCKET	800-1000			

GOLD & SILVER DECORATED 1910

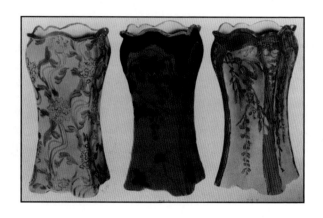

COMPLIMENTS OF THE OHIO HISTORICAL SOCIETY

X	DESCRIPTION	SECONDARY MARKET	PRICE PAID	DATE BOUGHT	CONDITION
	756-9X23 UMBRELLA	2000-2500			
	715-R UMBRELLA	2000-2500			
	715-Y UMBRELLA	2000-2500			
	717-10X231/2 UMBRELLA	1500-2500			
	712-91/2X221/2 UMBRELLA	1000-1500			
	712-91/2X221/2 UMBRELLA	1000-1500			

GOLD & SILVER DECORATED 1910

X	DESCRIPTION	SECONDARY MARKET	PRICE PAID	DATE BOUGHT	CONDITION
	711-8¹/²X11X26 UMBRELLA	3500-4500			
	711-8¹/²X11X26 UMBRELLA	3500-4500			
	717-10X24 UMBRELLA	3000-4000			
	717-10X24 UMBRELLA	3500-4500			
	429B-10¹/²X26 JARD. & PED.	3000-4000			
	429L-10¹/²X26 JARD. & PED.	3000-4000			
	429A-10¹/²X26 JARD. & PED.	3500-4500			

GOOD NIGHT CANDLESTICK 1910

X	DESCRIPTION	SECONDARY MARKET	PRICE PAID	DATE BOUGHT	CONDITION
	CANDLESTICK	400-450			

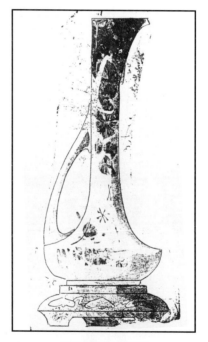

ARTIST DRAWING

GREEN 1910

COMPLIMENTS OF THE OHIO HISTORICAL SOCIETY

X	DESCRIPTION	SECONDARY MARKET	PRICE PAID	DATE BOUGHT	CONDITION
	658-12X34 JARD. & PEDESTAL	1200-1400			
	658-10X28 JARD. & PEDESTAL	1000-1200			
	740-22 UMBRELLA	1000-1200			
	741-10X21 UMBRELLA	1000-1200			
	741-10X21 UMBRELLA	1000-1200			

GREEN 1910

PICTURES NOT SHOWN:

X	DESCRIPTION	SECONDARY MARKET	PRICE PAID	DATE BOUGHT	CONDITION
	550-4 JARDINIERE	100-125			
	550-6 JARDINIERE	150-200			
	550-7 JARDINIERE	200-225			
	550-8 JARDINIERE	225-275			
	550-9 JARDINIERE	275-300			
	550-10 JARDINIERE	300-325			
	550-12 JARDINIERE	350-400			
	550-14 JARDINIERE	400-450			
	558-6 JARDINIERE	150-200			
	558-8 JARDINIERE	225-275			
	558-10 JARDINIERE	300-325			
	558-12 JARDINIERE	350-400			
	560-6 JARDINIERE	150-200			
	560-8 JARDINIERE	225-275			
	560-9 JARDINIERE	275-300			
	560-10 JARDINIERE	300-325			
	565-8 JARDINIERE	225-275			
	565-9 JARDINIERE	275-300			
	565-10 JARDINIERE	300-325			
	565-12 JARDINIERE	350-400			
	550-10X28 JARD. & PEDESTAL	1000-1200			
	550-12X33 JARD. & PEDESTAL	1200-1500			
	552-10X28 JARD. & PEDESTAL	1000-1200			
	552-12X33 JARD. & PEDESTAL	1200-1500			
	220-9 FERN DISH	225-250			
	221-61/2 FERN DISH	75-100			
	226-4 FERN DISH	50-75			
	226-5 FERN DISH	50-75			
	226-6 FERN DISH	75-100			
	61/2X11 WINDOW BOX	300-400			
	8X12 WINDOW BOX	400-500			
	81/2X16 WINDOW BOX	600-700			
	#1-10 CEMETARY VASE	400-500			
	#2-12 CEMETARY VASE	500-600			
	1208-12X61/2 WALL POCKET	300-400			
	1209-10X5 WALL POCKET	300-400			
	1210-10 WALL POCKET	600-700			
	1210-12 WALL POCKET	750-850			
	1211-10 WALL POCKET	600-700			
	1211-12 WALL POCKET	750-850			

HOLLAND BEFORE 1900

COMPLIMENTS OF THE OHIO HISTORICAL SOCIETY

X	DESCRIPTION	SECONDARY MARKET	PRICE PAID	DATE BOUGHT	CONDITION
	#8 MUG	175-200			
	#9 MUG	175-200			
	#15 MUG	175-200			
	#1 PITCHER	275-325			
	#856 MUG	175-200			
	#6 MUG	175-200			
	#16 MUG	175-200			
	#2 PITCHER	275-325			

COMPLIMENTS OF THE OHIO HISTORICAL SOCIETY

X	DESCRIPTION	SECONDARY MARKET	PRICE PAID	DATE BOUGHT	CONDITION
	WATER GLASS	100-125			
	CHAMBER POT	375-425			
	SMALL PITCHER	225-250			
	COMBINETTE	600-700			
	MUG	175-200			
	SOAP DISH	175-225			
	LARGE PITCHER	300-350			
	WASH BASIN	300-350			

HOLLAND BEFORE 1900

X	DESCRIPTION	SECONDARY MARKET	PRICE PAID	DATE BOUGHT	CONDITION
	TANKARD	250-300			
	MUG	75-100			

HOLLY 1908

COMPLIMENTS OF MARK BASSETT

X	DESCRIPTION	SECONDARY MARKET	PRICE PAID	DATE BOUGHT	CONDITION
	INDIVIDUAL TEAPOT	300-350			
	3 1/2 CREAMER	125-150			
	205-4 PLANTER	175-200			
NOT SHOWN					
	CHILD'S MUG	200-250			
	#1004 CANDLESTICK	150-200			
	#365 CANDLESTICK	150-200			
	#316-6 FERN DISH	100-150			
	#316-7 FERN DISH	125-175			
	#3 ASHTRAY	125-175			
	#5 ASHTRAY	125-175			
	DRESSER SET	450-550			
	SMOKER SET	800-1000			
	LEMONADE SET	1200-1500			
	#8 TEA SET	400-500			

HOME ART 1908

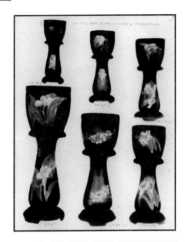

COMPLIMENTS OF THE OHIO HISTORICAL SOCIETY

X	DESCRIPTION	SECONDARY MARKET	PRICE PAID	DATE BOUGHT	CONDITION
	476-6X18$^{1/2}$ JARD. & PEDESTAL	1000-1200			
	476-7X20$^{1/2}$ JARD. & PEDESTAL	1200-1500			
	476-8X23$^{1/2}$ JARD. & PEDESTAL	1000-1200			
	476-12X37 JARD. & PEDESTAL	2000-2500			
	476-1029$^{1/2}$ JARD. & PEDESTAL	1500-2000			
	476-9X26$^{3/4}$ JARD. & PEDESTAL	1000-1200			

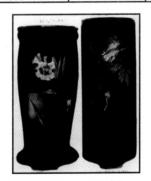

X	DESCRIPTION	SECONDARY MARKET	PRICE PAID	DATE BOUGHT	CONDITION
	724 UMBRELLA	500-600			
	723 UMBRELLA	500-600			
	424-12X32 UMBRELLA	1200-1500			
	715-9X23 UMBRELLA	1000-1200			
	910-10X22 UMBRELLA	1000-1500			

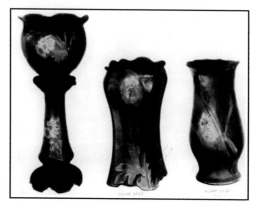

COMPLIMENTS OF THE OHIO HISTORICAL SOCIETY

COMPLIMENTS OF THE OHIO HISTORICAL SOCIETY

X	DESCRIPTION	SECONDARY MARKET	PRICE PAID	DATE BOUGHT	CONDITION
	723-8X20 JARD. & PED.	2000-2500			
	462-7 JARDINIERE	400-500			
	438-8 JARDINIERE	500-600			
	476-3 PLANTER	200-300			
	437-8 JARDINIERE	400-500			
	476-9X12 JARD. & PED.	2000-2500			

HYDE PARK ASHTRAY 1940-1954

X	DESCRIPTION	SECONDARY MARKET	PRICE PAID	DATE BOUGHT	CONDITION
	#1900 ASHTRAY (GREEN)	50-75			
	#1900 ASHTRAY (YELLOW)	50-75			
	#1910 ASHTRAY W/STAND	150-175			
	#1930 ASHTRAY	50-75			

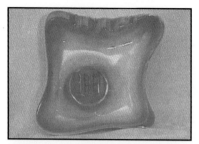
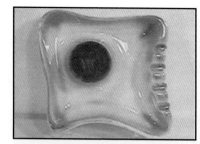

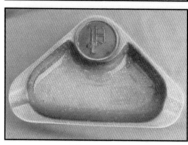

X	DESCRIPTION	SECONDARY MARKET	PRICE PAID	DATE BOUGHT	CONDITION
	#1930 ASHTRAY (BROWN)	50-75			
	#1930 ASHTRAY (YELLOW)	50-75			
	#1930 ASHTRAY (ORANGE)	50-75			
	#1935 ASHTRAY (GREEN)	75-100			
	#1935 ASHTRAY (BROWN)	75-100			
	#1940 ASHTRAY	50-75			
	#1945 ASHTRAY	50-75			
	#1950 ASHTRAY	50-75			

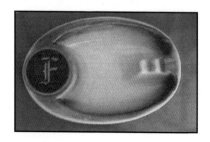

HYDE PARK ASHTRAY 1940-1954

 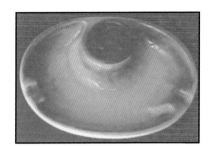

X	DESCRIPTION	SECONDARY MARKET	PRICE PAID	DATE BOUGHT	CONDITION
	#1950 ASHTRAY (GREEN)	50-75			
	#1950 ASHTRAY (WHITE)	50-75			
	#1950 ASHTRAY (SPECKLED GREEN)	50-75			
	#9150 ASHTRAY (WESTINGHOUSE)	75-100			
	#1955 ASHTRAY	50-75			
	#1961 ASHTRAY	75-100			

HYDE PARK ASHTRAY 1940-1954

 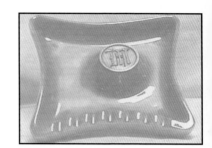

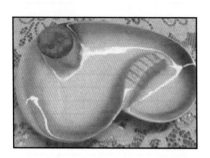 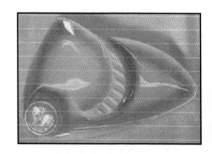

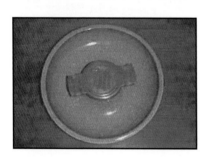 

X	DESCRIPTION	SECONDARY MARKET	PRICE PAID	DATE BOUGHT	CONDITION
	#1970 ASHTRAY	50-75			
	#1971 ASHTRAY	50-75			
	#1975 ASHTRAY	50-75			
	#1976 ASHTRAY	50-75			
	#1980 ASHTRAY	50-75			
	#1981 ASHTRAY	50-75			

HYDE PARK ASHTRAY 1940-1954

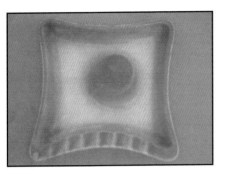 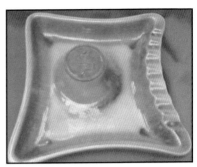

X	DESCRIPTION	SECONDARY MARKET	PRICE PAID	DATE BOUGHT	CONDITION
	#1990 ASHTRAY (TAN)	50-75			
	#1990 ASHTRAY (GREEN)	50-75			
	#1992 ASHTRAY	75-100			
	#1940 ASHTRAY W/STRIKER	100-125			
	RED ASHTRAY	50-75			

HYDE PARK CIGARETTE BOX 1940-1954

 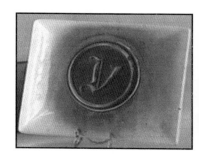

X	DESCRIPTION	SECONDARY MARKET	PRICE PAID	DATE BOUGHT	CONDITION
	#1510 HUMIDOR (LIGHT GREEN)	75-100			
	#1510 HUMIDOR (WHITE)	75-100			
	#1510 HUMIDOR (DARK)	75-100			
	4X8 RECTANGULAR BOX	75-100			

IDEAL PITCHER 1920'S

COMPLIMENTS OF THE OHIO HISTORICAL SOCIETY

X	DESCRIPTION	SECONDARY MARKET	PRICE PAID	DATE BOUGHT	CONDITION
	1-5 OUNCE	50-75			
	2-3/4 PINTS	75-100			
	3-13/4 PINTS	100-125			
	4-31/4 PINTS	125-150			
	7-15 PINTS	225-250			
	6-71/2 PINTS	200-225			
	5-3 PINTS	175-200			

IMPERIAL 1905

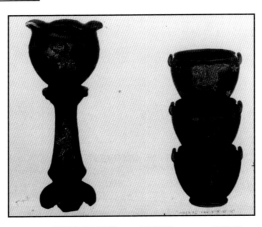

X	DESCRIPTION	SECONDARY MARKET	PRICE PAID	DATE BOUGHT	CONDITION
	424-12x32 JARD. & PEDESTAL	2000-3000			
	444-8 JARDINIERE	500-600			
	444-9 JARDINIERE	600-700			
	444-10 JARDINIERE	700-800			
	444-12 JARDINIERE	800-900			

IMPERIAL I 1916–1919

X	DESCRIPTION	SECONDARY MARKET	PRICE PAID	DATE BOUGHT	CONDITION
	31-9 VASE	175-225			
	291-7 BASKET	225-275			
	29-8 TRIPLE VASE	175-225			
	1223-10 WALL POCKET	300-400			
	30-81/2 TRIPLE VASE	175-225			
	1221-7 WATER PITCHER	250-300			
	1222-9 DOUBLE WALL POCKET	275-325			
	71-8 BOWL	100-125			
	156-12 VASE	200-250			
	71-71/2 BOWL	100-150			

X	DESCRIPTION	SECONDARY MARKET	PRICE PAID	DATE BOUGHT	CONDITION
	151-8 VASE	125-175			
	150-8 VASE	125-175			
	333-7 HANGING BASKET W/LINER	300-350			
	333-6 HANGING BASKET W/LINER	225-300			
	152-8 VASE	150-175			
	370-12 WINDOW BOX W/LINER	225-275			
	370-10 WINDOW BOX W/LINER	175-225			
	253-7 PEDESTAL BOWL W/LINER	175-200			
	251-6 BOWL W/LINER	125-150			
	251-7 BOWL W/LINER	150-175			

IMPERIAL I 1916-1919

COMPLIMENTS OF THE OHIO HISTORICAL SOCIETY

X	DESCRIPTION	SECONDARY MARKET	PRICE PAID	DATE BOUGHT	CONDITION
	591-6 JARDINIERE	100-150			
	591-7 JARDINIERE	175-225			
	591-10 JARDINIERE	250-300			
	591-12 JARDINIERE	500-600			
	591-9 JARDINIERE	400-500			
	591-8 JARDINIERE	300-400			
	591-10 JARDINIERE PEDESTAL	1500-2500			
	759-20 UMBRELLA	650-750			
	163-18 FLOOR VASE	600-700			
	162-18 FLOOR VASE	600-700			

IMPERIAL II 1924

GEORGE KRAUSE COLLECTION

X	DESCRIPTION	SECONDARY MARKET	PRICE PAID	DATE BOUGHT	CONDITION
	1262 WALL POCKET	350-450			
	1263 WALL POCKET	450-550			
	1264 WALL POCKET	600-700			
	466-4 VASE	300-325			
	469-6 VASE	275-325			
	476-8 VASE	500-600			
	470-5 1/2 VASE	400-500			
	467-5 VASE	200-300			
	199-4 1/2 BOWL	300-400			
	201-4 BOWL	450-500			
	200-4 1/2 BOWL	175-200			
	479-8 VASE	500-550			
	202-6 BOWL	400-450			
	481-8 1/2 VASE	700-800			
	203-5 BOWL	500-550			
	206-8 BOWL	700-800			

IMPERIAL II 1924

X	DESCRIPTION	GEORGE KRAUSE COLLECTION SECONDARY MARKET	PRICE PAID	DATE BOUGHT	CONDITION
	475-9 VASE	400-450			
	472-7 VASE	400-500			
	480-8 BOWL	600-700			
	20 ASHTRAY	150-225			
	205-8 BOWL	400-450			
	478-8 VASE	500-550			
	471-7 BOWL	300-375			
	1077-4 CANDLESTICK	300-400			
	207-8X12 COMPOTE	350-450			
	1076-2 1/2 CANDLESTICK	200-250			
	204-8 BOWL	250-300			
	474-7 VASE	325-400			
	484-11 VASE	800-900			
	483-10 VASE	750-850			
	482-11 VASE	850-950			
	473-7 1/2 VASE	550-600			
	468-5 VASE	200-275			
	477-9 1/2 VASE	500-600			

INDIAN EARLY TEENS

COMPLIMENTS OF THE OHIO HISTORICAL SOCIETY

#6 MUG	150-200			
#8 MUG	150-200			
#9 MUG	150-200			
#15 MUG	150-200			
#16 MUG	150-200			
#15 MUG	150-200			
#1A TANKER	225-275			
#1B TANKER	225-275			

IRIS 1939

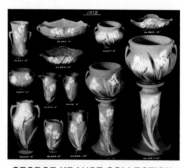

GEORGE KRAUSE COLLECTION

X	DESCRIPTION	SECONDARY MARKET	PRICE PAID	DATE BOUGHT	CONDITION
	927-10 VASE	325-425			
	364-14 CONSOLE	225-325			
	363-12 CONSOLE	200-300			
	647-6 JARDINIERE	300-375			
	362-10 CONSOLE	200-250			
	647-5 JARDINIERE	200-250			
	925-9 VASE	250-300			
	921-8 VASE	200-250			
	929-15 FLOOR VASE	800-1000			
	924-9 VASE	250-350			
	928-12 VASE	400-500			
	647-8 JARD. & PED.	900-1200			
	647-10 JARD. & PED.	1200-1500			

IRIS 1939

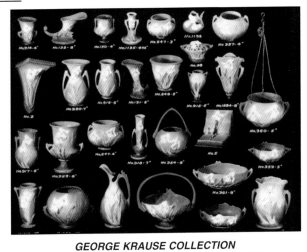

GEORGE KRAUSE COLLECTION

X	DESCRIPTION	SECONDARY MARKET	PRICE PAID	DATE BOUGHT	CONDITION
	914-4 VASE	100-150			
	132-8 CORNUCOPIA	150-200			
	130-4 VASE	100-125			
	1135-4 1/2 CANDLESTICK	300-400			
	647-3 JARDINIERE	100-125			
	1134 CANDLESTICK	150-200			
	357-4 JARDINIERE	125-150			
	2 WALL HANGER	600-700			
	920-7 VASE	200-225			
	916-6 VASE	125-150			
	131-6 CORNUCOPIA	150-175			
	648-5 PLANTER	150-200			
	38 FROG	125-150			
	915-5 VASE	100-125			
	1284-8 WALL POCKET	400-500			
	917-6 VASE	150-200			
	923-8 URN	300-350			
	647-4 JARDINIERE	125-150			
	918-7 VASE	200-225			
	354-8 BASKET	325-425			
	5 BOOKENDS	250-300			
	360-5 HANGING BASKET	300-350			
	919-7 VASE	175-225			
	358-6 BOWL	250-300			
	926-10 EWER	300-325			
	355-10 BASKET	375-475			
	361-8 CONSOLE	175-225			
	359-5 CONSOLE	150-175			
	360-6 CONSOLE	175-200			
	922-8 VASE	250-300			

IRIS TURN OF THE CENTURY

COMPLIMENTS OF THE OHIO HISTORICAL SOCIETY

X	DESCRIPTION	SECONDARY MARKET	PRICE PAID	DATE BOUGHT	CONDITION
	450-7 JARDINIERE	350-400			
	450-8 JARDINIERE	375-425			
	450-9 JARDINIERE	425-450			
	450-10 JARDINIERE	450-500			
	450-12 JARDINIERE	500-600			
	450-12X36 JARD. & PEDESTAL	2000-2500			

IVORY (OLD) 1910

COMPLIMENTS OF THE OHIO HISTORICAL SOCIETY

X	DESCRIPTION	SECONDARY MARKET	PRICE PAID	DATE BOUGHT	CONDITION
	506-8 JARDINIERE	325-375			
	506-9 JARDINIERE	400-450			
	506-10 JARDINIERE	550-600			
	508-7 JARDINIERE	300-350			
	508-8 JARDINIERE	325-375			
	508-10 JARDINIERE	500-600			
	504-7 JARDINIERE	300-350			
	504-9 JARDINIERE	400-450			
	504-10 JARDINIERE	500-600			
	505-7 JARDINIERE	300-350			
	505-8 JARDINIERE	325-375			

IVORY (OLD) 1910

CONTINUED FROM PAGE 189

X	DESCRIPTION	SECONDARY MARKET	PRICE PAID	DATE BOUGHT	CONDITION
	505-10 JARDINIERE	500-600			
	503-8 JARDINIERE	325-375			
	503-9 JARDINIERE	400-450			
	503-10 JARDINIERE	500-600			
	508-7 JARDINIERE	300-350			
	508-8 JARDINIERE	325-375			
	508-9 JARDINIERE	400-450			

IVORY 1933

GEORGE KRAUSE COLLECTION

X	DESCRIPTION	SECONDARY MARKET	PRICE PAID	DATE BOUGHT	CONDITION
	575-8 JARDINIERE	125-175			
	222-12 VASE	150-175			
	103-15 VASE	200-300			
	249-12 CONSOLE	100-125			
	701-10 VASE	100-150			
	105-9X12 PIN TRAY	150-200			
	364-4 1/2 X10 1/2 WINDOW BOX	150-175			
	275-12X8 PEDESTAL DISH	100-125			
	617-10 JARD. & PED.	800-1000			
	277-8X12 BOWL	75-100			
	743-14 VASE	200-250			
	702 VASE	150-175			
	273-12X5X4 WINDOW BOX	100-150			

IVORY 1933

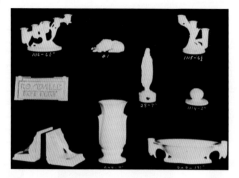

GEORGE KRAUSE COLLECTION

X	DESCRIPTION	SECONDARY MARKET	PRICE PAID	DATE BOUGHT	CONDITION
	1116-6 1/4 CANDLESTICK	700-800			
	1 DOG FIGURAL	1000-1200			
	1115-6 1/2 CANDLESTICK	300-350			
	ROSEVILLE SIGN	1200-1500			
	28-9 NUDE FIGURAL	2000-2500			
	1114-2 CANDLESTICK	150-200			
	2-4 1/4 BOOKENDS	125-150			
	698-9 VASE	100-150			
	303-13 1/2 COMPOTE				
	W/CANDLESTICK	200-225			

GEORGE KRAUSE COLLECTION

X	DESCRIPTION	SECONDARY MARKET	PRICE PAID	DATE BOUGHT	CONDITION
	1111-4 1/2 CANDLESTICK	100-150			
	1122-5 CANDLESTICK	100-125			
	301-10 CONSOLE	125-150			
	115-7 VASE	75-100			
	1112-5 1/2 CANDLESTICK	250-300			
	266-12 CONSOLE	125-150			
	266-8 CONSOLE	100-125			
	302-14X6 WINDOW BOX	150-175			
	836-12 VASE	150-200			
	837-14 VASE	200-225			
	1315-15 EWER	225-275			
	119-10 VASE	100-150			

IVORY 1933

GEORGE KRAUSE COLLECTION

X	DESCRIPTION	SECONDARY MARKET	PRICE PAID	DATE BOUGHT	CONDITION
	548-4 JARDINIERE	50-75			
	1114-2 CANDLESTICK	100-125			
	15-3 1/2 FROG	50-75			
	236-3 JARDINIERE	50-75			
	24-3 1/2 SHELL DISH	50-75			
	24-5 1/2 SHELL DISH	75-100			
	3645-5 JARD. W/LINER	75-100			
	630-4 PLANTER	50-75			
	1096-4 CANDLESTICK	150-175			
	550-4 BOWL	50-75			
	17-3 ASHTRAY	75-100			
	315-4 BOWL	75-100			
	1273-6 WALL POCKET	175-200			
	115-7 VASE	75-100			
	126-6 CORNUCOPIA	75-100			
	1122-5 VASE	100-150			
	365-6 CONSOLE	75-100			
	3-4 1/2 X5 1/2 WALL SHELF	175-200			
	679-6 VASE	50-75			
	1115-6 1/2 CANDLESTICK	300-350			
	942-8 VASE	100-150			
	580-4 PLANTER W/DISH	100-150			
	152-6 DISH	100-125			
	2-4 3/4 BOOKEND	125-150			
	368-10 CONSOLE	100-125			
	238-5 BOWL	75-100			
	366-7 DISH	100-125			
	575-4 JARDINIERE	150-175			
	580-5 PLANTER W/DISH	75-100			
	266-8 DISH	125-150			
	367-8 DISH	100-125			
	260-8 PLANTER	75-100			
	378-3 1/2x10 WINDOW BOX	100-150			
	575-5 JARDINIERE	100-125			
	580-6 PLANTER W/DISH	100-125			
	932-7 VASE	50-75			
	106-7 CORNUCOPIA	50-75			
	931-6 VASE	50-75			
	737-7 VASE	100-125			
	930-6 VASE	75-100			
	993-7 VASE	75-100			

IVORY 1933

CONTINUED FROM PAGE 192

X	DESCRIPTION	SECONDARY MARKET	PRICE PAID	DATE BOUGHT	CONDITION
	110-7 CORNUCOPIA	50+-75			
	575-6 JARDINIERE	125-150			
	259-6 BOWL	100-125			
	105-8 VASE	125-150			
	108-21/2-6 VASE	100-150			
	836-8 VASE	150-200			
	356-8 BASKET	125-150			
	935-8 VASE	100-150			
	934-8 VASE	100-150			
	274-6 BOWL	100-125			

GEORGE KRAUSE COLLECTION

X	DESCRIPTION	SECONDARY MARKET	PRICE PAID	DATE BOUGHT	CONDITION
	943-10 VASE	150-175			
	337-10 BASKET	100-125			
	938-9 VASE	125-150			
	937-9 VASE	125-150			
	941-10 EWER	200-250			
	939-10 VASE	150-200			
	940-10 VASE	150-200			
	119-10 VASE	100-125			
	314-14 CONSOLE	150-175			
	266-12 CONSOLE	100-125			
	836-12 VASE	150-175			
	837-14 VASE	175-200			
	722-14 VASE	200-250			
	A764-10X14 SAND JAR	300-350			
	A602-8 JARD. & PED.	450-550			
	A602-10 JARD. & PED.	600-800			

IVORY 1933

GEORGE KRAUSE COLLECTION

X	DESCRIPTION	SECONDARY MARKET	PRICE PAID	DATE BOUGHT	CONDITION
	17-41/2 FROG	50-75			
	1093-4 CANDLESTICK	100-125			
	1103-41/2 CANDLESTICK	100-125			
	1098-41/2 CANDLESTICK	100-125			
	1095 CANDLESTICK	150-175			
	3645-5 BOWL	75-100			
	1096-4 DOUBLE VASE	150-175			
	1101-41/2 CORNUCOPIA	100-125			
	1070-31/2 CANDLESTICK	100-150			
	15-31/2 FROG	50-75			
	734-7 VASE	100-125			
	14-4 PEDESTAL DISH	125-175			
	103-6 URN	125-150			
	24-51/2 SHELL DISH	50-75			
	105-8 VASE	125-175			
	5-7 VASE	75-100			
	24-31/2 SHELL DISH	50-75			
	735-7 VASE	100-125			
	24-71/2 SHELL DISH	100-125			
	106-7 CORNUCOPIA	50-75			
	371-6 VASE	100-125			
	679-6 VASE	100-125			
	238-5 BOWL	75-100			
	696-8 VASE	100-150			
	17-3 ASHTRAY	75-100			
	733-6 VASE	50-75			
	236-3 BOWL	50-75			
	110-7 CORNUCOPIA	50-100			

IVORY 1933

JIM JOHNSON COLLECTION

	733 ORIAN MOLD	125-150			

JOHN & NANCY WEAVER
(Founder of Roseville)

ROBERT P. WINDISH
(Last President of Roseville)

		GEORGE KRAUSE COLLECTION			
X	**DESCRIPTION**	**SECONDARY MARKET**	**PRICE PAID**	**DATE BOUGHT**	**CONDITION**
	549-4 PLANTER	75-100			
	152-6 DISH	100-125			
	550-4 BOWL	50-75			
	272-10 COMPOTE	75-100			
	630-4 PLANTER	50-75			
	580-4 PLANTER W/DISH	75-100			
	99-5 DISH	50-75			
	378-3 1/2X10 WINDOW BOX	100-150			
	111 TRIPLE CORNUCOPIA	125-175			
	267-6X12 CONSOLE	125-175			
	260-8 PLANTER	75-100			
	109-8 VASE	100-125			
	274-6 PED. BOWL	100-125			
	548-4 BOWL	50-75			
	119-6 DISH	75-125			
	97-3 1/2X5 PED. BOWL	75-125			
	12-4 1/2X8 PED. BOWL	100-125			

IVORY 1933

GEORGE KRAUSE COLLECTION

X	DESCRIPTION	SECONDARY MARKET	PRICE PAID	DATE BOUGHT	CONDITION
	316-10 VASE	150-175			
	586-8 VASE	100-150			
	44-8 VASE	50-75			
	345-8 VASED	100-125			
	346-9 VASE	100-150			
	317-10 VASE	125-175			
	157-5 BOWL	75-100			
	17 ASHTRAY	75-100			
	167-12 CONSOLE	100-150			
	159-6 BOWL	75-125			
	467-5 VASE	75-100			
	161-7 DISH	100-125			
	1063-3 CANDLESTICK	75-100			
	196-12x5x3$\frac{1}{2}$ CONSOLE	100-150			
	1065-4 CANDLESTICK	100-125			
	15-3$\frac{1}{2}$ FROG	50-75			
	585-4 VASE	75-100			
	335-8 VASE	125-150			
	341-5 VASE	75-100			
	168-10 COMPOTE	100-150			
	311-7 VASE	75-100			
	318-8 VASE	125-175			

IVORY 1933

GEORGE KRAUSE COLLECTION

X	DESCRIPTION	SECONDARY MARKET	PRICE PAID	DATE BOUGHT	CONDITION
	695-8 VASE	75-125			
	738-9 VASE	100-150			
	694-7 VASE	75-100			
	374-8 VASE	100-125			
	697-8 VASE	100-150			
	736-8 VASE	100-150			
	337-10 BASKET	150-175			
	372-6 VASE	100-125			
	737-7 VASE	100-125			
	739-9 VASE	125-150			
	740-10 VASE	125-150			
	108-2¹/2 X 6 URN	100-150			
	741-10 VASE	125-175			
	259-6 VASE	100-125			
	742-12 VASE	150-200			
	699-9 VASE	100-125			
	316-10 VASE	100-175			
	346-9 VASE	100-150			

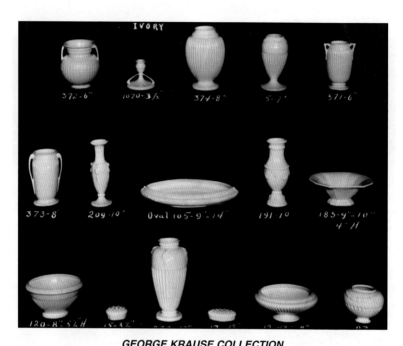

X	DESCRIPTION	GEORGE KRAUSE COLLECTION SECONDARY MARKET	PRICE PAID	DATE BOUGHT	CONDITION
	372-6 VASE	100-125			
	1070-3 1/2 CANDLESTICK	100-125			
	374-8 VASE	100-150			
	5-7 VASE	75-100			
	371-6 VASE	100-125			
	373-8 VASE	100-125			
	209-10 VASE	125-175			
	105-9X14 OVAL DISH	150-200			
	191-10 VASE	125-175			
	183-9X4 CONSOLE	125-150			
	183-10X4 CONSOLE (N/S)	150-175			
	120-8X5 1/2 BOWL	150-200			
	15-3 1/2 FROG	50-75			
	222-12 VASE	150-200			
	17-4 1/2 FROG	75-100			
	12-4 1/2X8 PEDESTAL DISH	100-125			
	97-3 1/2X5 1/2 BOWL	75-125			

IVORY 1933

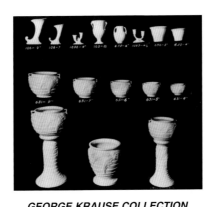

GEORGE KRAUSE COLLECTION

X	DESCRIPTION	SECONDARY MARKET	PRICE PAID	DATE BOUGHT	CONDITION
	106-9 CORNUCOPIA	50-75			
	106-7 CORNUCOPIA	50-75			
	1096-4 DOUBLE VASE	150-175			
	105-8 VASE	125-150			
	679-6 VASE	50-75			
	1095-4½ DOUBLE CANDLESTICK	150-175			
	630-5 PLANTER	75-100			
	630-4 PLANTER	50-75			
	631-9 JARDINIERE	150-175			
	631-7 JARDINIERE	125-150			
	631-6 JARDINIERE	100-125			
	631-5 JARDINIERE	75-100			
	631-4 JARDINIERE	50-75			
	631-10 JARD. & PED.	700-800			
	771-10X15 SAND JAR	300-400			
	631-8 JARD. & PED.	500-600			

IVORY TINT 1912-1914

COMPLIMENTS OF THE OHIO HISTORICAL SOCIETY

X	DESCRIPTION	SECONDARY MARKET	PRICE PAID	DATE BOUGHT	CONDITION
	BLUE MUG	100-125			
	GOLD MUG	100-125			
	PINK MUG	100-125			
	GREEN MUG	100-125			
	BLUE TANKER	300-350			
	GOLD TANKER	300-350			
	PINK TANKER	300-350			
	GREEN TANKER	300-350			

IVORY TINT 1912–1914

X	DESCRIPTION	SECONDARY MARKET	PRICE PAID	DATE BOUGHT	CONDITION
	PINK CREAMER	50-100			
	GREEN TEAPOT	200-250			
	GOLD CREAMER	50-100			
	BLUE TEAPOT	200-250			
	PINK SUGAR	50-100			
	GREEN SUGAR	50-100			
	GOLD SUGAR	50-100			
	BLUE SUGAR	50-100			
	PINK TEAPOT	200-250			
	GREEN CREAMER	50-100			
	GOLD TEAPOT	200-250			
	BLUE CREAMER	50-100			

IXIA   1937

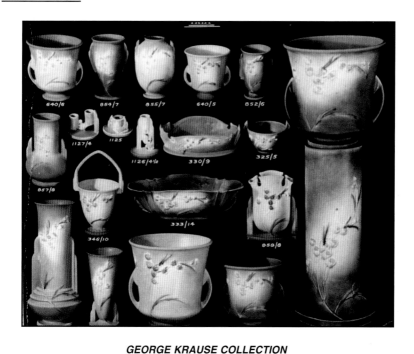

GEORGE KRAUSE COLLECTION

X	DESCRIPTION	SECONDARY MARKET	PRICE PAID	DATE BOUGHT	CONDITION
	640-6 JARDINIERE	250-300			
	854-7 VASE	150-200			
	855-7 VASE	175-200			
	640-5 JARDINIERE	175-200			
	852-6 VASE	125-150			
	857-8 VASE	200-275			
	1127-4 DOUBLE CANDLESTICK	275-300			
	1125 CANDLESTICK	100-125			
	1126-4 1/2 CANDLESTICK	175-225			
	330-9 CONSOLE	150-175			
	325-5 BOWL	100-125			
	346-10 BASKET	250-325			
	333-14 CONSOLE	300-350			
	858-8 VASE	200-250			
	865-15 FLOOR VASE	550-750			
	859-9 VASE	200-250			
	610-9 JARDINIERE	500-525			
	640-7 JARDINIERE	325-375			
	640-10 JARD. & PED.	1500-2000			

IXIA 1937

GEORGE KRAUSE COLLECTION

X	DESCRIPTION	SECONDARY MARKET	PRICE PAID	DATE BOUGHT	CONDITION
	331-9 CONSOLE	175-200			
	327-6 VASE	250-300			
	329-7 CONSOLE	150-175			
	357-5 HANGING BASKET	325-375			
	326-4 BOWL	125-175			
	853-6 VASE	125-150			
	640-4 JARDINIERE	125-150			
	34 FROG	125-150			
	1128 TRIPLE CANDLESTICK	325-400			
	641-5 PLANTER W/DISH	250-300			
	856-8 VASE	200-225			
	328-11½ BOWL & CANDLESTICK	250-300			
	332-12 CONSOLE	200-300			
	864-12 VASE	375-425			
	860-9 VASE	250-275			
	861-10 VASE	275-300			
	863-10 VASE	350-400			
	862-10 VASE	300-350			
	640-8 JARD. & PED.	1000-1500			

JEANETTE 1915

X	DESCRIPTION	SECONDARY MARKET	PRICE PAID	DATE BOUGHT	CONDITION
	VASE	1100-1500			

PICTURES NOT SHOWN:

	545-6 JARDINIERE	200-250			
	545-8 JARDINIERE	250-275			
	545-10 JARDINIERE	275-300			
	545-10X30 JARD. & PED.	1500-1200			
	723-9X21 UMBRELLA	1000-1500			
	#909 CUSPIDOR	300-350			
	#626 CUSPIDOR	300-350			

JONQUIL 1931

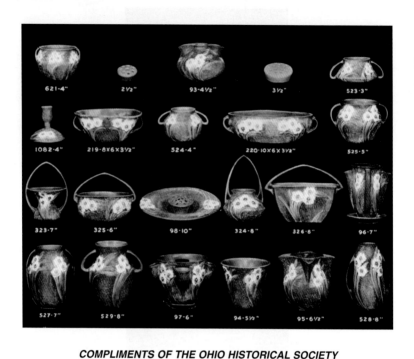

COMPLIMENTS OF THE OHIO HISTORICAL SOCIETY

X	DESCRIPTION	SECONDARY MARKET	PRICE PAID	DATE BOUGHT	CONDITION
	621-4 JARDINIERE	150-200			
	2½ FROG	50-100			
	93-4½ TRIPLE PLANTER	175-250			
	3½ FROG	75-125			
	1082-4 CANDLESTICK	250-300			
	219-8X6X3½ WINDOW BOX	275-325			
	524-4 BOWL	150-200			
	220-10x6x3½ WINDOW BOX	325-400			
	525-5 JARDINIERE	200-225			
	323-7 BASKET	350-450			
	325-6 BASKET	450-550			
	98-10 CONSOLE & FROG	275-375			
	324-8 BASKET	450-550			
	326-8 BASKET	350-450			
	96-7 VASE	325-375			
	527-7 VASE	250-300			
	529-8 VASE	300-350			
	97-6 STRAWBERRY POT	450-500			
	94-5½ PLANTER	275-325			
	95-6½ VASE	400-500			
	528-8 VASE	250-325			

JONQUIL 1931

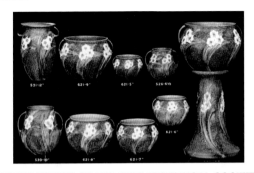

COMPLIMENTS OF THE OHIO HISTORICAL SOCIETY

X	DESCRIPTION	SECONDARY MARKET	PRICE PAID	DATE BOUGHT	CONDITION
	531-12 VASE	800-900			
	621-9 JARDINIERE	500-600			
	621-5 JARDINIERE	175-225			
	526-61/2 VASE	250-325			
	530-10 VASE	650-750			
	621-8 JARDINIERE	400-500			
	621-7 JARDINIERE	374-475			
	621-6 JARDINIERE	325-375			
	621-18X10 JARD. & PED.	2500-3500			

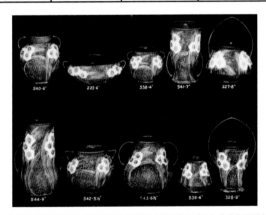

COMPLIMENTS OF THE OHIO HISTORICAL SOCIETY

X	DESCRIPTION	SECONDARY MARKET	PRICE PAID	DATE BOUGHT	CONDITION
	540-6 VASE	250-325			
	223-6 CONSOLE	275-325			
	538-4 VASE	175-250			
	541-7 VASE	350-425			
	327-8 BASKET	450-500			
	544-9 VASE	300-400			
	542-51/2 BOWL	275-325			
	543-61/2 VASE	300-350			
	539-4 BOWL	175-225			
	328-9 BASKET	550-650			

JUVENILE WARE   1916

X	DESCRIPTION	SECONDARY MARKET	PRICE PAID	DATE BOUGHT	CONDITION
	13 BOWL	150-200			
	6 INDIV. CREAMER	125-150			
	6 DBL HANDLED MUG	175-200			
	5 MUG	100-125			
	14 CEREAL BOWL	150-175			
	7 MUG	200-225			
	8 CUP & SAUCER	125-150			
	9-9 DIVIDED DISH	300-400			
	6 BOWL	175-200			
	13 INDIV. CREAMER	200-250			
	8-6¼ ROLLED PLATE	250-275			
	7-7⅞ PLATE	150-200			
	6-6 ROLLED PLATE	200-250			

JUVENILE WARE   1916

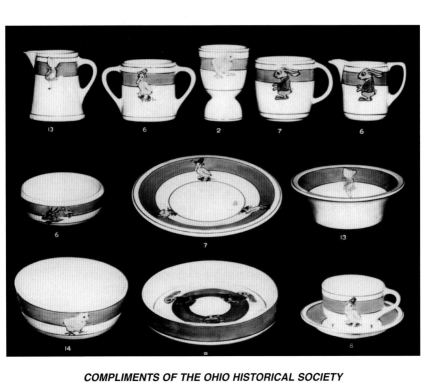

X	DESCRIPTION	SECONDARY MARKET	PRICE PAID	DATE BOUGHT	CONDITION
	13 CREAMER	150-200			
	6-DBL HANDLED MUG	175-200			
	2 EGG CUP	200-250			
	7 MUG	200-225			
	6 IND. CREAMER	125-150			
	6 BOWL	175-200			
	7 DISH	150-200			
	13 BOWL	150-200			
	14 CEREAL BOWL	175-200			
	8 ROLLED PLATE	250-275			
	8 CUP & SAUCER	125-150			

JUVENILE WARE 1916

COMPLIMENTS OF THE OHIO HISTORICAL SOCIETY

X	DESCRIPTION	SECONDARY MARKET	PRICE PAID	DATE BOUGHT	CONDITION
	7 CUP & SAUCER	125-150			
	51 CUSTARD	75-100			
	1 EGG	200-250			
	2 EGG	250-300			
	2 MUG	150-175			
	1 SOAP	250-275			
	3 MUG	100-125			
	1 SODA	225-275			
	1 MUG	125-175			
	6 CUP & SAUCER	150-175			
	4-53/4" PLATE	100-125			
	2-63/4" PLATE	125-150			
	5-61/8" DUTCH PLATE	100-125			
	1-71/2" PLATE	125-150			
	5-61/2" PLATE	100-125			
	6 BREAD & MILK	100-125			
	4 BREAD & MILK	150-175			
	1 BREAD & MILK	100-125			
	3 BREAD & MILK	125-150			
	8 BREAD & MILK	150-175			
	5 BREAD & MILK	150-175			
	2 BREAD & MILK	125-150			
	7 BREAD & MILK	125-150			
	3-81/4" PLATE	150-175			
	9 BREAD & MILK	125-150			
	1 EWER & BASON	300-400			
	1 CHAMBER	250-275			
	2 CHAMBER	225-250			

JUVENILE WARE   1916

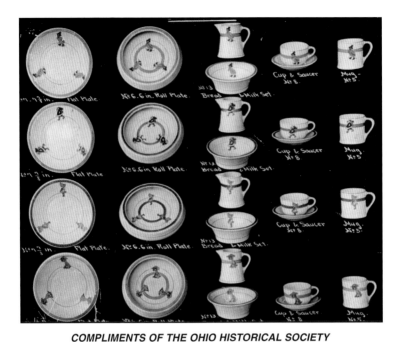

X	DESCRIPTION	SECONDARY MARKET	PRICE PAID	DATE BOUGHT	CONDITION
	7-7⅞" FLAT PLATE	125-150			
	6-6" ROLLED PLATE	100-125			
	13 BREAD & MILK SET	100-125			
	8 CUP & SAUCER	100-125			
	5 MUG	10-125			
	7-7⅞" FLAT PLATE	300-400			
	6-6" ROLL PLATE	250-300			
	13 BREAD & MILK SET	300-400			
	8 CUP & SAUCER	250-300			
	5 MUG	200-250			
	7-7⅞" FLAT PLATE	125-150			
	6-6" ROLL PLATE	100-125			
	13 BREAD & MILK SET	100-125			
	8 CUP & SAUCER	100-125			
	5 MUG	100-125			
	7-7⅞" FLAT PLATE	200-225			
	6-6" ROLL PLATE	175-200			
	13 BREAD & MILK SET	125-150			
	8 CUP & SAUCER	175-200			
	5 MUG	175-200			

KETTLE & SKILLET 1940s

X	DESCRIPTION	SECONDARY MARKET	PRICE PAID	DATE BOUGHT	CONDITION
	DISH	50-75			
	SKILLET	50-75			
	BEAN POT	50-75			

LAMPS

X	DESCRIPTION	SECONDARY MARKET	PRICE PAID	DATE BOUGHT	CONDITION
	BANADA	500-600			
	CARNELIAN II	400-500			
	CHERRY BLOSSOM	700-800			

LAMPS

  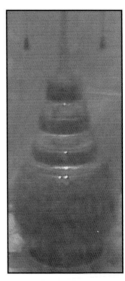

X	DESCRIPTION	SECONDARY MARKET	PRICE PAID	DATE BOUGHT	CONDITION
	FLORENTINE	300-400			
	(BLUE) FREESIA	350-450			
	(RUST) FREESIA	350-450			
	FUCHSIA	500-600			
	FUTURA BALLOON	800-1000			
	FUTURA BALLOON	700-800			

LAMPS

X	DESCRIPTION	SECONDARY MARKET	PRICE PAID	DATE BOUGHT	CONDITION
	FUTURA	800-900			
	IMPERIAL II	400-500			
	IXIA	450-550			
	(BLUE) LUFFA	400-500			
	(RUST) LUFFA	400-500			
	MONTICELLO	300-400			

LAMPS

X	DESCRIPTION	SECONDARY MARKET	PRICE PAID	DATE BOUGHT	CONDITION
	ORIAN	450-550			
	ROSECRAFT PANEL NUDE	700-800			
	ROSECRAFT PANEL FLORAL	600-700			
	ROSECRAFT COLOR	350-450			
	ROSECRAFT COLOR	300-400			
	ROZANE EGYPTO	900-1200			

LAMPS

X	DESCRIPTION	SECONDARY MARKET	PRICE PAID	DATE BOUGHT	CONDITION
	RUSSO	300-400			
	SAVANA	600-700			
	SUNFLOWER	500-600			
	SUNFLOWER	500-600			
	SUNFLOWER	600-700			
	PRIMROSE	300-400			

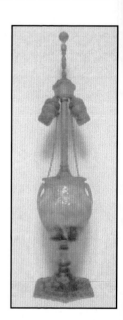

LAMPS

CONTINUED FROM PAGE 203

X	DESCRIPTION	SECONDARY MARKET	PRICE PAID	DATE BOUGHT	CONDITION
	(GOLD) TUSCANY	350-450			
	(RED) TUSCANY	350-450			
	(BLUE) TUSCANY	350-450			

X	DESCRIPTION	SECONDARY MARKET	PRICE PAID	DATE BOUGHT	CONDITION
	VICTORIAN ART	400-500			
	VICTORIAN ART	400-500			
	VICTORIAN ART	500-600			

LAMPS

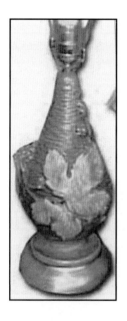

X	DESCRIPTION	SECONDARY MARKET	PRICE PAID	DATE BOUGHT	CONDITION
	WINDSOR	300-400			
	IMPERIAL II	450-500			
	LUFFA	400-500			
	BUSHBERRY	600-700			
	MAGNOLIA	300-350			
	FERALLA	600-700			

LAMPS

GORDON HOPPE COLLECTION

X	DESCRIPTION	SECONDARY MARKET	PRICE PAID	DATE BOUGHT	CONDITION
	FLORENTINE II	400-500			
	(UNKNOWN)	350-450			
	PANEL	400-500			
	CARNELIAN II	500-600			
	SUNFLOWER	500-600			

LAMPS

GORDON HOPPE COLLECTION

EARLY VELMOSS	600-700			
CHERRY BLOSSOM	700-800 EA.			

UNKNOWN LAMPS

X	DESCRIPTION	SECONDARY MARKET	PRICE PAID	DATE BOUGHT	CONDITION
	#1 LAMP	700-800			
	#2 LAMP	400-500			
	#3 LAMP	350-400			

UNKNOWN LAMPS

X	DESCRIPTION	SECONDARY MARKET	PRICE PAID	DATE BOUGHT	CONDITION
	#4 LAMP	500-600			
	#5 LAMP	600-700			
	#6 LAMP	400-500			
	#7 LAMP	450-550			
	#8 LAMP	700-800			

UNKNOWN LAMPS

X	DESCRIPTION	SECONDARY MARKET	PRICE PAID	DATE BOUGHT	CONDITION
	#9 LAMP	550-650			
	#10 LAMP	750-850			
	#11 LAMP	350-450			
	#12 LAMP	550-650			
	#13 LAMP	450-500			
	#14 LAMP	350-450			

UNKNOWN LAMPS

#15 LAMP	400-500			
#16 LAMP	350-450			

GORDON HOPPE COLLECTION

X	DESCRIPTION	SECONDARY MARKET	PRICE PAID	DATE BOUGHT	CONDITION
	BROWN LAMP	600-700			
	GREEN LAMP	600-700			

GORDON HOPPE COLLECTION

LANDSCAPE EARLY TEENS

X	DESCRIPTION	SECONDARY MARKET	PRICE PAID	DATE BOUGHT	CONDITION
	LARGE CASSEROLE	200-225			
	COFFEE POT	350-450			
	CREAMER	75-100			
	INDIV. COFFEE POT	125-150			
	SUGAR	75-100			
	CUSTARD CUP	50-75			

COMPLIMENTS OF THE OHIO HISTORICAL SOCIETY

X	DESCRIPTION	SECONDARY MARKET	PRICE PAID	DATE BOUGHT	CONDITION
	604-5 JARDINIERE	125-175			
	605-5 PLANTER	175-200			
	604-6 JARDINIERE	200-250			
	604-9 JARDINIERE	400-500			
	604-7 JARDINIERE	275-325			
	761-20 UMBRELLA	800-1000			
	604-10 JARD. & PED.	1400-1800			
	604-8 JARD. & PED.	1200-1400			

LA ROSE 1924

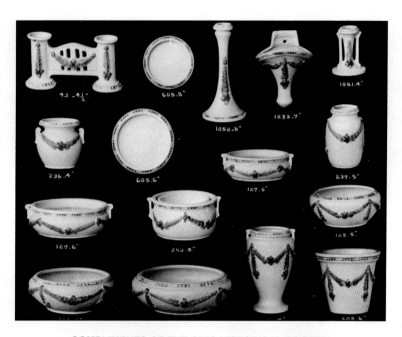

X	DESCRIPTION	SECONDARY MARKET	PRICE PAID	DATE BOUGHT	CONDITION
	43-4 1/2 BRIDGE	150-200			
	605-5 PLATE	175-225			
	1052-8 CANDLESTICKS	250-350			
	1233-7 WALL POCKET	325-425			
	1051-4 CANDLESTICK	175-225			
	236-4 URN	150-200			
	605-6 PLATE	200-250			
	127-5 CONSOLE	125-175			
	237-5 VASE	150-200			
	127-6 CONSOLE	100-150			
	259-5 PLANTER W/LINER	200-250			
	128-5 PLANTER	125-175			
	128-6 PLANTER	125-175			
	128-7 PLANTER	150-200			
	240-7 VASE	175-225			
	605-6 PLANTER	200-225			

LA ROSE 1924

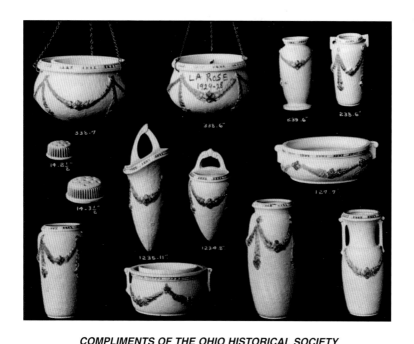

COMPLIMENTS OF THE OHIO HISTORICAL SOCIETY

X	DESCRIPTION	SECONDARY MARKET	PRICE PAID	DATE BOUGHT	CONDITION
	38-7 HANGING BASKET W/LINER	300-400			
	338-6 HANGING BASKET W/LINER	250-300			
	239-6 VASE	175-225			
	238-6 VASE	150-200			
	14-2 1/2 FROG	75-100			
	14-3 1/2 FROG	75-100			
	1235-11 WALL POCKET	400-500			
	1234-8 WALL POCKET	350-450			
	127-7 CONSOLE	125-150			
	241-8 VASE	200-250			
	259-6 PLANTER W/LINER	200-250			
	243-10 VASE	250-300			
	242-8 VASE	225-275			

LAUREL 1934

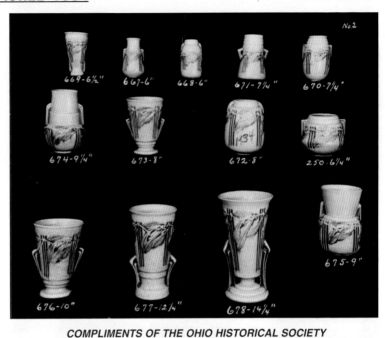

X	DESCRIPTION	SECONDARY MARKET	PRICE PAID	DATE BOUGHT	CONDITION
	669-6 1/2 VASE	200-300			
	667-6 VASE	250-350			
	668-6 VASE	350-450			
	671-7 1/4 VASE	200-300			
	670-7 1/4 VASE	275-375			
	674-9 1/4 VASE	300-400			
	673-8 VASE	275-375			
	672-8 VASE	325-425			
	250-6 1/4 JARDINIERE	200-275			
	676-10 VASE	300-400			
	677-12 1/4 VASE	400-500			
	678-14 1/4 VASE	650-750			
	675-9 VASE	300-400			
	CANDLESTICKS	200-300 EA.			
	673-8 BLEND. VASE	275-375			

226

LEMONADE SETS EARLY 1900s

Lemonade Sets.

COMPLIMENTS OF THE OHIO HISTORICAL SOCIETY

X	DESCRIPTION	SECONDARY MARKET	PRICE PAID	DATE BOUGHT	CONDITION
	DUTCH TUMBLER	100-150			
	DUTCH PITCHER	200-300			
	DUTCH COMP. SET	600-700			
	CONVENTIONAL TUMBLER	50-75			
	CONVENTIONAL PITCHER	100-200			
	CONVENTIONAL COMP. SET	400-500			

PICTURES NOT SHOWN:

	LANDSCAPE TUMBLER SET	100-150			
	LANDSCAPE PITCHER	200-300			
	LANDSCAPE COMPLETE SET	600-700			

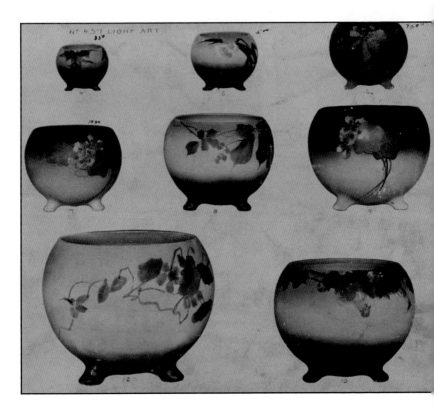

COMPLIMENTS OF THE OHIO HISTORICAL SOCIETY

X	DESCRIPTION	SECONDARY MARKET	PRICE PAID	DATE BOUGHT	CONDITION
	457-4 JARDINIERE	125-150			
	457-5 JARDINIERE	150-175			
	457-6 JARDINIERE	175-200			
	457-7 JARDINIERE	200-225			
	457-8 JARDINIERE	225-250			
	457-9 JARDINIERE	250-275			
	457-12 JARDINIERE	350-400			
	457-10 JARDINIERE	300-350			

LODGE LINE   EARLY TEENS

COMPLIMENTS OF THE OHIO HISTORICAL SOCIETY

X	DESCRIPTION	SECONDARY MARKET	PRICE PAID	DATE BOUGHT	CONDITION
	EAGLE #16 MUG	125-150			
	EAGLE #856 MUG	125-150			
	EAGLE #6 MUG	125-150			
	EAGLE #8 MUG	125-150			
	EAGLE #9 MUG	125-150			
	EAGLE #15 MUG	125-150			
	EAGLE TANKER	250-350			
	ELK #856 MUG	100-125			
	ELK #6 MUG	100-125			
	ELK #8 MUG	100-125			
	ELK #9 MUG	100-125			
	ELK #16 MUG	100-125			
	ELK #15 MUG	100-125			
	ELK TANKER	200-300			

PICTURES NOT SHOWN:

	DESCRIPTION	SECONDARY MARKET	PRICE PAID	DATE BOUGHT	CONDITION
	OSMOND TEMPLE #16 MUG	150-200			
	OSMOND TEMPLE #856 MUG	150-200			

LODGE LINE   EARLY TEENS

CONTINUED FROM PAGE 230

X	DESCRIPTION	SECONDARY MARKET	PRICE PAID	DATE BOUGHT	CONDITION
	OSMOND TEMPLE #6 MUG	150-200			
	OSMOND TEMPLE #8 MUG	150-200			
	OSMOND TEMPLE #9 MUG	150-200			
	OSMOND TEMPLE #9 MUG	150-200			
	OSMOND TEMPLE #15 MUG	150-200			
	OSMOND TEMPLE TANKER	300-400			
	DUTCH #16 MUG	100-125			
	DUTCH #856 MUG	100-125			
	DUTCH #6 MUG	100-125			
	DUTCH #8 MUG	100-125			
	DUTCH #9 MUG	100-125			
	DUTCH #15 MUG	100-125			
	DUTCH TANKER	200-250			
	MONK #16 MUG	150-200			
	MONK #856 MUG	150-200			
	MONK #6 MUG	150-200			
	MONK #8 MUG	150-200			
	MONK #9 MUG	150-200			
	MONK #15 MUG	150-200			
	MONK TANKER	300-400			
	KNIGHTS OF PYTHIAS #16 MUG	150-200			
	KNIGHTS OF PYTHIAS #856 MUG	150-200			
	KNIGHTS OF PYTHIAS #6 MUG	150-200			
	KNIGHTS OF PYTHIAS #8 MUG	150-200			
	KNIGHTS OF PYTHIAS #9 MUG	150-200			
	KNIGHTS OF PYTHIAS #15 MUG	150-200			
	KNIGHTS OF PYTHIAS TANKER	300-400			
	MOOSE #16 MUG	100-125			
	MOOSE #856 MUG	100-125			
	MOOSE #6 MUG	100-125			
	MOOSE #8 MUG	100-125			
	MOOSE #9 MUG	100-125			
	MOOSE #15 MUG	100-125			
	MOOSE TANKER	200-250			
	ALADDIN PATROL #16 MUG	150-200			
	ALADDIN PATROL #856 MUG	150-200			
	ALADDIN PATROL #6 MUG	150-200			
	ALADDIN PATROL #8 MUG	150-200			
	ALADDIN PATROL #9 MUG	150-200			
	ALADDIN PATROL #15 MUG	150-200			
	ALADDIN PATROL TANKER	300-400			

HOSTER FLAG ON STEINS

	8 ounce	125-150			
	10 ounce	150-175			
	12 ounce	175-200			

LOMBARDY 1924

COMPLIMENTS OF THE OHIO HISTORICAL SOCIETY

X	DESCRIPTION	SECONDARY MARKET	PRICE PAID	DATE BOUGHT	CONDITION
	1257-8 WALL POCKET	275-325			
	342-5 HANG. BASKET	500-600			
	342-6 HANG. BASKET	600-700			
	1256-8 WALL POCKET	275-325			
	175-7 CONSOLE	250-275			
	175-6 CONSOLE	200-225			
	175-5 CONSOLE	175-200			
	15-2 1/2 FROG	75-100			
	15-3 1/2 FROG	100-125			
	350-6 VASE	200-225			
	350-9 VASE	300-325			
	350-10 VASE	350-400			

COMPLIMENTS OF THE OHIO HISTORICAL SOCIETY

X	DESCRIPTION	SECONDARY MARKET	PRICE PAID	DATE BOUGHT	CONDITION
	613-6 JARDINIERE	150-200			
	613-7 JARDINIERE	200-250			
	613-8 JARDINIERE	250-300			
	613-9 JARDINIERE	300-350			
	613-10 JARDINIERE	350-400			
	613-12 JARDINIERE	400-450			

LOTUS 1951

GEORGE KRAUSE COLLECTION

X	DESCRIPTION	SECONDARY MARKET	PRICE PAID	DATE BOUGHT	CONDITION
	3" CANDLESTICKS	100-125			
	9" ROUND BOWL	100-150			
	10"X8" SQ. VASE	200-250			
	7" WALL POCKET	200-250			
	10" CYLINDRICAL VASE	200-250			
	10" OBLONG BOWL	275-300			

LUFFA 1934

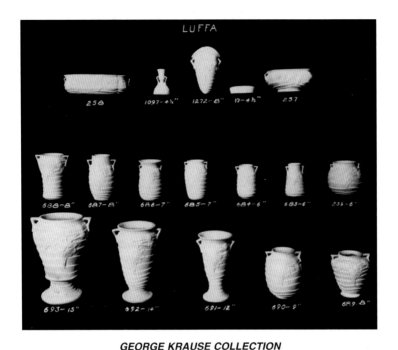

GEORGE KRAUSE COLLECTION

X	DESCRIPTION	SECONDARY MARKET	PRICE PAID	DATE BOUGHT	CONDITION
	258 WINDOW BOX	200-225			
	1097-4 1/2 CANDLESTICK	150-200			
	1272-8 WALL POCKET	300-400			
	17-4 1/2 FROG	75-100			
	257 CONSOLE	125-175			
	688-8 VASE	225-275			
	687-8 VASE	300-325			
	686-7 VASE	275-300			
	685-7 VASE	225-275			
	684-6 VASE	200-250			
	683-6 VASE	175-200			
	236-6 PLANTER	100-150			
	693-15 FLOOR VASE	500-600			
	692-14 FLOOR VASE	425-500			
	691-12 VASE	400-500			
	690-9 VASE	300-400			
	689-8 VASE	250-300			

LUFFA   1934

GEORGE KRAUSE COLLECTION

X	DESCRIPTION	SECONDARY MARKET	PRICE PAID	DATE BOUGHT	CONDITION
	631-9 JARDINIERE	300-400			
	631-7 JARDINIERE	275-300			
	631-6 JARDINIERE	250-275			
	631-5 JARDINIERE	200-225			
	631-4 JARDINIERE	125-150			
	631-10 JARD. & PED.	1200-1500			
	771-10X15 SAND JAR	900-1000			
	631-8 JARD. & PED.	1000-1200			

POTTER AT WORK

LUSTRE 1921

X	DESCRIPTION	SECONDARY MARKET	PRICE PAID	DATE BOUGHT	CONDITION
	1026-10 CANDLESTICK	250-300			
	1021-12 CANDLESTICK	325-350			
	1028-12 CANDLESTICK	325-375			
	87-7 PLANTER	125-175			
	175-6 URN	100-125			
	175-8 URN	150-175			
	86-8 PLANTER	150-200			
	310-9 BASKET	400-500			
	311-9½ BASKET	400-500			
	308-9 BASKET	450-500			
	84-10 DISH	125-175			
	177-12 VASE	200-275			
	85-12 DISH	175-200			
	86-10 DISH	150-200			
	179-14 VASE	250-350			

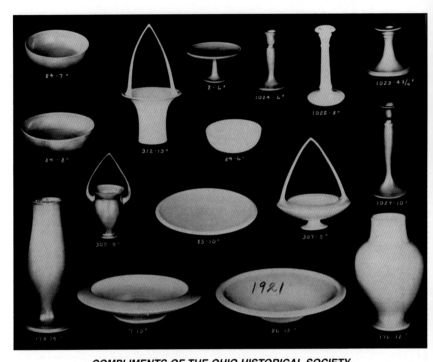

X	DESCRIPTION	SECONDARY MARKET	PRICE PAID	DATE BOUGHT	CONDITION
	84-7 DISH	125-175			
	8-6 PEDESTAL DISH	100-150			
	1024-6 CANDLESTICK	150-200			
	1025-8 CANDLESTICK	200-225			
	1023-4³/4 CANDLESTICK	125-150			
	84-8 DISH	125-175			
	312-13 BASKET	450-500			
	84-6 DISH	100-150			
	309-9 BASKET	350-400			
	85-10 DISH	125-175			
	307-9 BASKET	400-500			
	1027-10 CANDLESTICK	250-300			
	178-14 VASE	200-300			
	7-10 PEDESTAL DISH	150-200			
	86-12 CONSOLE	175-200			
	176-12 VASE	175-200			

LUSTRE 1921

X	DESCRIPTION	SECONDARY MARKET	PRICE PAID	DATE BOUGHT	CONDITION
	1019-8 CANDLESTICKS	125-175			
	5-8 PEDESTAL DISH	150-200			
	34-8 VASE	100-125			
	1020-10 CANDLESTICKS	200-250			
	6-10 COMPOTE	150-200			
	35-10 VASE	100-125			
	15-2½ FROG	50-75			
	295-6 BASKET	200-250			
	15-3½ FROG	75-100			
	82-4 BOWL	100-125			
	299-9 BASKET	350-400			
	294-6 BASKET	300-350			
	297-7½ BASKET	250-350			
	77-5 BOWL	75-100			
	76-5 DISH	75-100			
	296-6 BASKET	200-250			
	169-6 VASE	100-125			
	78-6 BOWL	100-125			
	80-7 DISH	100-150			
	170-7 VASE	100-150			
	298-8 BASKET	350-400			
	81-7 DISH	100-125			
	79-6 DISH	100-125			
	300-14 BASKET	400-500			
	83-5 BOWL	125-150			
	172-9 VASE	125-175			
	173-10 VASE	150-200			
	171-8 VASE	125-150			
	174-14 VASE	250-300			

MAGNOLIA 1943

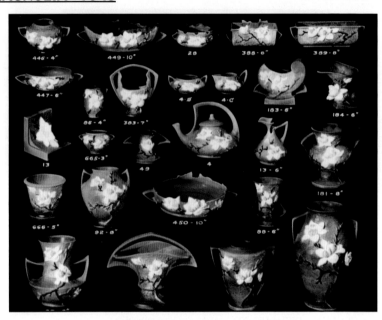

GEORGE KRAUSE COLLECTION

X	DESCRIPTION	SECONDARY MARKET	PRICE PAID	DATE BOUGHT	CONDITION
	446-4 BOWL	125-150			
	449-10 CONSOLE	175-225			
	28 ASHTRAY	150-175			
	388-6 WINDOW BOX	125-175			
	389-8 WINDOW BOX	150-200			
	447-6 CONSOLE	100-125			
	86-4 VASE	100-125			
	383-7 BASKET	175-225			
	4-S SUGAR	75-100			
	4-C CREAMER	75-100			
	183-6 VASE	100-150			
	184-6 CORNUCOPIA	100-150			
	13 BOOKENDS	225-275			
	665-3 BOWL	75-100			
	49 FROG	100-125			
	4 TEAPOT	300-400			
	13-6 EWER	150-200			
	181-8 VASE	150-175			
	666-5 PLANTER W/DISH	175-225			
	92-8 VASE	175-225			
	450-10 CONSOLE	175-225			
	88-6 VASE	100-150			
	93-9 VASE	175-225			
	385-10 BASKET	250-300			
	94-9 VASE	175-225			
	97-14 VASE	300-400			

MAGNOLIA 1943

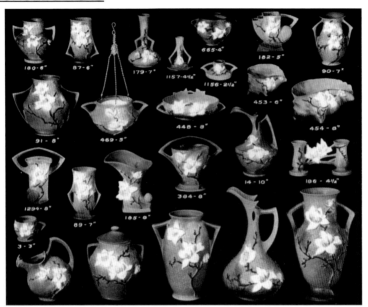

GEORGE KRAUSE COLLECTION

X	DESCRIPTION	SECONDARY MARKET	PRICE PAID	DATE BOUGHT	CONDITION
	180-6 VASE	100-125			
	87-6 VASE	100-125			
	179-7 VASE	125-150			
	1157-4 1/2 CANDLESTICK	125-175			
	665-4 JARDINIERE	100-125			
	1156-2 1/2 CANDLESTICK	75-100			
	182-5 TRIPLE VASE	100-150			
	453-6 SHELL	175-225			
	90-7 VASE	100-150			
	91-8 VASE	175-225			
	469-5 HANG. BASKET	175-275			
	448-8 CONSOLE	150-200			
	454-8 SHELL	175-250			
	1294-8 BASKET	225-325			
	89-7 VASE	100-150			
	185-8 CORNUCOPIA	125-175			
	384-8 BASKET	200-275			
	14-10 EWER	200-300			
	186-4 1/2 BRIDGE	125-175			
	3-3 MUG	75-100			
	1327 PITCHER	300-400			
	2-8 COOKIE JAR	300-500			
	96-12 VASE	350-400			
	15-15 EWER	400-500			
	98-15 FLOOR VASE	400-500			

MAGNOLIA   1943

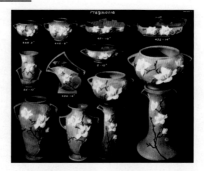

X	DESCRIPTION	SECONDARY MARKET	PRICE PAID	DATE BOUGHT	CONDITION
	665-5 JARDINIERE	100-125			
	446-6 BOWL	150-175			
	451-12 CONSOLE	175-225			
	452-14 CONSOLE	200-250			
	95-10 VASE	200-275			
	386-12 BASKET	325-375			
	5-10 CONSOLE	175-225			
	100-18 FLOOR VASE	600-800			
	99-16 FLOOR VASE	500-700			
	665-8 JARD. & PED.	800-1200			
	665-10 JARD. & PED.	1500-1700			

MATT COLOR   1920

X	DESCRIPTION	SECONDARY MARKET	PRICE PAID	DATE BOUGHT	CONDITION
	609-6 VASE	100-125			
	607-4 VASE	100-125			
	236-3 BOWL	100-125			
	608-6 VASE	100-125			
	548-4 JARDINIERE	100-125			
	236-4 BOWL	100-125			
	624-4 PLANTER	75-100			
	549-4 PLANTER	75-100			
	625-5 JARDINIERE	100-125			
	22 ASHTRAY	75-125			
	550-4 JARDINIERE	75-125			
	364-5 BOWL	125-175			

MATT GREEN   1910

COMPLIMENTS OF THE OHIO HISTORICAL SOCIETY

X	DESCRIPTION	SECONDARY MARKET	PRICE PAID	DATE BOUGHT	CONDITION
	504-7 JARDINIERE	550-650			
	504-9 JARDINIERE	900-1100			
	504-10 JARDINIERE	1200-1500			
	502-6 JARDINIERE	275-325			
	502-8 JARDINIERE	400-500			
	502-10 JARDINIERE	800-900			
	506-8 JARDINIERE	650-750			
	506-9 JARDINIERE	800-900			
	506-10 JARDINIERE	1100-1300			
	508-7 JARDINIERE	500-600			
	508-8 JARDINIERE	650-750			
	508-10 JARDINIERE	1100-1300			
	507-7 JARDINIERE	400-450			
	507-8 JARDINERE	500-600			
	507-9 JARDINIERE	550-650			
	503-8 JARDINIERE	650-750			
	503-9 JARDINIERE	800-900			
	503-10 JARDINIERE	1100-1300			
	501-4 JARDINIERE	200-300			
	501-5 JARDINIERE	300-400			
	501-6 JARDINIERE	400-500			
	501-7 JARDINIERE	500-600			
	501-8 JARDINIERE	650-750			
	501-9 JARDINIERE	800-900			
	501-10 JARDINIERE	1100-1300			
	505-7 JARDINIERE	400-450			
	505-8 JARDINIERE	500-600			
	505-10 JARDINIERE	600-700			

MATT GREEN 1910

COMPLIMENTS OF THE OHIO HISTORICAL SOCIETY

X	DESCRIPTION	SECONDARY MARKET	PRICE PAID	DATE BOUGHT	CONDITION
	463-8 JARDINIERE	400-550			
	463-7 JARDINIERE	275-325			
	463-6 JARDINIERE	150-200			
	463-5 JARDINIERE	125-150			
	463-4 JARDINIERE	100-125			
	463-9 JARDINIERE	550-600			
	463-10 JARDINIERE	650-750			
	463-12 JARDINIERE	800-900			

COMPLIMENTS OF THE OHIO HISTORICAL SOCIETY

X	DESCRIPTION	SECONDARY MARKET	PRICE PAID	DATE BOUGHT	CONDITION
	3645-5 HANG. BASKET	200-250			
	3684-4 HANG. BASKET	200-250			
	3656-5 HANG. BASKET	200-250			
	3676-6 HANG. BASKET	200-250			
	549-4 PLANTER	75-100			
	5.4-6 VASE	100-125			
	5.6-9 VASE	150-200			
	548-3 BOWL	50-75			
	548-4 BOWL	75-100			
	7 BRIDGE	125-150			
	5.7-12 VASE	250-300			
	5.8-15 VASE	450-550			
	4546-10 JARD. & PED.	2000-2500			
	5.5-8 VASE	125-150			
	5.10-18 FLOOR VASE	600-700			

MATT GREEN 1910

X	DESCRIPTION	SECONDARY MARKET	PRICE PAID	DATE BOUGHT	CONDITION
	2-12 VASE	300-400			
	2-16 VASE	500-600			
	1-16 VASE	800-1000			
	1-12 VASE	500-600			
	2-24 VASE	1200-1500			
	2-18 VASE	800-1000			
	1-18 VASE	1100-1300			
	1-24 VASE	1800-2000			

X	DESCRIPTION	SECONDARY MARKET	PRICE PAID	DATE BOUGHT	CONDITION
	3-12 VASE	400-500			
	3-16 VASE	700-800			
	4-16 VASE	700-800			
	4-12 VASE	400-500			
	3-24 VASE	1500-1800			
	3-18 VASE	900-1100			
	4-18 VASE	900-1100			
	4-24 VASE	1500-1800			

MATT GREEN 1910

X	DESCRIPTION	SECONDARY MARKET	PRICE PAID	DATE BOUGHT	CONDITION
	456-5 JARDINIERE	200-250			
	456-6 JARDINIERE	250-300			
	456-7 JARDINIERE	300-350			
	456-8 JARDINIERE	350-400			
	456-9 JARDINIERE	400-450			
	456-10X27 JARD. & PED.	2020-2500			
	456-12X31 JARD. & PED.	3500-4500			

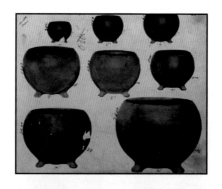

X	DESCRIPTION	SECONDARY MARKET	PRICE PAID	DATE BOUGHT	CONDITION
	457-4 JARDINIERE	125-150			
	457-5 JARDINIERE	150-175			
	457-6 JARDINIERE	175-200			
	457-9 JARDINIERE	200-225			
	457-8 JARDINIERE	225-300			
	457-7 JARDINIERE	300-350			
	457-10 JARDINIERE	450-550			
	457-12 JARDINIERE	550-650			

MATT GREEN 1910

X	DESCRIPTION	SECONDARY MARKET	PRICE PAID	DATE BOUGHT	CONDITION
	468-5 JARDINIERE	125-150			
	468-6 JARDINIERE	150-175			
	468-7 JARDINIERE	175-200			
	468-8 JARDINIERE	200-225			
	468-9 JARDINIERE	225-250			
	468-10 JARDINIERE	250-275			
	468-12 JARDINIERE	325-425			
	456-5 JARDINIERE	125-150			
	456-6 JARDINIERE	150-175			
	456-7 JARDINIERE	175-200			
	456-8 JARDINIERE	200-225			
	456-9 JARDINIERE	225-250			
	456-10 JARDINIERE	250-275			
	456-12 JARDINIERE	325-425			
	501-4 JARDINIERE	200-300			
	501-5 JARDINIERE	300-400			
	501-6 JARDINIERE	400-500			
	501-7 JARDINIERE	500-600			
	501-8 JARDINIERE	650-750			
	501-9 JARDINIERE	800-900			
	501-10 JARDINIERE	1100-1300			
	507-7 JARDINIERE	400-450			
	507-8 JARDINIERE	500-600			
	507-9 JARDINIERE	550-650			
	457-4 JARDINIERE	125-150			
	457-5 JARDINIERE	150-175			
	457-6 JARDINIERE	250-300			
	457-7 JARDINIERE	350-400			
	457-8 JARDINIERE	500-600			
	457-9 JARDINIERE	650-750			
	457-10 JARDINIERE	800-900			
	457-12 JARDINIERE	1000-1200			
	462-3 JARDINIERE	75-100			
	462-4 JARDINIERE	100-125			
	462-5 JARDINIERE	125-150			
	462-6 JARDINIERE	150-200			

MATT GREEN 1910

CONTINUED FROM PAGE 246

X	DESCRIPTION	SECONDARY MARKET	PRICE PAID	DATE BOUGHT	CONDITION
	462-7 JARDINIERE	275-300			
	462-8 JARDINIERE	400-550			
	462-9 JARDINIERE	550-600			
	462-10 JARDINIERE	650-750			
	462-12 JARDINIERE	800-900			
	463-4 JARDINIERE	100-125			
	463-5 JARDINIERE	125-150			
	463-6 JARDINIERE	150-200			
	463-7 JARDINIERE	275-375			
	463-8 JARDINIERE	400-550			
	463-9 JARDINIERE	550-600			
	463-10 JARDINIERE	650-750			
	463-12 JARDINIERE	800-900			
	502-6 JARDINIERE	275-325			
	502-8 JARDINIERE	500-600			
	502-10 JARDINIERE	800-900			
	508-7 JARDINIERE	500-600			
	508-8 JARDINIERE	650-750			
	508-10 JARDINIERE	1100-1300			
	506-8 JARDINIERE	650-750			
	506-9 JARDINIERE	800-900			
	506-10 JARDINIERE	1100-1300			
	506-12 JARDINIERE	1300-1500			
	503-8 JARDINIERE	650-750			
	503-9 JARDINIERE	800-900			
	503-10 JARDINIERE	1100-1300			
	504-7 JARDINIERE	550-650			
	504-9 JARDINIERE	900-1100			
	504-10 JARDINIERE	1200-1500			

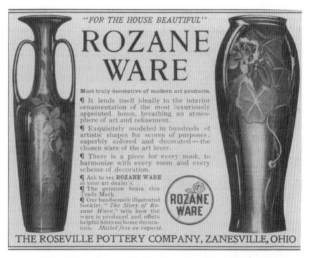

1904 Ad for The Rozane Ware Line

MATT GREEN 1910

X	DESCRIPTION	SECONDARY MARKET	PRICE PAID	DATE BOUGHT	CONDITION
	6" FERN DISH W/LINER	75-100			
	7" FERN DISH W/LINER	125-150			
	8" FERN DISH W/LINER	150-200			
	9" FERN DISH W/LINER	225-250			
	963-4X9 1/2 JARD. & PEDESTAL	400-500			
	102-5 HANG. BASKET	300-350			
	102-4 HANG. BASKET	250-300			
	102-6 HANG. BASKET	400-500			
	102-7 HANG. BASKET	650-750			

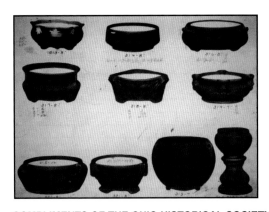

X	DESCRIPTION	SECONDARY MARKET	PRICE PAID	DATE BOUGHT	CONDITION
	313-6 FERN DISH W/LINER	125-150			
	313-7 FERN DISH W/LINER	150-200			
	313-8 FERN DISH W/LINER	225-250			
	314-6 FERN DISH W/LINER	75-100			
	314-7 FERN DISH W/LINER	125-150			
	314-8 FERN DISH W/LINER	150-200			

MATT GREEN 1910

CONTINUED FROM PAGE 248

X	DESCRIPTION	SECONDARY MARKET	PRICE PAID	DATE BOUGHT	CONDITION
	314-9 FERN DISH W/LINER	225-250			
	316-6 FERN DISH W/LINER	125-150			
	316-7 FERN DISH W/LINER	150-200			
	316-8 FERN DISH W/LINER	225-250			
	317-6 FERN DISH W/LINER	150-200			
	317-7 FERN DISH W/LINER	225-250			
	317-8 FERN DISH W/LINER	250-300			
	318-6 FERN DISH W/LINER	125-150			
	318-7 FERN DISH W/LINER	150-200			
	318-8 FERN DISH W/LINER	225-250			
	319-6 FERN DISH W/LINER	150-175			
	319-7 FERN DISH W/LINER	225-250			
	319-8 FERN DISH W/LINER	250-300			
	319-12 FERN DISH W/LINER	400-500			
	320-6 FERN DISH W/LINER	100-200			
	320-8 FERN DISH W/LINER	200-300			
	320-12 FERN DISH W/LINER	350-400			
	321-5 FERN DISH W/LINER	125-150			
	321-7 FERN DISH W/LINER	200-250			
	321-8 FERN DISH W/LINER	250-300			
	321-10 FERN DISH W/LINER	300-350			
	315-7 FERN DISH W/LINER	350-375			
	963 JARD. & PED.	400-500			

PICTURES NOT SHOWN:

	DESCRIPTION	SECONDARY MARKET	PRICE PAID	DATE BOUGHT	CONDITION
	208-7 FERN DISH	125-150			
	209-6 FERN DISH	75-100			
	210-4X8 FERN DISH	175-200			
	211-3 1/2 X6 FERN DISH	100-125			
	212-10 1/2 FERN DISH	200-250			
	213-3 1/2 FERN DISH	50-75			
	213-4 1/2 FERN DISH	50-75			
	213-5 1/2 FERN DISH	50-75			
	214-5 FERN DISH	50-75			
	215-4 FERN DISH	50-75			
	215-5 FERN DISH	50-75			
	216-4 SQ. FERN DISH	75-100			
	217-5 SQ. FERN DISH	75-100			
	218-3 SQ. FERN DISH	50-75			
	218-4 SQ. FERN DISH	50-75			
	218-5 SQ. FERN DISH	50-75			
	E-11 FOOTED FERNERY	100-125			
	315-4 HANG. BASKET	250-300			
	315-5 HANG. BASKET	300-350			
	315-6 HANG. BASKET	350-375			
	315-8 HANG. BASKET	500-600			
	315-9 HANG. BASKET	550-650			
	315-10 HANG. BASKET	650-750			
	3694 HANG. BASKET	300-350			

MATT GREEN 1910

CONTINUED FROM PAGE 249

X	DESCRIPTION	SECONDARY MARKET	PRICE PAID	DATE BOUGHT	CONDITION
	3704 HANG. BASKET	300-350			
	326-10 WALL POCKET	250-300			
	328-10 WALL POCKET	250-300			
	1201-15 WALL POCKET	500-600			
	1205-10 WALL POCKET	250-300			
	1202-15 WALL POCKET	500-600			
	1206-10 WALL POCKET	250-300			
	1203-10 WALL POCKET	250-300			
	1206-12 WALL POCKET	300-400			
	1203-12 WALL POCKET	300-400			
	1204-10 WALL POCKET	250-300			
	1204-12 WALL POCKET	300-400			
	3-18 VASE	175-225			
	E68 BIRDS IN FOLIAGE	250-300			
	#1-3X3 FROG	75-100			
	#1-3X4 FROG	75-100			
	#1-3X6 FROG	75-100			
	#1-4X3 FROG	75-100			
	#1-4X4 FROG	75-100			
	#1-4X6 FROG	75-100			
	#1-6X3 FROG	100-125			
	#1-6X4 FROG	100-125			
	#1-6X6 FROG	125-150			
	#2-3X3 FROG	75-100			
	#2-3X4 FROG	75-100			
	#2-3X6 FROG	75-100			
	#2-4X3 FROG	75-100			
	#2-4X4 FROG	75-100			
	#2-4X6 FROG	75-100			
	#4-3 FROG	50-75			
	#5-6 FROG	50-75			
	#6-4 FROG	50-75			
	#3 BRIDGE	150-200			
	#7 BRIDGE	150-200			
	#10 BRIDGE	150-200			
	1004 CANDLESTICK	100-175			
	1005 CANDLESTICK	100-175			
	1006 CANDLESTICK	100-175			
	1010 CANDLESTICK	100-175			
	#18 ASHTRAY	125-175			
	#19 ASHTRAY	125-175			
	#20 ASHTRAY	125-175			
	466-20 JARDINIERE	1200-1500			
	546-8 JARDINIERE	350-400			
	550-4 JARDINIERE	200-250			
	550-6 JARDINIERE	300-350			
	550-8 JARDINIERE	350-400			
	550-9 JARDINIERE	400-450			
	550-10 JARDINIERE	450-500			
	550-12 JARDINIERE	500-600			

MATT GREEN 1910

CONTINUED FROM PAGE 250

X	DESCRIPTION	SECONDARY MARKET	PRICE PAID	DATE BOUGHT	CONDITION
	550-14 JARDINIERE	600-700			
	558-6 JARDINIERE	300-350			
	558-8 JARDINIERE	350-400			
	558-10 JARDINIERE	450-500			
	558-12 JARDINIERE	500-600			
	559-8 JARDINIERE	350-400			
	559-10 JARDINIERE	450-500			
	452-14X33 JARD. & PEDESTAL	3500-4000			
	456-14X44 JARD. & PEDESTAL	4500-5500			
	462-10X27 JARD. & PEDESTAL	2000-2500			
	462-12X33 JARD. & PEDESTAL	3500-4500			
	468-10X29 JARD. & PEDESTAL	2250-2750			
	468-12X35 JARD. & PEDESTAL	3500-4500			
	552-10X28 JARD. & PEDESTAL	2000-2500			
	552-12X33 JARD. & PEDESTAL	3500-4500			
	531-10X28 JARD. & PEDESTAL	2000-2500			
	534-10X29 JARD. & PEDESTAL	2000-2500			
	547-10X28 JARD. & PEDESTAL	2000-2500			
	739-10X19 UMBRELLA	750-1000			
	728-10X 20 UMBRELLA	750-1000			
	741-10X21 UMBRELLA	750-1000			
	204-3 ROUND FERN DISH	50-75			
	204-4 ROUND FERN DISH	75			
	204-5 ROUND FERN DISH	75-100			
	205-3 ROUND FERN DISH	50-75			
	205-5 ROUND FERN DISH	75			
	202-4 SQ. FERN DISH	50-75			
	202-5 SQ. FERN DISH	50-75			
	202-6 SQ. FERN DISH	75-100			

GEORGE KRAUSE COLLECTION

X	DESCRIPTION	SECONDARY MARKET	PRICE PAID	DATE BOUGHT	CONDITION
	1101-5 CREAMER	75-100			
	1102-5 CREAMER	75-100			
	1103-6 PITCHER	75-100			
	1105-8 PITCHER	100-125			
	1004-9 VASE	100-125			
	1107-12 PITCHER	150-175			
	1106-10 PITCHER	125-150			
	1006-12 VASE	100-150			
	1003-8 VASE	75-100			
	1017-12 VASE	175-200			
	1016-10 VASE	150-175			

GEORGE KRAUSE COLLECTION

X	DESCRIPTION	SECONDARY MARKET	PRICE PAID	DATE BOUGHT	CONDITION
	1119-9 SHELL	75-100			
	1151 SHELL CANDLESTICK	50-75			
	1120-12 SHELL	150-175			
	1118-6 SHELL	50-100			
	1012-10 BASKET	125-150			
	1011-12 COMPOTE	150-175			
	1009-8 BOWL	150-175			
	1010-10 BOWL	75-100			
	116-10 WINDOW BOX	100-125			
	1114-8 WINDOW BOX	75-100			

MAYFAIR   LATE 1940s

GEORGE KRAUSE COLLECTION

X	DESCRIPTION	SECONDARY MARKET	PRICE PAID	DATE BOUGHT	CONDITION
	1111-5 PLANTER	50-75			
	1109-8 BOWL	50-75			
	1110-4 BOWL	50-75			
	90-4 PLANTER	50-75			
	1121 IND. COFFEE	125-150			
	71-4 PLANTER	50-75			
	1018-6 CORNUCOPIA	100-125			
	1122 IND. TEAPOT	150-175			
	1112-8 PLANTER	75-100			
	72-5 PLANTER	50-75			
	1014-8 WALL POCKET	175-200			
	1113-8 PLANTER	75-100			
	1117-5 PLANTER W/DISH	75-100			
	73-6 PLANTER	50-75			
	1115-10 PLANTER	100-125			

MEDALLION   BEFORE 1916

X	DESCRIPTION	SECONDARY MARKET	PRICE PAID	DATE BOUGHT	CONDITION
	HAIR SAVER	75-100			
	IND. TEAPOT	100-150			
	CREAMER	75-100			

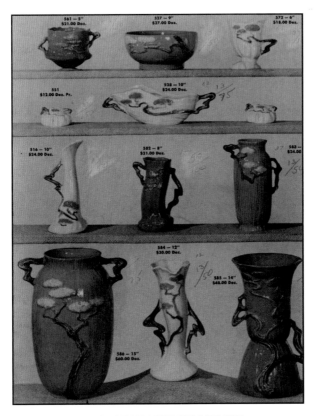

GEORGE KRAUSE COLLECTION

X	DESCRIPTION	SECONDARY MARKET	PRICE PAID	DATE BOUGHT	CONDITION
	561-5 HANG. BASKET	150-175			
	527-9 PLANTER	200-250			
	572-6 VASE	100-150			
	551 CANDLESTICK	50-75			
	528-10 CONSOLE	125-175			
	516-10 VASE	150-200			
	582-8 VASE	125-150			
	583-10 VASE	200-250			
	586-15 FLOOR VASE	300-400			
	584-12 VASE	200-250			
	585-14 VASE	250-300			

MING TREE 1949

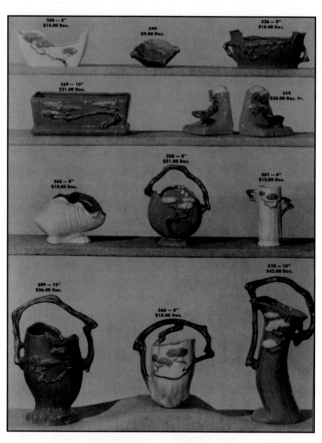

X	DESCRIPTION	SECONDARY MARKET	PRICE PAID	DATE BOUGHT	CONDITION
	568-8 PLANTER	100-150			
	599 ASHTRAY	75-100			
	526-9 CONSOLE	100-150			
	569-10 WINDOW BOX	175-200			
	559 BOOKENDS	100-125			
	563-8 CONCH SHELL	100-150			
	508-8 BASKET	175-225			
	581-6 VASE	100-150			
	509-12 BASKET	225-300			
	566-8 WALL POCKET	225-275			
	510-14 VASE	250-300			

MOCK ORANGE   1950

GEORGE KRAUSE COLLECTION

X	DESCRIPTION	SECONDARY MARKET	PRICE PAID	DATE BOUGHT	CONDITION
	900-4 JARDINIERE	75-100			
	979-7 VASE	100-150			
	980-6 VASE	100-125			
	961-5 HANG. BASKET	300-350			
	953-6 WINDOW BOX	100-150			
	954-7 PLANTER	125-150			
	926-6 BOWL	100-150			
	916-6 EWER	100-125			
	927-6 FOOTED BOWL	150-200			
	957-8 FOOTED BOWL	100-150			
	908-6 BASKET	150-200			
	956-8 WINDOW BOX	150-175			
	968-8 WINDOW BOX	125-175			
	921-6 CORNUCOPIA	100-150			
	952-5 PLANTER	100-150			
	941-5 BOWL	125-150			

MOCK ORANGE   1950

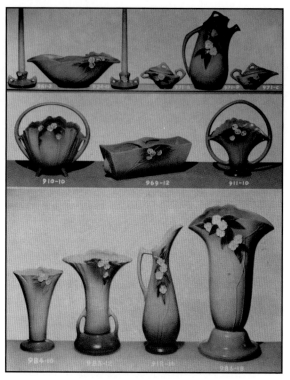

GEORGE KRAUSE COLLECTION

X	DESCRIPTION	SECONDARY MARKET	PRICE PAID	DATE BOUGHT	CONDITION
	951-2 CANDLESTICK	75-100			
	934-12 CONSOLE	175-200			
	971-S SUGAR	100-150			
	971-P PITCHER	200-300			
	971-C CREAMER	100-150			
	910-10 BASKET	200-250			
	969-12 WINDOW BOX	125-175			
	911-10 BASKET	225-325			
	984-10 VASE	125-150			
	985-12 VASE	150-175			
	918-16 EWER	350-450			
	986-18 FLOOR VASE	400-500			

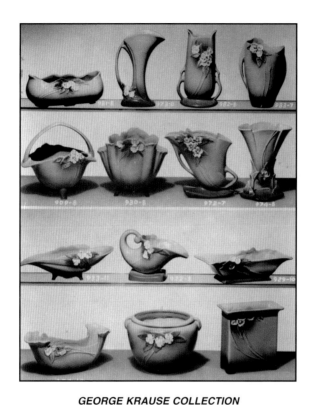

GEORGE KRAUSE COLLECTION

X	DESCRIPTION	SECONDARY MARKET	PRICE PAID	DATE BOUGHT	CONDITION
	931-8 VASE	100-150			
	973-8 VASE	100-150			
	982-8 VASE	100-150			
	983-7 VASE	100-125			
	909-8 BASKET	175-225			
	930-8 VASE	100-125			
	972-7 VASE	100-125			
	974-8 VASE	125-150			
	933-11 COMPOTE	150-200			
	922-8 CORNUCOPIA	150-175			
	929-10 CONSOLE	175-225			
	932-10 CONSOLE	125-175			
	901-6 JARDINIERE	125-150			
	981-7 WINDOW PLANTER	125-175			

MODERN ART/GOLD   1905

X	DESCRIPTION	SECONDARY MARKET	PRICE PAID	DATE BOUGHT	CONDITION
	429B-10½X26 JARD. & PEDESTAL	800-1000			
	429C-10½X26 JARD. & PEDESTAL	800-1000			
	429A-10½X26 JARD. & PEDESTAL	800-1000			
	429 GOLD 10½X26 JARD. & PEDESTAL	800-1000			
	429 GREEN 10½X26 JARD. & PEDESTAL	800-1000			
	429 BLUE 10½X26 JARD. & PEDESTAL	800-1000			
	429 RED 10½X26 JARD. & PEDESTAL	800-1000			

MODERN ART/GOLD 1905

X	DESCRIPTION	SECONDARY MARKET	PRICE PAID	DATE BOUGHT	CONDITION
	429-1-11X26 JARD. & PEDESTAL	800-1000			
	429-2-11X26 JARD. & PEDESTAL	800-1000			
	429-3-11X26 JARD. & PEDESTAL	800-1000			
	410-38 JARD. & PED.	1000-1200			
	410-22 JARD. & PED.	500-700			
	411-38 JARD. & PED.	1000-1200			
	411-22 JARD. & PED.	500-700			

MODERNE 1936

X	DESCRIPTION	SECONDARY MARKET	PRICE PAID	DATE BOUGHT	CONDITION
	1112-5½ TRIPLE CANDLESTICK	200-300			
	1111-4½ CANDLESTICK	150-200			
	302-14 CONSOLE	250-350			
	792-7 TRIPLE VASE	150-200			
	298-6 PEDESTAL PLANTER	150-200			
	295-6 PEDESTAL PLANTER	100-150			
	1110 CANDLESTICK	100-150			
	296-6 PLANTER	100-150			
	793-7 VASE	150-200			
	788-6 VASE	125-175			
	791-8 VASE	150-200			
	800-10 VASE	175-225			
	803-14 VASE	300-400			
	801-10 VASE	175-200			
	795-8 VASE	175-200			
	790-7 VASE	125-150			

GEORGE KRAUSE COLLECTION

X	DESCRIPTION	SECONDARY MARKET	PRICE PAID	DATE BOUGHT	CONDITION
	300-9 CONSOLE	100-150			
	789-6 VASE	125-175			
	301-10 CONSOLE	175-200			
	799-9 VASE	150-200			
	297-6 PED. DISH	150-200			
	27 FROG	200-250			
	299-6 BOWL	150-200			
	787-6 VASE	100-150			
	794-7 VASE	150-200			
	797-8 VASE	175-225			
	802-12 VASE	250-300			
	798-9 VASE	175-225			
	796-8 VASE	175-225			
	26-7 FROG	175-200			

MONTACELLO WARE

561-7" · 556-5" · 559-5" · 333-6" · 563-8"

565-10" · 555-4" · 562-7" · 332-6" · 564-9"

COMPLIMENTS OF THE OHIO HISTORICAL SOCIETY

X	DESCRIPTION	SECONDARY MARKET	PRICE PAID	DATE BOUGHT	CONDITION
	561-7 VASE	375-475			
	556-5 VASE	275-375			
	559-6 JARDINIERE	250-350			
	333-6 BASKET	450-550			
	563-8 VASE	450-550			
	565-10 VASE	500-600			
	555-4 VASE	200-300			
	562-7 VASE	400-500			
	332-6 BASKET	550-650			
	564-9 VASE	500-600			
	557-5 VASE	300-375			
	1085-41/2 CANDLESTICK	300-400			
	225-10 CONSOLE	250-350			
	558-5 VASE	300-400			
	560-6 VASE	350-450			

MORNING GLORY 1935

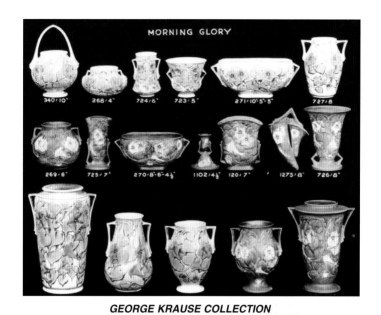

MORNING GLORY

GEORGE KRAUSE COLLECTION

X	DESCRIPTION	SECONDARY MARKET	PRICE PAID	DATE BOUGHT	CONDITION
	340-10 BASKET	750-850			
	268-4 BOWL	400-450			
	724-6 VASE	600-700			
	723-5 PLANTER	400-500			
	271-10X5X5 WINDOW BOX	450-600			
	727-8 VASE	500-600			
	269-6 BOWL	450-550			
	725-7 VASE	400-500			
	270-8X6X4$1/2$ WINDOW BOX	400-500			
	1102-4$1/2$ CANDLESTICK	250-350			
	120-7 PILLOW VASE	450-550			
	1275-8 WALL POCKET	800-1000			
	726-8 VASE	600-700			
	732-14 VASE	1500-1700			
	730-10 VASE	700-800			
	729-9 VASE	700-800			
	728-9 VASE	700-800			
	731-12 VASE	1000-1200			

MOSS 1936

GEORGE KRAUSE COLLECTION

X	DESCRIPTION	SECONDARY MARKET	PRICE PAID	DATE BOUGHT	CONDITION
	291-5 DISH	150-200			
	1109-2 CANDLESTICK	100-200			
	24 FROG	125-140			
	25 FROG	150-175			
	291-6 DISH	175-200			
	1278-8 WALL POCKET	600-800			
	773-5 PLANTER	200-300			
	1107 CANDLESTICK	175-200			
	1108 TRIPLE CANDLESTICK	400-600			
	291-7 DISH	175-225			
	294-12 WINDOW BOX	300-350			
	292-8 CONSOLE	225-250			
	293-10 CONSOLE	200-300			
	353-5 HANG. BASKET	350-450			
	637-5 PLANTER W/DISH	250-300			
	1279-4 WALL POCKET	1000-1200			
	778-7 VASE	225-300			
	781-8 VASE	250-350			

X	DESCRIPTION	SECONDARY MARKET	PRICE PAID	DATE BOUGHT	CONDITION
	774-6 VASE	250-300			
	775-6 VASE	175-225			
	776-7 VASE	200-300			
	777-7 VASE	225-235			
	783-9 VASE	350-400			
	782-9 VASE	325-375			
	781-8 VASE	250-300			
	289-4 JARDINIERE	150-225			
	635-5 JARDINIERE	150-200			
	779-8 URN	150-200			
	784-10 URN	550-600			
	785-12 URN	600-650			
	786-14 URN	650-700			

MOSS   1936

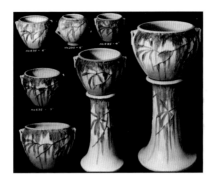

GEORGE KRAUSE COLLECTION

X	DESCRIPTION	SECONDARY MARKET	PRICE PAID	DATE BOUGHT	CONDITION
	635-6 JARDINIERE	200-250			
	290-6 JARDINIERE	200-300			
	635-4 JARDINIERE	150-200			
	635-7 JARDINIERE	200-300			
	635-9 JARDINIERE	400-500			
	635-8 JARD. & PED.	1000-1500			
	635-10 JARD. & PED.	1500-2500			

MOSTIQUE   1915

COMPLIMENTS OF THE OHIO HISTORICAL SOCIETY

X	DESCRIPTION	SECONDARY MARKET	PRICE PAID	DATE BOUGHT	CONDITION
	334-6 HANG. BASKET	225-325			
	164-10 VASE	175-225			
	164-6 VASE	125-175			
	164-8 VASE	150-200			
	631 CUSPIDOR	250-300			
	334-8 HANG. BASKET	275-375			
	73-5 FERN DISH	75-100			
	72-6 FERN DISH	75-100			
	73-7 FERN DISH	100-125			
	72-8 FERN DISH	100-125			
	1224-12 WALL POCKET	250-350			
	1224-10 WALL POCKET	175-225			
	164-10 VASE	200-300			
	164-15 VASE	350-450			

MOSTIQUE 1915

COMPLIMENTS OF THE OHIO HISTORICAL SOCIETY

X	DESCRIPTION	SECONDARY MARKET	PRICE PAID	DATE BOUGHT	CONDITION
	253-5 PLANTER	100-150			
	593-7 PLANTER	100-175			
	253-6 PLANTER	100-150			
	592-8 PLANTER	150-200			
	592-6 PLANTER	100-150			
	592-10 PLANTER	200-250			
	593-12 PLANTER	200-350			
	593-9 PLANTER	200-250			

PICTURES NOT SHOWN:

	573-7 JARDINIERE	100-175			
	573-8 JARDINIERE	175-200			
	573-9 JARDINIERE	200-250			
	573-10 JARDINIERE	250-300			
	573-12 JARDINIERE	350-400			
	571-10X28 JARD. & PEDESTAL	1000-1500			
	573-1-X29 JARD. & PEDESTAL	1000-1500			
	573-12X33 JARD. & PEDESTAL	1500-2000			
	752-10X20 UMBRELLA	750-1250			

MOSTIQUE 1915

COMPLIMENTS OF THE OHIO HISTORICAL SOCIETY

X	DESCRIPTION	SECONDARY MARKET	PRICE PAID	DATE BOUGHT	CONDITION
	131-4 FERN DISH	75-100			
	131-5 FERN DISH	75-100			
	131-6 FERN DISH	100-125			
	131-7 FERN DISH	125-150			
	606-6 JARDINIERE	150-200			
	606-7 JARDINIERE	200-225			
	606-8 JARDINIERE	225-250			
	606-9 JARDINIERE	300-350			
	606-10 JARD. & PED.	900-1100			

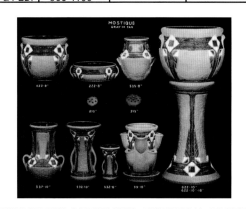

COMPLIMENTS OF THE OHIO HISTORICAL SOCIETY

X	DESCRIPTION	SECONDARY MARKET	PRICE PAID	DATE BOUGHT	CONDITION
	622-8 JARDINIERE	400-500			
	222-8 FERN DISH	100-150			
	535-8 VASE	175-225			
	21/2 FROG	50-75			
	31/2 FROG	50-75			
	537-10 VASE	200-250			
	532-10 VASE	175-225			
	532-6 VASE	125-150			
	99-10 STRAWBERRY PLANTER	500-600			
	622-10X18 JARD & PED.	1000-1600			

MOSTIQUE 1915

X	DESCRIPTION	SECONDARY MARKET	PRICE PAID	DATE BOUGHT	CONDITION
	622-7 JARDINIERE	225-275			
	221-6 DISH	75-100			
	532-8 VASE	150-200			
	533-8 VASE	125-175			
	534-8 VASE	200-250			
	532-12 VASE	225-275			
	536-12 VASE	150-175			
	100-10 STRAWBERRY PLANTER	500-600			
	1083-4 CANDLESTICK	175-200			
	622-9 JARDINIERE	350-400			

X	DESCRIPTION	SECONDARY MARKET	PRICE PAID	DATE BOUGHT	CONDITION
	3-6 VASE	100-125			
	8-8 VASE	125-175			
	21-10 VASE	125-175			
	9-8 VASE	150-200			
	7-8 VASE	150-175			
	11-6 VASE	125-150			
	26-12 VASE	300-350			
	15-10 VASE	150-175			
	22-10 VASE	150-200			
	30-12 VASE	325-350			

MOSTIQUE 1915

X	DESCRIPTION	SECONDARY MARKET	PRICE PAID	DATE BOUGHT	CONDITION
	19-10 VASE	200-250			
	2-6 VASE	100-150			
	14-8 VASE	100-150			
	5-6 VASE	100-150			
	1-6 VASE	100-125			
	17-10 VASE	200-250			
	27-12 VASE	325-375			
	24-10 VASE	200-250			
	20-10 VASE	175-225			
	29-12 VASE	300-350			

X	DESCRIPTION	SECONDARY MARKET	PRICE PAID	DATE BOUGHT	CONDITION
	12-8 VASE	150-200			
	13-8 VASE	150-200			
	11-8 VASE	150-200			
	4-6 VASE	100-125			
	10-8 VASE	150-200			
	18-10 VASE	200-250			
	25-12 VASE	300-350			
	16-10 VASE	200-250			
	23-10 VASE	200-250			
	28-12 VASE	300-350			

MOWA   1917 OR 1934

COMPLIMENTS OF THE OHIO HISTORICAL SOCIETY

X	DESCRIPTION	SECONDARY MARKET	PRICE PAID	DATE BOUGHT	CONDITION
	246-2 3/4 DISH	125-150			
	245-6 VASE	200-225			
	658-7 1/4 VASE	175-200			
	657-6 3/4 VASE	150-175			
	656-6 VASE	125-150			
	1093-4 CANDLESTICK	300-325			
	659-8 VASE	250-275			
	660-8 1/4 VASE	250-275			
	661-9 1/4 VASE	275-325			
	662-9 VASE	300-325			
	663-10 VASE	325-350			
	666-15 VASE	800-1000			
	665-14 1/2 VASE	600-700			
	664-12 1/4 VASE	400-450			
	246-3 DISH	150-175			

NORMANDY 1924-1928

COMPLIMENTS OF THE OHIO HISTORICAL SOCIETY

X	DESCRIPTION	SECONDARY MARKET	PRICE PAID	DATE BOUGHT	CONDITION
	341-5 HANG. BASKET	350-400			
	341-6 HANG. BASKET	400-500			
	609-7 JARDINIERE	275-325			
	609-8 JARDINIERE	300-350			
	609-9 JARDINIERE	350-400			
	609-10 JARDINIERE	450-500			
	609-10 JARDINIERE & PEDESTAL	1400-1500			

NOVA 1949-1950

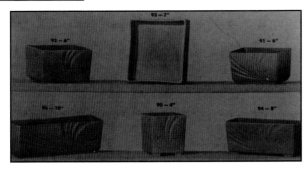

GEORGE KRAUSE COLLECTION

X	DESCRIPTION	SECONDARY MARKET	PRICE PAID	DATE BOUGHT	CONDITION
	92-6 PLANTER	50-75			
	93-7 DISH	50-75			
	91-6 PLANTER	50-75			
	96-10 WINDOW BOX	100-125			
	90-4 PLANTER	50-75			
	94-8 WINDOW BOX	75-100			

NOVELTY STEINS

COMPLIMENTS OF THE OHIO HISTORICAL SOCIETY

X	DESCRIPTION	SECONDARY MARKET	PRICE PAID	DATE BOUGHT	CONDITION
	9-1 STEINS	150-200			
	6-2 STEINS	150-200			
	856-3 STEINS	150-200			
	16-4 STEINS	150-200			
	15-5 STEINS	150-200			
	15-6 STEINS	150-200			
	9-7 STEINS	150-200			
	16-8 STEINS	150-200			
	8-9 STEINS	150-200			
	6-10 STEINS	150-200			
	8-11 STEINS	150-200			
	856-12 STEINS	150-200			

NURSERY   EARLY TEENS

CHARLOTTE BUCHANAN COLLECTION

X	DESCRIPTION	SECONDARY MARKET	PRICE PAID	DATE BOUGHT	CONDITION
	HIGGLEDY PIGGLEDY	200-300			
	LITTLE JACK HORNER	200-300			

NOT SHOWN:

	LITTLE BO PEEP	200-300			
	TOM THE PIPERS SON	200-300			
	LITTLE MISS MUFFET	200-300			
	TOM THUMB	200-300			
	HICKORY DICKORY DOCK	200-300			

PICTURES NOT SHOWN:

	#1 BREAD & MILK SET	150-175			
	#2 BREAD & MILK SET	150-175			
	#3 BREAD & MILK SET	150-175			
	#4 BREAD & MILK SET	150-175			
	#5 BREAD & MILK SET	150-175			
	#6 CUP & SAUCER	100-125			
	#181 CASSEROLE	175-200			
	CUSTARD	75-100			
	RAMEKINS	75-100			
	CHILD'S MUG #1	125-175			
	CHILD'S MUG #2	150-175			
	SODA MUG	225-275			
	INDIVID. TEAPOT	300-350			
	#2 TEASET	400-500			
	#8 TEASET	400-500			
	BABY PLATE #1	100-125			
	BABY PLATE #2-7"	100-125			
	BABY PLATE #3-8 1/4"	125-150			
	CREAMER #10 1/4 PT.	125-150			
	CREAMER #13 1/4 PT.	125-150			
	CREAMER #10 1/2 PT.	150-175			
	CREAMER #14 1/2 PT.	150-175			
	1004 GOODNIGHT				
	CANDLESTICK	400-450			

OPAC ENAMELS   BEFORE 1900

X	DESCRIPTION	SECONDARY MARKET	PRICE PAID	DATE BOUGHT	CONDITION
	463-8 JARDINIERE	250-275			
	463-7 JARDINIERE	225-250			
	463-6 JARDINIERE	200-225			
	463-5 JARDINIERE	175-200			
	463-4 JARDINIERE	150-175			
	463-9 JARDINIERE	275-300			
	463-10 JARDINIERE	300-400			
	463-12 JARDINIERE	400-500			

ORAIN 1935

GEORGE KRAUSE COLLECTION

X	DESCRIPTION	SECONDARY MARKET	PRICE PAID	DATE BOUGHT	CONDITION
	743-14 VASE	400-550			
	741-10 VASE	300-400			
	739-9 VASE	200-275			
	740-10 VASE	200-300			
	742-12 VASE	300-450			
	274-6 BOWL	200-250			
	734-7 VASE	125-200			
	735-7 VASE	150-250			
	1276-8 WALL POCKET	600-700			
	736-8 VASE	150-250			
	738-9 VASE	200-275			
	733-6 VASE	150-250			
	273-12X5X4$1/2$ WINDOW BOX	200-250			
	1108-4$1/2$ CANDLESTICK	175-250			
	272-10 COMPOTE	175-275			
	737-7 VASE	175-200			

PASADENA PLANTERS   CIRCA 1952

GEORGE KRAUSE COLLECTION

X	DESCRIPTION	SECONDARY MARKET	PRICE PAID	DATE BOUGHT	CONDITION
	L2B PLANTER	90-130			
	L10-8 PLANTER	60-120			
	L11-10 PLANTER	100-150			
	L12-12 PLANTER	125-175			
	L14-4 PLANTER	50-100			
	L15-5 PLANTER	75-125			
	L16-7 PLANTER	75-125			
	L17-9 PLANTER	100-150			
	L18-6 PLANTER	50-100			
	L19-8 PLANTER	100-150			
	L20-10 PLANTER	100-150			
	L21-12 PLANTER	100-150			
	L22-4 PLANTER	100-150			
	L23-5 PLANTER	125-175			
	L24-3 PLANTER	100-150			
	L24-6 PLANTER	125-175			

ARTIST DRAWING

PASADENA PLANTERS   CIRCA 1952

X	DESCRIPTION	SECONDARY MARKET	PRICE PAID	DATE BOUGHT	CONDITION
	L26-7 PLANTER	50-100			
	L27-5 PLANTER	50-100			
	L28-6 PLANTER	100-150			
	L29-7 PLANTER	75-125			
	L30-3 PLANTER	75-125			
	L31-4 PLANTER	75-125			
	L32-5 PLANTER	100-150			
	L33-6 PLANTER	100-150			
	L34-8 PLANTER	100-150			
	L35-10 PLANTER	100-150			
	L36-4 PLANTER	100-150			
	L37-5 PLANTER	75-125			
	L38-6 PLANTER	75-125			

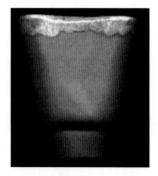

L-36

PAULEO 1914

BOB BETTINGER COLLECTION   *HARDY HUDSON COLLECTION*

X	DESCRIPTION	SECONDARY MARKET	PRICE PAID	DATE BOUGHT	CONDITION
	LAMP	900-1200			
	LAMP	900-1200			
	LAMP	800-900			
	VASE	600-700			

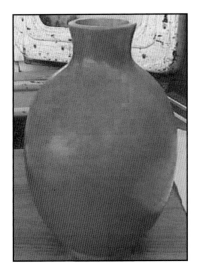

PAULEO 1914

X	DESCRIPTION	SECONDARY MARKET	PRICE PAID	DATE BOUGHT	CONDITION
	VASE	1000-1300			
	VASE	1000-1300			
	VASE	900-1200			
	VASE	750-1250			

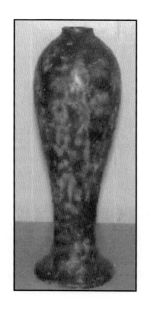

PEONY 1942

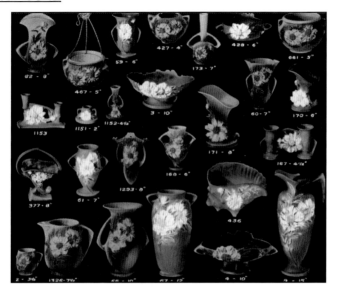

GEORGE KRAUSE COLLECTION

X	DESCRIPTION	SECONDARY MARKET	PRICE PAID	DATE BOUGHT	CONDITION
	62-8 VASE	175-225			
	467-5 HANG. BASKET	200-275			
	59-6 VASE	100-150			
	427-4 JARDINIERE	100-125			
	173-7 VASE	100-125			
	428-6 CONSOLE	125-175			
	661-5 JARDINIERE	150-175			
	1153 DOUBLE CANDLESTICK	200-250			
	1151-2 CANDLESTICK	100-125			
	1152-41/2 CANDLESTICK	125-150			
	3-10 COMPOTE	275-325			
	171-8 CORNUCOPIA	150-175			
	60-7 VASE	125-150			
	170-6 CORNUCOPIA	100-175			
	377-8 BASKET	150-200			
	61-7 VASE	125-150			
	1293-8 WALL POCKET	225-325			
	168-6 VASE	150-200			
	436 SHELL	175-275			
	167-41/2 BRIDGE	100-175			
	2-31/2 MUG	100-125			
	1326-71/2 PITCHER	225-325			
	66-10 VASE	225-275			
	67-12 VASE	275-325			
	4-10 COMPOTE	225-275			
	9-15 EWER	400-475			

PEONY 1942

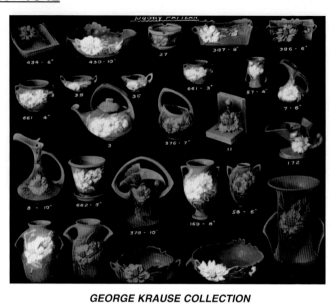

GEORGE KRAUSE COLLECTION

X	DESCRIPTION	SECONDARY MARKET	PRICE PAID	DATE BOUGHT	CONDITION
	434-6 PIN TRAY	150-200			
	430-10 CONSOLE	150-200			
	27 ASHTRAY	150-175			
	387-8 WINDOW BOX	150-175			
	386-6 WINDOW BOX	125-150			
	661-4 JARDINIERE	100-125			
	3S SUGAR	100-125			
	3 TEAPOT	300-325			
	3C CREAMER	100-125			
	661-3 JARDINIERE	100-125			
	57-4 VASE	100-125			
	7-6 EWER	125-150			
	376-7 BASKET	200-225			
	11 BOOKEND	225-250			
	172 DOUBLE CORNUCOPIA	150-200			
	8-10 EWER	225-275			
	662-5 PLANTER W/DISH	150-175			
	378-10 BASKET	225-325			
	169-8 VASE	150-200			
	58-6 VASE	100-150			
	65-9 VASE	175-225			
	64-9 VASE	175-225			
	429-8 CONSOLE	150-175			
	431-10 CONSOLE	175-200			
	68-14 VASE	350-375			

PEONY   1942

GEORGE KRAUSE COLLECTION

X	DESCRIPTION	SECONDARY MARKET	PRICE PAID	DATE BOUGHT	CONDITION
	427-6 BOWL	125-175			
	661-6 JARDINIERE	200-250			
	432-12 CONSOLE	200-250			
	433-14 CONSOLE	250-300			
	63-8 VASE	150-175			
	379-12 BASKET	325-375			
	435-10 PIN TRAY	150-200			
	70-18 FLOOR VASE	450-500			
	69-15 VASE	350-450			
	661-8 JARD. & PED.	1000-1200			
	661-10 JARD. & PED.	1300-1500			

PERSIAN 1908

X	DESCRIPTION	SECONDARY MARKET	PRICE PAID	DATE BOUGHT	CONDITION
	523-4 JARDINIERE W/LINER	200-250			
	523-5 JARDINIERE W/LINER	250-300			
	523-7 JARDINIERE W/LINER	300-350			
	523-9 JARDINIERE W/LINER	350-400			
	523-6 JARDINIERE	400-450			
	523-8 JARDINIERE W/LINER	500-600			
	523-10 JARDINIERE W/LINER	600-700			

PICTURES NOT SHOWN:

	557-6 JARDINIERE	250-300			
	557-8 JARDINIERE	400-500			
	557-10 JARDINIERE	550-600			

PERSIAN 1908

X	DESCRIPTION	SECONDARY MARKET	PRICE PAID	DATE BOUGHT	CONDITION
	462-7 JARDINIERE	350-400			
	462-6 JARDINIERE	300-350			
	462-5 JARDINIERE	250-300			
	315-8 HANG. BASKET	650-750			
	462-9 JARDINIERE	500-550			
	462-8 JARDINIERE	450-550			
	462-10X271/2 JARD. & PEDESTAL	1800-2200			
	462-12X33 JARD. & PEDESTAL	2250-2750			

PERSIAN 1908

X	DESCRIPTION	SECONDARY MARKET	PRICE PAID	DATE BOUGHT	CONDITION
	315-4 HANG. BASKET	325-425			
	315-5 HANG. BASKET	325-425			
	315-6 HANG. BASKET	425-525			
	315-7 HANG. BASKET	550-650			
	315-8 HANG. BASKET	650-700			
	JARDINIERE & PEDESTAL	2500-3000			

HARDY HUDSON COLLECTION

PINECONE 1935

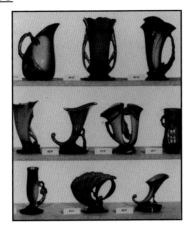

GEORGE KRAUSE COLLECTION

X	DESCRIPTION	SECONDARY MARKET	PRICE PAID	DATE BOUGHT	CONDITION
	415-2QT PITCHER	500-800			
	491-10 VASE	500-750			
	485-10 VASE	500-700			
	490-8 VASE	350-450			
	422-8 VASE	250-325			
	473-8 VASE	300-400			
	480-7 VASE	150-225			
	479-7 VASE	200-300			
	472-6 VASE	375-450			
	421-6 CORNUCOPIA	150-250			
	414-5 VASE	175-250			
	466 WALL POCKET	400-600			
	459B BOOKENDS	350-450			

GEORGE KRAUSE COLLECTION

X	DESCRIPTION	SECONDARY MARKET	PRICE PAID	DATE BOUGHT	CONDITION
	492-12 VASE	800-1200			
	493-12 VASE	350-450			
	416-18 EWER	1200-1800			
	405-8 JARD. & PED.	900-1200			
	406-10 JARD. & PED.	1000-1500			

PINECONE 1935

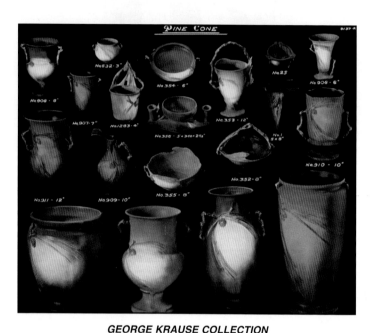

GEORGE KRAUSE COLLECTION

X	DESCRIPTION	SECONDARY MARKET	PRICE PAID	DATE BOUGHT	CONDITION
	908-8 URN	300-400			
	907-7 VASE	300-400			
	632-3 JARDINIERE	150-200			
	1283-4 WALL POCKET	1000-1500			
	354-6 DISH	150-200			
	356-5X3$1/2$X2$1/2$				
	CONSOLE & CANDLESTICKS	400-600			
	353-12 BASKET	400-600			
	25 ASHTRAY	150-250			
	1-5x8 WALL SHELF	700-900			
	906-6 VASE	200-300			
	911-12 VASE	700-800			
	909-10 EWER	350-500			
	355-8 CONSOLE	175-225			
	352-8 BASKET	800-1000			
	910-10 VASE	500-600			
	776-14 SAND JAR	2000-3000			
	912-15 VASE	2000-2800			
	913-18 FLOOR VASE	2000-2500			
	777-20 FLOOR VASE	2800-3800			

PINECONE   1935

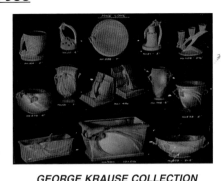

GEORGE KRAUSE COLLECTION

X	DESCRIPTION	SECONDARY MARKET	PRICE PAID	DATE BOUGHT	CONDITION
	124-5 VASE	250-325			
	20-4 FROG	150-200			
	288-7 DISH	400-500			
	21-5 FROG	175-225			
	1106-5 1/2 TRIPLE VASE	500-700			
	278-4 BOWL	250-325			
	121-7 VASE	200-300			
	1-4 3/4 BOOKENDS	400-600			
	748-6 VASE	250-350			
	633-5 PLANTER W/ DISH	300-450			
	379-9X3X3 1/2 WINDOW BOX	400-600			
	380-10X5 1/2 WINDOW BOX	1200-1500			
	279-9X6 COMPOTE	275-325			

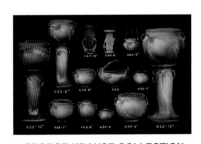

GEORGE KRAUSE COLLECTION

X	DESCRIPTION	SECONDARY MARKET	PRICE PAID	DATE BOUGHT	CONDITION
	747-10 VASE	450-550			
	746-8 VASE	250-350			
	352-5 HANG. BASKET	800-1200			
	632-8 JARD. & PED.	550-750			
	632-6 JARDINIERE	300-400			
	339 BASKET	500-700			
	632-5 JARDINIERE	200-300			
	632-10 JARD. & PED.	900-1200			
	632-7 JARDINIERE	400-500			
	745-6 VASE	225-300			
	632-4 JARDINIERE	200-275			
	632-9 JARDINIERE	600-900			
	632-12 JARD. & PED.	1500-2000			

PINECONE 1935

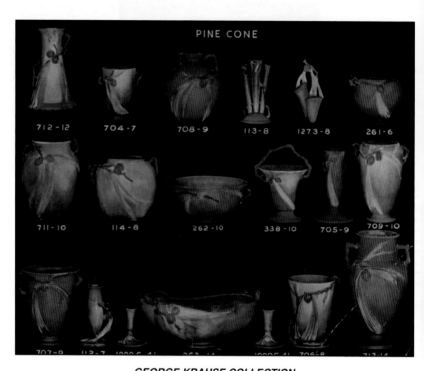

PINE CONE

712-12   704-7   708-9   113-8   1273-8   261-6

711-10   114-8   262-10   338-10   705-9   709-10

707-9   113-7   1099C-4½   263-14   1099C-4½   706-8   713-14

GEORGE KRAUSE COLLECTION

X	DESCRIPTION	SECONDARY MARKET	PRICE PAID	DATE BOUGHT	CONDITION
	712-12 VASE	400-600			
	704-7 VASE	250-325			
	708-9 VASE	800-1000			
	113-8 TRIPLE VASE	275-325			
	1273-8 WALL POCKET	350-450			
	261-6 BOWL	250-350			
	711-10 VASE	500-700			
	114-8 VASE	350-500			
	262-10 CONSOLE	350-500			
	338-10 BASKET	350-550			
	705-9 VASE	300-400			
	709-10 VASE	500-700			
	707-9 VASE	400-500			
	112-7 VASE	200-300			
	1099C-4½ CANDLESTICK	275-400			
	263-14 CONSOLE	350-450			
	706-8 VASE	350-400			
	713-14 VASE	700-1000			

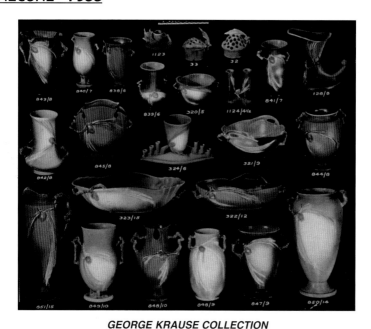

PINECONE 1935

GEORGE KRAUSE COLLECTION

X	DESCRIPTION	SECONDARY MARKET	PRICE PAID	DATE BOUGHT	CONDITION
	843-8 VASE	400-500			
	840-7 VASE	300-400			
	838-6 VASE	200-300			
	1123 CANDLESTICK	200-300			
	839-6 VASE	200-300			
	33 FROG	200-300			
	320-5 BOWL	150-225			
	32 FROG	175-250			
	1124-4½ DBL. VASE	500-600			
	841-7 VASE	300-400			
	128-8 CORNUCOPIA	225-325			
	842-8 VASE	325-375			
	845-10 PILLOW VASE	400-500			
	324-6 CENTERPIECE	500-600			
	321-9 CONSOLE	400-600			
	844-8 VASE	300-450			
	323-15 CONSOLE	400-600			
	322-12 CONSOLE	450-550			
	851-15 EWER	700-900			
	849-10 VASE	500-600			
	848-10 VASE	400-500			
	848-9 VASE	300-400			
	847-9 VASE	350-500			
	850-14 VASE	600-800			

PINECONE 1935

GEORGE KRAUSE COLLECTION

X	DESCRIPTION	SECONDARY MARKET	PRICE PAID	DATE BOUGHT	CONDITION
	126-6 CORNUCOPIA	225-275			
	804-10 VASE	300-400			
	261-6 DISH W/LINER	250-350			
	805-12 VASE	600-800			
	806-12 VASE	600-800			
	807-15 FLOOR VASE	800-1000			

GEORGE KRAUSE COLLECTION

X	DESCRIPTION	SECONDARY MARKET	PRICE PAID	DATE BOUGHT	CONDITION
	428-8 DISH	200-300			
	426-6 DISH	225-275			
	427-8 DISH	275-325			
	441-4 CANDLESTICK	200-250			
	425-6 FERN DISH	250-275			
	430-12 PINTRAY	300-450			
	432-12 FOOTED DISH	375-475			
	433-12 FERN DISH	375-475			
	431-15 WINDOW BOX	325-425			
	429-10 BOAT	350-450			
	411-10 BASKET	400-500			
	410-10 BASKET	375-475			
	409 BASKET	350-450			
	408-6 BASKET	300-400			

GEORGE KRAUSE COLLECTION

X	DESCRIPTION	SECONDARY MARKET	PRICE PAID	DATE BOUGHT	CONDITION
	455-6 PLANTER	150-200			
	462 DOUBLE SERVING TRAY	375-475			
	468-8 WINDOW BOX	350-450			
	458-5 BOWL	350-400			
	454-7 BOWL	200-250			
	441-4 BOWL	200-250			
	456-6 PLANTER	175-225			
	497 CANDY DISH	150-250			
	457-7 PLANTER	250-325			
	499 ASHTRAY	125-225			
	498 CIGARETTE CUP	250-350			
	461 HANG. BASKET	350-450			
	400-4 JARDINIERE	125-175			
	469-12 WINDOW BOX	350-450			
	401-6 JARDINIERE	250-350			

POPPY 1938

GEORGE KRAUSE COLLECTION

X	DESCRIPTION	SECONDARY MARKET	PRICE PAID	DATE BOUGHT	CONDITION
	642-4 JARDINIERE	100-150			
	334-4 BOWL	150-200			
	1130-5 CANDLESTICKS	250-275			
	1129 CANDLESTICK	200-250			
	35 FROG	175-200			
	358-5 HANG. BASKET	350-400			
	870-8 VASE	175-250			
	867-6 VASE	125-175			
	336-5 BOWL	100-150			
	12841-8 WALL POCKET	450-550			
	871-8 VASE	200-250			
	866-6 VASE	125-175			
	868-7 VASE	150-200			
	338-10 CONSOLE	175-225			
	339-12 CONSOLE	250-300			
	337-8 CONSOLE	150-250			
	348-12 BASKET	400-500			
	335-6 JARDINIERE	200-225			
	642-6 JARDINIERE	250-300			
	642-7 JARDINIERE	300-350			
	642-8 JARD. & PED.	1200-1500			

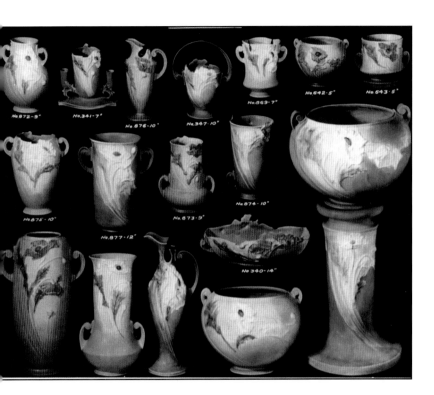

X	DESCRIPTION	SECONDARY MARKET	PRICE PAID	DATE BOUGHT	CONDITION
	872-9 VASE	175-275			
	341-7 CENTERPIECE	375-400			
	876-10 EWER	375-475			
	347-10 BASKET	350-450			
	869-7 VASE	150-225			
	642-5 JARDINIERE	150-200			
	643-5 PLANTER	150-200			
	875-10 VASE	300-350			
	877-12 VASE	400-450			
	873-9 VASE	175-275			
	874-10 VASE	275-375			
	340-14 CONSOLE	250-325			
	879-18 FLOOR VASE	500-700			
	878-15 VASE	400-500			
	880-18 EWER	600-800			
	642-9 JARDINIERE	500-600			
	642-10 JARD. & PED.	1800-2000			

PRIMROSE 1936

GEORGE KRAUSE COLLECTION

X	DESCRIPTION	SECONDARY MARKET	PRICE PAID	DATE BOUGHT	CONDITION
	22-4 FROG	150-200			
	1105-4 1/2 CANDLESTICK	225-325			
	287-12X7 CONSOLE	175-225			
	286-9 CONSOLE	150-200			
	762-7 VASE	150-175			
	761-6 VASE	150-175			
	285-6 VASE	150-175			
	760-6 VASE	125-150			
	769-9 VASE	225-300			
	766-8 VASE	200-250			
	767-8 VASE	225-250			
	771-12 VASE	325-425			

GEORGE KRAUSE COLLECTION

X	DESCRIPTION	SECONDARY MARKET	PRICE PAID	DATE BOUGHT	CONDITION
	125-6 CORNUCOPIA	125-150			
	1113-5 1/2 TRIPLE CANDLESTICK	300-400			
	260-5 BOWL W/LINER	150-175			
	341-10 BASKET	300-400			
	636-5 PLANTER W/DISH	200-250			
	354-5 HANG. BASKET	300-350			
	381-10 WINDOW BOX	325-425			

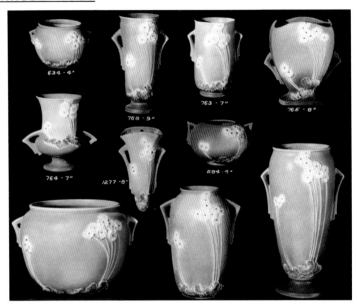

		GEORGE KRAUSE COLLECTION			
X	**DESCRIPTION**	**SECONDARY MARKET**	**PRICE PAID**	**DATE BOUGHT**	**CONDITION**
	634-4 JARDINIERE	100-125			
	768-9 VASE	225-275			
	763-7 VASE	150-175			
	765-8 VASE	200-275			
	764-7 VASE	175-225			
	1277-8 WALL POCKET	350-450			
	284-4 BOWL	125-175			
	634-8 JARDINIERE	425-475			
	770-10 VASE	250-300			
	772-14 VASE	500-700			

1929 Ad For Roseville Pottery

PRIMROSE   1936

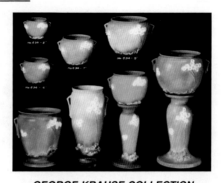

GEORGE KRAUSE COLLECTION

X	DESCRIPTION	SECONDARY MARKET	PRICE PAID	DATE BOUGHT	CONDITION
	634-5 JARDINIERE	150-175			
	634-6 JARDINIERE	200-250			
	634-7 JARDINIERE	250-300			
	634-9 JARDINIERE	350-450			
	772-10X14 SAND JAR	500-600			
	773-10X21 FLOOR VASE	700-800			
	634-8 JARD. & PED.	1000-1200			
	634-10 JARD. & PED.	1300-1500			

QUAKER   EARLY TEENS

BOB BETTINGER COLLECTION

X	DESCRIPTION	SECONDARY MARKET	PRICE PAID	DATE BOUGHT	CONDITION
	MUG	175-200			
	TANKER	300-400			
	HUMIDOR	375-425			

RAMEKIN 1905

COMPLIMENTS OF THE OHIO HISTORICAL SOCIETY

X	DESCRIPTION	SECONDARY MARKET	PRICE PAID	DATE BOUGHT	CONDITION
	204-3 PT	100-125			
	7" SPECIAL	100-150			
	193-1/2 OVAL 8"	150-175			
	194-1/2 OVAL 9"	200-225			
	174-7	100-125			

RAYMOR 1953

#150 & #151

#152

#153

#154

#155

#156

X	DESCRIPTION	SECONDARY MARKET	PRICE PAID	DATE BOUGHT	CONDITION
	#150 CUP	25-35			
	#151 SAUCER	10-25			
	#152 DINNER PLATE	25-35			
	#153 SALAD PLATE	25-35			
	#154 BREAD & BUTTER PLATE	15-20			
	#155 LUG SOUP	20-30			
	#156 IND. COVERED RAMEKIN	40-50			
	#157 COVERED SUGAR	40-50			
	#158 CREAMER	40-50			
	#159 STAND FOR SUGAR & CREAMER	40-50			
	#160 VEGETABLE BOWL	20-30			
	#161 SALAD BOWL	35-45			

RAYMOR 1953

#157

#158

#159

#160

#161

#162

#163

#164

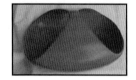
#166

#168 & 169

X	DESCRIPTION	SECONDARY MARKET	PRICE PAID	DATE BOUGHT	CONDITION
	#162 CORN SERVER	20-30			
	#163 PLATTER	50-75			
	#164 CHOP PLATTER	50-75			
	#165 DIVIDED VEGETABLE BOWL	50-75			
	#166 HNLD FRUIT BOWL	75-100			
	#167-6 PC. CONDIMENT SET	200-275			
	#168 SALT SHAKER	15-25			
	#169 PEPPER SHAKER	15-25			
	#170 VINEGAR CRUET	40-50			
	#171 OIL CRUET	40-50			
	#172 COVERED JAM/RELISH	50-75			
	#173 CONDIMENT STAND ONLY	50-75			

RAYMOR   1953

#170

#171

#172

#174

#179

#176

#177

#181

#183

#184

X	DESCRIPTION	SECONDARY MARKET	PRICE PAID	DATE BOUGHT	CONDITION
	#174 TEAPOT	200-250			
	#175 TEAPOT TRIVET	50-60			
	#176 LG. COFFEE POT & STAND	350-450			
	#177 CELERY & OLIVE DISH	75-100			
	#178 STEAK PLATTER W/WELL	100-150			
	#179 HANDLED COFFEE TUMBLER	50-60			
	#180 3PC. CHEESE & RELISH SET	100-150			
	#181 COVEREd BUTTER DISH	50-75			
	#182 RELISH & SANDWICH TRAY	50-75			
	#183 MED. CASSEROLE	50-75			
	#184 MED. CASSEROLE TRIVET	25-50			
	#185 LG. CASSEROLE	125-175			

RAYMOR 1953

#187

#188

#189

#190

X	DESCRIPTION	SECONDARY MARKET	PRICE PAID	DATE BOUGHT	CONDITION
	#186 LG CASSEROLE TRIVET	50-75			
	#187 4QT. BEAN POT	100-150			
	#188 BEAN POT TRIVET	25-50			
	#189 WATER PITCHER	150-200			
	#190 GRAVY BOAT	50-75			
	#191 PICKLE DISH	25-50			
	#192 LUG FRUIT	15-25			
	#193 3QT BEAN POT	100-125			
	#194 2QT BEAN POT	75-100			
	#195 IND. BEAN POT	25-50			
	#196 4QT HANDLED CASSEROLE	150-175			
	#197 - 2$1/2$ QT HANDLED CASSEROLE	100-125			

#191

#192

#193 & #194

RAYMOR   1953

#198

#199

X	DESCRIPTION	SECONDARY MARKET	PRICE PAID	DATE BOUGHT	CONDITION
	#198 - 1 1/2 QT HANDLED CASSEROLE	50-75			
	#199 IND. CASSEROLE	25-50			
	#200 SHIRRED EGG	50-60			
	#201 DBL STACKED WARMER	75-100			
	#202 BUN WARMER	200-300			
	#203 ASHTRAY	75-100			

#201

#202

#203

RAYMOR KITCHENWARE 1954

GEORGE KRAUSE COLLECTION

X	DESCRIPTION	SECONDARY MARKET	PRICE PAID	DATE BOUGHT	CONDITION
	#12-10" MIXING BOWL	125-150			
	#11-8" MIXING BOWL	75-100			
	#10-6" MIXING BOWL	50-75			
	#15-5½" PITCHER 2PT.	100-125			
	#16-6½" PITCHER 3½ PT.	125-150			
	#17-7½" PITCHER 6PT.	150-200			
	#14C CREAMER	50-75			
	#14P TEAPOT	200-250			
	#14S SUGAR	50-75			
	#13-11" GREEN FRUIT BOWL	100-125			
	#13-11" BLUE FRUIT BOWL	100-125			
	#13-11" GOLD FRUIT BOWL	100-125			

RAYMOR GOURMET 1954

GEORGE KRAUSE COLLECTION

X	DESCRIPTION	SECONDARY MARKET	PRICE PAID	DATE BOUGHT	CONDITION
	#19-5QT BEAN POT	150-200			
	#18-2½QT BEAN POT	125-150			
	#12-6QT MIXING BOWL	150-200			
	#11-3QT MIXING BOWL	100-150			
	#10-1½QT MIXING BOWL	75-100			
	#9-1QT MIXING BOWL	50-75			
	#20-2QT CASSEROLE	175-225			
	#21-2½ QT. CASSEROLE	100-150			
	#22-5QT CASSEROLE	75-100			

X	DESCRIPTION	SECONDARY MARKET	PRICE PAID	DATE BOUGHT	CONDITION
	9" JARDINIERE	250-300			
	7" JARDINIERE	150-200			

NOT SHOWN

	DESCRIPTION	SECONDARY MARKET	PRICE PAID	DATE BOUGHT	CONDITION
	11" JARD. & PEDESTAL	2000-2500			
	6" JARDINIERE	100-150			
	8" JARDINIERE	200-250			
	10" JARDINIERE	300-400			

1904 Ad for
The Rozane
Ware

ROSECRAFT BLACK   1916–1919

X	DESCRIPTION	SECONDARY MARKET	PRICE PAID	DATE BOUGHT	CONDITION
	45-8 VASE	100-150			
	44-8 VASE	100-150			
	598-4 PLANTER W/DISH	75-100			
	598-5 PLANTER W/DISH	75-100			
	598-6 PLANTER W/DISH	100-125			
	598-7 PLANTER W/DISH	125-150			
	1236-9 WALL POCKET	200-250			
	158-5 JARDINIERE	125-150			
	1029-3½ CANDLESTICK	125-150			
	46-5 BRIDGE	150-175			
	338-12 VASE	250-300			
	309-8 VASE	100-150			
	311-7 VASE	100-150			
	308-7 VASE	100-150			
	124-5 FERN DISH	50-75			
	124-6 FERN DISH	50-100			
	124-7 FERN DISH	75-100			
	124-6 FERN DISH	50-100			
	74-5 FERN DISH	50-75			
	74-6 FERN DISH	50-75			
	74-7 FERN DISH	75-100			
	74-8 FERN DISH	75-100			
	315-10 VASE	100-125			
	335-8 VASE	200-225			
	318-8 VASE	150-200			
	314-9 VASE	125-150			
	319-12 VASE	200-225			
	319-10 VASE	200-225			
	336-9 VASE	200-225			
	339-15 VASE	250-300			
	337-10 VASE	225-250			
	316-10 VASE	175-200			

ROSECRAFT BLENDED   1917

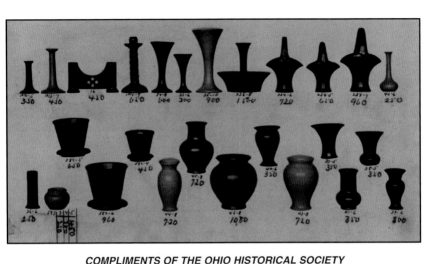

COMPLIMENTS OF THE OHIO HISTORICAL SOCIETY

X	DESCRIPTION	SECONDARY MARKET	PRICE PAID	DATE BOUGHT	CONDITION
	1012-5 VASE	75-100			
	1013-7 VASE	125-150			
	16 BRIDGE	150-175			
	1014-9 CANDLESTICK	200-225			
	34-8 VASE	100-125			
	33-6 VASE	75-100			
	35-10 VASE	125-150			
	236-8 BOWL W/VASE	150-225			
	234-6 BASKET	200-250			
	234-5 BASKET	150-200			
	234-7 BASKET	225-275			
	42-6 VASE	100-150			
	582-5 PLANTER W/DISH	100-125			
	582-4 PLANTER W/DISH	75-100			
	45-8 VASE	100-125			
	40-6 VASE	75-100			
	37-5 VASE	75-100			
	38-5 VASE	75-100			
	36-6 VASE	75-100			
	583-3 JARDINIERE	75-100			
	583-4 JARDINIERE	100-125			
	583-5 JARDINIERE	125-150			
	582-6 PLANTER W/DISH	125-150			
	44-8 VASE	125-150			
	46-8 VASE	125-150			
	43-8 VASE	125-150			
	41-8 VASE	125-150			
	39-6 VASE	100-125			

ROSECRAFT COLOR 1916

X	DESCRIPTION	SECONDARY MARKET	PRICE PAID	DATE BOUGHT	CONDITION
	166-8 VASE	100-150			
	165-6 VASE	100-150			
	1018-10 CANDLESTICK	300-350			
	1017-8 CANDLESTICK	200-250			
	32-8 VASE	125-175			
	33-10 VASE	150-225			
	167-10 VASE	200-225			
	74-6 FERN DISH	100-150			
	74-5 FERN DISH	100-150			
	168-12 VASE	200-300			
	74-8 FERN DISH	100-150			
	74-7 FERN DISH	100-150			
	3-8 COMPOTE	200-300			
	75-10 DISH	150-200			
	4-10 COMPOTE	175-225			
	75-8 DISH	150-175			

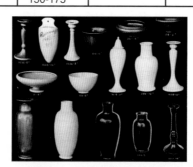

X	DESCRIPTION	SECONDARY MARKET	PRICE PAID	DATE BOUGHT	CONDITION
	1035-8 CANDLESTICK	250-300			
	1225-10 WALL POCKET	250-350			
	1036-8 CANDLESTICK	225-275			
	109-6 DISH	100-150			
	10-5 FERN DISH	100-150			
	108-5 DISH	100-150			
	11-8 COMPOTE	150-200			
	10-6 DISH	100-150			
	4-11 URN	200-300			
	186-10 VASE	150-200			
	1038-10 CANDLESTICK	325-375			
	187-12 VASE	200-300			
	211-12 VASE	225-275			
	210-12 VASE	200-250			
	185-8 VASE	150-200			
	1037-10 CANDLESTICK	350-375			

ROSECRAFT COLOR   1916

X	DESCRIPTION	SECONDARY MARKET	PRICE PAID	DATE BOUGHT	CONDITION
	319-8 BASKET	300-400			
	224-6 VASE	125-175			
	74-6 BOWL	100-150			
	223-5 1/2 VASE	100-175			
	15-2 1/2 FROG	50-100			
	244-6 VASE	125-175			
	45-8 VASE	125-175			
	125-5 JARDINIERE	150-175			
	1036-8 CANDLESTICK	225-275			
	187-12 VASE	200-300			
	11-8 COMPOTE	150-200			
	225-12 VASE	200-300			

X	DESCRIPTION	SECONDARY MARKET	PRICE PAID	DATE BOUGHT	CONDITION
	175-6 VASE	125-175			
	87-6 BOWL	100-150			
	245-6 VASE	125-175			
	247-6 VASE	125-175			
	83-5 BOWL	125-175			
	44-8 VASE	100-125			
	310-9 BASKET	300-400			
	251-10 VASE	175-225			
	248-8 VASE	150-200			
	175-8 VASE	150-200			
	227-12 VASE	250-300			

COMPLIMENTS OF THE OHIO HISTORICAL SOCIETY

X	DESCRIPTION	SECONDARY MARKET	PRICE PAID	DATE BOUGHT	CONDITION
	1237-10 WALL POCKET	300-350			
	46-5 BRIDGE	150-200			
	598-5 PLANTER W/DISH	200-250			
	1225-10 WALL POCKET	250-300			
	185-8 VASE	150-200			
	1029-3 1/4 CANDLESTICK	125-175			
	1236-9 WALL POCKET	300-400			
	15-3 1/2 FROG	50-100			
	249-8 VASE	150-200			
	1234-6 FERN DISH	100-150			
	94-5 BOWL	125-175			
	250-10 VASE	175-225			

1931 Ad for
Roseville
Pottery

ROSECRAFT HEXAGON   1924–1928

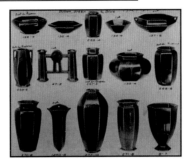

COMPLIMENTS OF THE OHIO HISTORICAL SOCIETY

X	DESCRIPTION	SECONDARY MARKET	PRICE PAID	DATE BOUGHT	CONDITION
	136-5 BOWL	150-200			
	135-4 FERN DISH	125-175			
	266-4 VASE	100-150			
	134-4 DISH	100-125			
	137-6 CONSOLE	125-175			
	269-6 VASE	200-250			
	47-5 BRIDGE	425-525			
	262-5 VASE	175-225			
	138-4 BOWL	200-250			
	268-6 VASE	200-225			
	270-8 VASE	300-400			
	1240-8 WALL POCKET	300-450			
	270-10 VASE	500-600			
	271-8 VASE	300-400			
	8-7 VASE	200-300			

ROSECRAFT PANEL   1920

GEORGE KRAUSE COLLECTION

X	DESCRIPTION	SECONDARY MARKET	PRICE PAID	DATE BOUGHT	CONDITION
	1057-8 FLORAL CANDLESTICK	350-375			
	293-8 FLORAL VASE	275-325			
	282-8 FLORAL VASE	200-250			
	291-8 FLORAL VASE	200-250			
	295-9 FLORAL URN	500-600			
	294-8 FLORAL URN	175-200			
	296-10 NUDE URN	800-1000			
	297-10 FLORAL URN	300-350			
	298-11" NUDE URN	700-800			
	299-12 FLORAL URN	400-500			

ROSECRAFT VINTAGE   1924

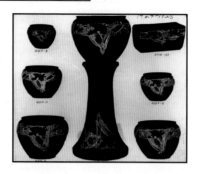

X	DESCRIPTION	SECONDARY MARKET	PRICE PAID	DATE BOUGHT	CONDITION
	607-6 JARDINIERE	175-200			
	372-10 WINDOW BOX	350-450			
	607-7 JARDINIERE	225-250			
	607-6 JARDINIERE	200-225			
	607-9 JARDINIERE	300-400			
	607-10 JARD. & PED.	1200-1800			
	607-8 JARDINIERE	250-300			

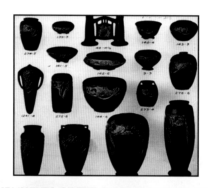

X	DESCRIPTION	SECONDARY MARKET	PRICE PAID	DATE BOUGHT	CONDITION
	274-5 VASE	150-200			
	139-3 DISH	100-150			
	48-41/2 BRIDGE	175-225			
	140-4 DISH	100-150			
	143-3 BOWL	75-100			
	141-5 DISH	100-150			
	142-6 FERN DISH	125-175			
	9-3 BOWL	150-200			
	1241-8 WALL POCKET	350-450			
	275-6 VASE	200-250			
	144-6 JARDINIERE	275-325			
	273-4 VASE	150-200			
	276-6 VASE	200-275			
	277-8 VASE	225-275			
	278-8 VASE	250-350			
	279-10 VASE	350-450			
	280-12 VASE	400-500			

ROYAL CAPRI 1952-1954

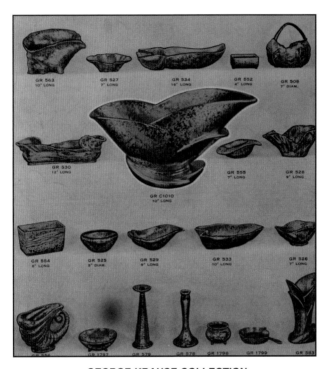

GEORGE KRAUSE COLLECTION

X	DESCRIPTION	SECONDARY MARKET	PRICE PAID	DATE BOUGHT	CONDITION
	GR563-10" SHELL	275-325			
	GR527-7" DISH	150-200			
	GR534-16" LEAF DISH	250-325			
	GR552-4" DISH	150-200			
	GR508-7" BASKET	175-225			
	GR530-12" PLANTER	175-250			
	GRC1010-10" PLANTER	275-375			
	GR555-7" PLANTER	175-250			
	GR528-9" PLANTER	150-200			
	GR554-6" WINDOW BOX	150-225			
	GR525-5" DISH	150-200			
	GR529-9" DISH	150-200			
	GR533-10" LEAF DISH	150-225			
	GR526-7" PLANTER	150-200			
	GR556-6" CORNUCOPIA	200-275			
	GR1797-5" FOOTED DISH	150-225			
	GR579-8" VASE	150-225			
	GR578-7" VASE	150-225			
	GR1798-3" BEAN POT	150-225			
	GR1799-5" SKILLET	175-225			
	GR583-9" VASE	225-275			

COMPLIMENTS OF THE OHIO HISTORICAL SOCIETY

X	DESCRIPTION	SECONDARY MARKET	PRICE PAID	DATE BOUGHT	CONDITION
	813-9³/4 VASE	900-1000			
	827-9 VASE	900-1200			
	821-8¹/2 VASE	800-1000			
	814-9¹/2 VASE	900-1200			
	845-11¹/2 VASE	1000-1500			
	831-9³/4 VASE	1000-1300			
	824-11¹/4 VASE	1200-1500			
	832-20 FLOOR VASE	2700-3200			
	826-21 FLOOR VASE	3000-3500			
	863-21 FLOOR VASE	3000-3500			

COMPLIMENTS OF THE OHIO HISTORICAL SOCIETY

X	DESCRIPTION	SECONDARY MARKET	PRICE PAID	DATE BOUGHT	CONDITION
	923B-5 VASE	300-375			
	924-4¹/2 VASE	300-400			
	922-4¹/2 VASE	250-350			
	929-4¹/2 VASE	275-325			
	925A-3¹/2 VASE	225-275			
	925B-3¹/2 VASE	225-325			
	930-5 EWER	300-400			
	923A-5 VASE	275-375			
	927-2¹/2 BOWL	225-275			
	926-3 BOWL	225-275			
	911-6¹/2 BOWL	325-375			
	913-6 VASE	325-375			
	915-7 VASE	375-425			
	914-6 VASE	325-375			
	918-7 VASE	375-425			
	912-6¹/2 VASE	350-400			
	816-15 VASE	1500-2000			
	921-11 TANKER	600-900			
	917-12¹/2 VASE	600-700			
	916-11 VASE	600-800			
	928-10 VASE	375-475			
	919-8 VASE	325-400			

ROZANE 1900s

COMPLIMENTS OF THE OHIO HISTORICAL SOCIETY

X	DESCRIPTION	SECONDARY MARKET	PRICE PAID	DATE BOUGHT	CONDITION
	848-63/4 VASE	325-425			
	872-51/2 VASE	325-425			
	809-51/4 VASE	275-375			
	904-5 PILLOW VASE	500-600			
	804-23/4 VASE	150-200			
	908-51/2 VASE	350-450			
	841-71/2 VASE	275-375			
	805-8 EWER	325-425			
	870-11 EWER	600-700			
	837-123/4 VASE	500-600			
	882-9 PILLOW VASE	3100-3700			
	823-61/2 VASE	250-350			
	853-51/2 VASE	250-350			
	843-7 VASE	550-650			

COMPLIMENTS OF THE OHIO HISTORICAL SOCIETY

X	DESCRIPTION	SECONDARY MARKET	PRICE PAID	DATE BOUGHT	CONDITION
	971-9 VASE	400-450			
	970-10 VASE	500-550			
	R5-101/2 VASE	400-500			
	R3-77 VASE	350-450			
	961-101/8 VASE	350-400			
	958-11/4 VASE	375-475			
	973-111/8 VASE	500-600			
	969-12 VASE	500-600			
	974-111/2 VASE	400-500			
	R7-12 VASE	325-400			
	R8-10 VASE	450-500			
	985-10 JARDINIERE	1000-1100			
	986-9 JARDINIERE	600-700			
	987-8 JARDINIERE	500-600			
	988-61/2 JARDINIERE	400-500			
	989-51/2 VASE	275-375			
	990-43/4 VASE	225-325			

ROZANE   1900s

COMPLIMENTS OF THE OHIO HISTORICAL SOCIETY

X	DESCRIPTION	SECONDARY MARKET	PRICE PAID	DATE BOUGHT	CONDITION
	903-9$^{1/2}$ VASE	350-400			
	871-8 VASE	300-400			
	901-9 URN	900-1100			
	876-8$^{1/2}$ VASE	350-450			
	896-8$^{1/4}$ VASE	450-550			
	888-4 PITCHER	450-550			
	817-4 VASE	275-375			
	860-4$^{3/4}$ VASE	250-350			
	846-4 VASE	250-300			
	864-8$^{1/2}$ PITCHER	450-550			
	886-5 MUG	300-400			
	856-4$^{1/2}$ MUG	300-400			
	897-5$^{1/2}$ TOBACCO JAR	1000-1400			
	900-6 DBL. HND. MUG	350-450			

315

ROZANE 1900s

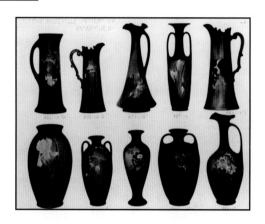

COMPLIMENTS OF THE OHIO HISTORICAL SOCIETY

X	DESCRIPTION	SECONDARY MARKET	PRICE PAID	DATE BOUGHT	CONDITION
	855-14$\frac{1}{2}$ TANKER	650-750			
	890-12$\frac{1}{2}$ TANKER	600-800			
	854-16 EWER	1100-1300			
	887-16 VASE	1100-1300			
	884-16$\frac{1}{2}$ TANKER	900-1200			
	891-14 VASE	1100-1300			
	818-12 VASE	800-900			
	807-13 VASE	600-700			
	898-13$\frac{1}{2}$ VASE	700-800			
	858-15 EWER	1100-1300			

	815-20 VASE	1600-2000			
	865-19 VASE	1500-1900			
	822-15$\frac{3}{4}$ VASE	1300-1700			

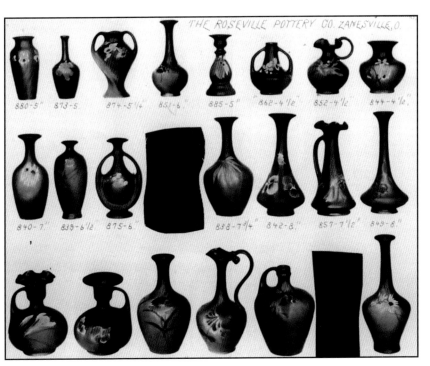

COMPLIMENTS OF THE OHIO HISTORICAL SOCIETY

X	DESCRIPTION	SECONDARY MARKET	PRICE PAID	DATE BOUGHT	CONDITION
	880-5 VASE	300-350			
	873-5 VASE	250-300			
	874-51/4 VASE	325-425			
	851-6 VASE	275-375			
	885-5 CANDLESTICK	275-375			
	862-41/2 VASE	250-300			
	852-41/2 EWER	325-425			
	844-41/2 VASE	175-225			
	840-7 VASE	275-375			
	839-61/2 VASE	275-375			
	875-6 VASE	325-375			
	838-73/4 VASE	300-375			
	842-8 VASE	375-475			
	857-71/2 EWER	350-400			
	849-8 VASE	350-450			
	883-6 VASE	300-400			
	881-6 VASE	300-400			
	836-71/2 VASE	350-425			
	906-8 EWER	550-650			
	889-7 JUG	400-500			
	868-9 VASE	400-500			

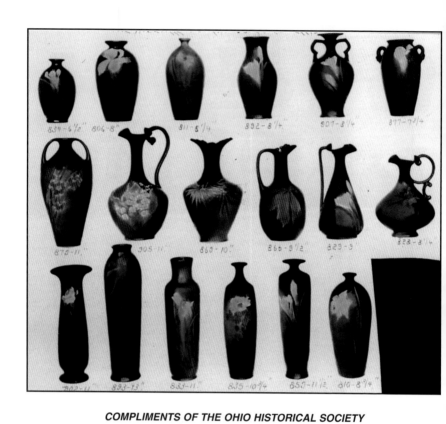

COMPLIMENTS OF THE OHIO HISTORICAL SOCIETY

X	DESCRIPTION	SECONDARY MARKET	PRICE PAID	DATE BOUGHT	CONDITION
	834-6½ VASE	325-375			
	806-8 VASE	325-425			
	811-8¼ VASE	325-425			
	892-8¼ VASE	325-425			
	907-8¼ VASE	325-425			
	877-7¾ VASE	350-425			
	879-11 VASE	375-475			
	905-11 EWER	550-650			
	869-10 VASE	375-475			
	866-9½ EWER	400-500			
	829-9 EWER	500-600			
	828-3½ EWER	625-725			
	902-11 VASE	550-650			
	893-12 VASE	600-700			
	833-11 VASE	450-550			
	835-10¾ VASE	350-450			
	859-11½ VASE	375-475			
	810-8¾ VASE	325-425			

ROZANE LINE 1917

X	DESCRIPTION	SECONDARY MARKET	PRICE PAID	DATE BOUGHT	CONDITION
	250-61/4 PEDESTAL VASE	250-350			
	360-6 HANG. BASKET	350-500			
	251-51/2 BASKET	250-300			
	R108-51/4 BASKET	125-175			
	102-12 VASE	200-300			
	R110-6 VASE	150-200			
	588-6 JARDINIERE	175-225			
	252-8 BASKET	250-300			
	16F FRUIT BOWL	150-200			
	367-10 WINDOW BOX	500-600			
	588-5 JARDINIERE	125-150			

X	DESCRIPTION	SECONDARY MARKET	PRICE PAID	DATE BOUGHT	CONDITION
	588-10 JARD. & PED	1200-1500			
	#2-8 PEDESTAL VASE	225-275			
	#1 PEDESTAL VASE	350-400			
	756-9X19 UMBRELLA STAND	700-900			
	588-8 JARDINIERE	300-400			

ROZANE CRYSTALIS 1905

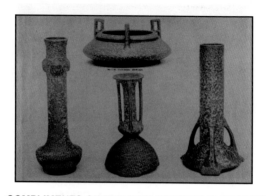

COMPLIMENTS OF THE OHIO HISTORICAL SOCIETY

X	DESCRIPTION	SECONDARY MARKET	PRICE PAID	DATE BOUGHT	CONDITION
	C2-5X12 BOWL	2500-3000			
	R64-141/4 PITCHER	2000-2500			
	C16-11 VASE	2000-2500			
	C23-14 VASE	2200-2600			

COMPLIMENTS OF THE OHIO HISTORICAL SOCIETY

X	DESCRIPTION	SECONDARY MARKET	PRICE PAID	DATE BOUGHT	CONDITION
	C20-81/2 VASE	2300-2800			
	C15-71/4 VASE	1500-1800			
	C25-8 VASE	1800-2000			
	C17-8 VASE	2000-2500			
	C13-11 VASE	2000-2500			
	C24-111/4 VASE	2000-2500			
	C19-121/4 VASE	2300-2800			
	C12-131/4 VASE	2500-3000			
	C26-14 VASE	2200-2600			
	C14-12 VASE	2300-2800			

ROZANE-DELLA ROBBIA 1906

COMPLIMENTS OF THE OHIO HISTORICAL SOCIETY

X	DESCRIPTION	SECONDARY MARKET	PRICE PAID	DATE BOUGHT	CONDITION
	D17 VASE	1800-2000			
	D11 VASE	1800-2000			
	D15 VASE	2000-2500			
	D7 VASE	2000-2200			
	D1 VASE	2000-2200			
	D9 VASE	1800-2000			
	D18 VASE	1300-1500			
	D4 VASE	1300-1500			
	D16 VASE	1300-1500			
	D10 VASE	2200-2500			
	D8 VASE	2200-2500			
	D3 VASE	2200-2500			
	D14 VASE	2200-2500			
	D12 VASE	2200-2500			
	D5 VASE	2000-2200			
	D8 VASE	2200-2500			
	D6 VASE	1800-2000			
	D13 VASE	2200-2500			

COMPLIMENTS OF THE OHIO HISTORICAL SOCIETY

X	DESCRIPTION	SECONDARY MARKET	PRICE PAID	DATE BOUGHT	CONDITION
	1 TEAPOT	1400-1600			
	3 TEAPOT	1400-1600			
	12 TEAPOT	1500-2000			
	11 TEAPOT	1500-2000			
	8 TEAPOT	1400-1800			
	2 TEAPOT	1400-1600			
	9 TEAPOT	1400-1800			
	7 TEAPOT	1400-1800			
	4 TEAPOT	2000-2500			
	6 TEAPOT	2000-2500			
	10 TEAPOT	1500-2000			
	5 TEAPOT	1400-1800			

ROZANE-DELLA ROBBIA   1906

COMPLIMENTS OF THE OHIO HISTORICAL SOCIETY

X	DESCRIPTION	SECONDARY MARKET	PRICE PAID	DATE BOUGHT	CONDITION
	23-7 PLANTER	2800-3000			
	23-8 PLANTER	3300-3600			
	23-6 PLANTER	2200-2500			
	29-9 1/4 VASE	7000-8000			
	24-11 1/4 VASE	1400-1600			
	36-11 VASE	1500-1700			

	21-13 1/4 VASE	8000-10000			
	15-14 VASE	7000-8000			
	53-14 TANKER	4000-5000			
	32-10 TANKER	3000-3500			

COMPLIMENTS OF THE OHIO HISTORICAL SOCIETY

X	DESCRIPTION	SECONDARY MARKET	PRICE PAID	DATE BOUGHT	CONDITION
	51-6 FERN DISH	2000-2200			
	51-8 FERN DISH	3000-3500			
	51-7 FERN DISH	2500-2800			
	16-12¼ VASE	7000-8000			
	69-13½ VASE	14000-16000			
	17-12 VASE	10000-12000			

	59-7 VASE	4000-6000			
	54-7 VASE	5000-6000			
	38-6½ VASE	3500-4000			
	45-9¼ VASE	4000-5000			
	27-9¼ VASE	4000-5000			
	62-10 VASE	7000-8000			
	9-10¼ VASE	4000-5000			
	8-10 VASE	6000-7000			
	32-9 VASE	3000-3500			

ROZANE–DELLA ROBBIA 1906

COMPLIMENTS OF THE OHIO HISTORICAL SOCIETY

X	DESCRIPTION	SECONDARY MARKET	PRICE PAID	DATE BOUGHT	CONDITION
	44-5 NUG	2000-3000			
	3-6$^{1/2}$ VASE	2500-3000			
	50-3$^{1/2}$ PLANTER	2000-3000			
	22-6 VASE	3000-3500			
	46-9$^{1/2}$ VASE	7000-8000			
	66-11$^{1/4}$ VASE	8000-9000			
	18-12 VASE	7000-8000			
	19-9 VASE	7000-8000			

	26-6$^{1/2}$ MUG	1500-2000			
	5-6 VASE	4000-5000			
	25-8 VASE	3000-3500			
	40-7$^{1/2}$ PITCHER	8000-10000			
	35-7$^{1/2}$ TOBACCO JAR	4000-4500			
	34-6$^{1/4}$ PITCHER	3500-4000			

COMPLIMENTS OF THE OHIO HISTORICAL SOCIETY

X	DESCRIPTION	SECONDARY MARKET	PRICE PAID	DATE BOUGHT	CONDITION
	60-41/2 MUG	1500-1800			
	56-4 COMPOTE	3000-3500			
	57-51/2 VASE	1500-1800			
	12-101/4 VASE	6000-7000			
	43-111/2 VASE	10000-12000			
	11-101/2 VASE	7000-8000			

	13-18 VASE	30000-35000			
	30-19 VASE	35000-40000			
	20-161/2 VASE	8000-10000			

ROZANE–DELLA ROBBIA   1906

X	DESCRIPTION	SECONDARY MARKET	PRICE PAID	DATE BOUGHT	CONDITION
	64-3 PLANTER	8000-10000			
	55-131/4 VASE	15000-20000			
	63-131/4 VASE	12000-15000			
	49-14 VASE	18000-22000			

	33-171/4 VASE	15000-18000			
	68-111/2 VASE	10000-12000			
	2-161/4 VASE	15000-18000			

COMPLIMENTS OF THE OHIO HISTORICAL SOCIETY

X	DESCRIPTION	SECONDARY MARKET	PRICE PAID	DATE BOUGHT	CONDITION
	48-11 1/4 VASE	6000-7000			
	52-16 VASE	10000-12000			
	47-16 VASE	15000-20000			
	37-14 1/4 VASE	8000-10000			
	65-11 1/4 VASE	8000-10000			

	DESCRIPTION	SECONDARY MARKET	PRICE PAID	DATE BOUGHT	CONDITION
	28-19 FLOOR VASE	20000-25000			
	67-17 1/2 VASE	14000-17000			
	1-18 VASE	18000-22000			
	61-20 FLOOR VASE	20000-25000			

ROZANE–DELLA ROBBIA 1906

X	DESCRIPTION	SECONDARY MARKET	PRICE PAID	DATE BOUGHT	CONDITION
	70-7 1/2 CHALICE	7000-8000			
	39-7 1/4 VASE	2500-3000			
	42-6 1/4 VASE	6000-7000			
	6-11 1/2 VASE	7000-8000			
	7-8 1/2 VASE	5000-6000			
	10-9 VASE	7000-8000			
	41-9 URN	8000-10000			

	58-10 1/2 VASE	6000-7000			
	4-15 VASE	9000-11000			
	2-16 VASE	15000-20000			
	14-15 VASE	9000-11000			

ROZANE EGYPTO 1905

X	DESCRIPTION	SECONDARY MARKET	PRICE PAID	DATE BOUGHT	CONDITION
	E19-5$^{1/2}$ VASE	325-375			
	E44-6 VASE	200-250			
	E30-4$^{1/4}$ MUG	150-200			
	E31-7 BASKET	175-225			
	E21-6$^{1/2}$ VASE	300-400			
	E17-6 VASE	350-400			
	E11-9$^{1/4}$ FERN DISH	400-500			
	E36-10$^{1/2}$ PITCHER	400-500			
	E12-10$^{1/2}$ VASE	500-600			
	E50-12 VASE	600-700			
	E46-12$^{1/2}$ URN	1500-2000			
	E35-10 ALADDIN LAMP	400-500			

X	DESCRIPTION	SECONDARY MARKET	PRICE PAID	DATE BOUGHT	CONDITION
	E57-3$^{1/2}$ PLANTER	150-200			
	E32-5$^{1/2}$ BASKET	200-275			
	E29-5$^{1/4}$ ALADDIN LAMP	300-325			
	E38-5$^{1/4}$ ALADDIN LAMP	250-300			
	E56-4$^{1/2}$ VASE	225-275			
	E33-5$^{1/4}$ PITCHER	250-300			
	E34-3$^{1/2}$ CREAMER	150-200			
	E51-12$^{1/2}$ EWER	800-1200			
	E41-13$^{1/4}$ VASE	500-600			
	E58-14$^{1/2}$ BASKET	1000-1200			
	E68-16$^{1/4}$ VASE	1800-2400			
	E59-15$^{1/2}$ BASKET	1000-1500			
	E47-12$^{1/2}$ VASE	600-700			
	E45-12$^{1/4}$ EWER	800-1000			

ROZANE EGYPTO 1905

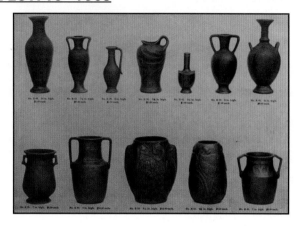

X	DESCRIPTION	SECONDARY MARKET	PRICE PAID	DATE BOUGHT	CONDITION
	E49-10 VASE	450-550			
	E53-71/2 VASE	250-300			
	E39-6 EWER	175-225			
	E20-71/2 EWER	275-325			
	E42-51/2 EWER	150-200			
	E52-8 VASE	275-325			
	E48-10 VASE	450-550			
	E38-7 VASE	250-300			
	E40-9 VASE	350-450			
	E10-81/2 VASE	600-700			
	E15-81/4 VASE	400-450			
	E43-7 VASE	350-400			

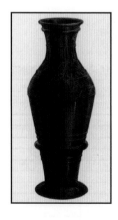

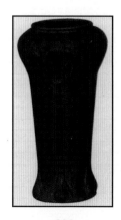

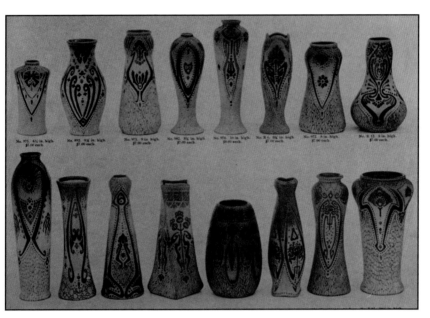

COMPLIMENTS OF THE OHIO HISTORICAL SOCIETY

X	DESCRIPTION	SECONDARY MARKET	PRICE PAID	DATE BOUGHT	CONDITION
	975-5$1/2$ VASE	1200-1500			
	892-8$1/4$ VASE	1800-2200			
	971-9 VASE	1800-2200			
	982-8$1/4$ VASE	1500-2000			
	970-10 VASE	2000-2500			
	R6-8$1/4$ VASE	1500-2000			
	972-8 VASE	1500-1800			
	R12-8 VASE	1800-2200			
	893-12$1/2$ VASE	3000-3500			
	961-10$1/2$ VASE	2000-2500			
	973-11$1/2$ VASE	2200-2600			
	R5-10$1/4$ VASE	2200-2600			
	R14-8$1/4$ VASE	2200-2600			
	R3-10$1/2$ VASE	2200-2600			
	974-11$1/2$ VASE	2200-2600			
	R15-10$1/2$ VASE	2500-3000			

ROZANE HAND DECORATED 1905-1910

X	DESCRIPTION	SECONDARY MARKET	PRICE PAID	DATE BOUGHT	CONDITION
	822-16 VASE	500-600			
	807-123/4 VASE	350-400			
	893-123/4 VASE	300-400			
	961-101/2 VASE	350-400			
	956-81/2 VASE	275-325			
	900-6 VASE	225-275			
	438A-7 JARDINIERE	250-275			
	438A-8 JARDINIERE	275-300			
	438A-9 JARDINIERE	300-325			
	438A-10 JARDINIERE	325-350			
	438A-12 JARDINIERE	400-450			
	438B-7 JARDINIERE	250-275			
	438B-8 JARDINIERE	275-300			
	438B-9 JARDINIERE	300-325			
	438B-10 JARDINIERE	325-350			
	438B-12 JARDINIERE	400-450			
	438C-7 JARDINIERE	400-450			
	438C-8 JARDINIERE	275-300			
	438C-9 JARDINIERE	300-325			
	438C-10 JARDINIERE	325-350			
	438C-12 JARDINIERE	400-450			
	438D-7 JARDINIERE	250-275			
	438D-8 JARDINIERE	275-300			
	438D-9 JARDINIERE	300-325			
	438D-10 JARDINIERE	325-350			
	438D-12 JARDINIERE	400-450			

ROZANE HOLLYWOOD WARE   1905

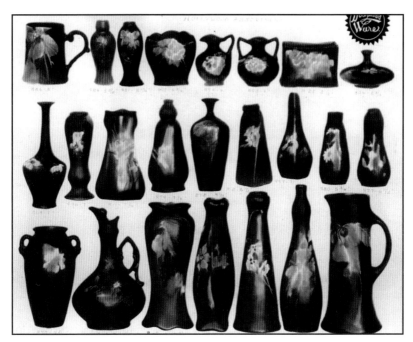

COMPLIMENTS OF THE OHIO HISTORICAL SOCIETY

X	DESCRIPTION	SECONDARY MARKET	PRICE PAID	DATE BOUGHT	CONDITION
	886-5 MUG	175-200			
	984-5³/8 VASE	125-150			
	981-5¹/4 VASE	125-150			
	990-4³/4 PLANTER	175-200			
	994-4 PITCHER	100-125			
	995-4 VASE	100-125			
	R22-3¹/2 WINDOW BOX	200-225			
	804-2³/4 VASE	125-150			
	268-9 VASE	225-250			
	976-7 VASE	175-200			
	R1-7¹/4 VASE	200-250			
	979-7¹/4 VASE	200-225			
	878-7¹/2 VASE	225-250			
	R2-6¹/2 VASE	175-200			
	999-7 VASE	175-200			
	980-5³/4 VASE	175-200			
	977-6¹/2 VASE	150-175			
	877-7³/4 VASE	200-225			
	940-9¹/2 EWER	450-550			
	R9-4-9³/4 VASE	275-325			
	973-11¹/2 VASE	400-500			
	969-12 VASE	400-500			
	921-11 TANKER	500-600			

ROZANE MARA   1904

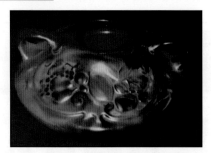

HARDY HUDSON COLLECTION

X	DESCRIPTION	SECONDARY MARKET	PRICE PAID	DATE BOUGHT	CONDITION
	PLANTER	550-650			
	K21 VASE	500-600			
	K24 VASE	550-650			
	K22 VASE	550-650			
	K15 VASE	700-800			
	K14 VASE	700-800			
	K11 VASE	600-700			
	K12 VASE	700-800			

ROZANE MARA   1904

X	DESCRIPTION	SECONDARY MARKET	PRICE PAID	DATE BOUGHT	CONDITION
	13" VASE	2500-3500			
	8¹/₂" VASE	1500-1800			
	13" VASE	2500-3500			

ROZANE MONGOL 1903

  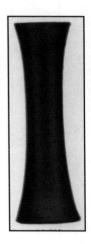 

X	DESCRIPTION	SECONDARY MARKET	PRICE PAID	DATE BOUGHT	CONDITION
	M-957 VASE	550-650			
	M-893 VASE	650-750			
	M-961 VASE	500-600			
	M-814 VASE	600-700			
	VASE	600-700			

MARVIN STOFFT COLLECTION

ROZANE MONGOL 1903

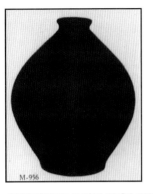

CONTINUED FROM PAGE 321

X	DESCRIPTION	SECONDARY MARKET	PRICE PAID	DATE BOUGHT	CONDITION
	M-956 VASE	600-700			
	M-962 VASE	900-1000			
	M-821 VASE	600-700			
	M-960 VASE	500-600			
	M-900 VASE	500-600			
	M-959 VASE	450-550			
	11" VASE	2500-3500			
	10 1/2" VASE	3000-4000			
	17" VASE	5000-6000			

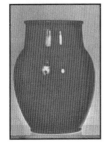

ROZANE OLYMPIC 1905

 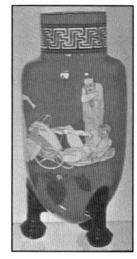 

BOB BETTINGER COLLECTION

X	DESCRIPTION	SECONDARY MARKET	PRICE PAID	DATE BOUGHT	CONDITION
	13" VASE	6500-7500			
	14 1/2" FOOTED URN	8000-9000			
	16" VASE	7000-8000			
	10 1/2" TANKER	12000-15000			
	7 1/2" JUG	5000-6000			

PICTURES NOT SHOWN:

	20' VASE	10000-15000			
	MUG	1500-2000			

ROZANE PATTERN 1941

X	DESCRIPTION	SECONDARY MARKET	PRICE PAID	DATE BOUGHT	CONDITION
	1 ORNAMENT FISH & WAVE	100-125			
	2 ORNAMENT FLAME	175-225			
	44 FROG	100-150			
	1-6 VASE	100-150			
	408-6 DISH	100-150			
	398-4 BOWL	75-100			
	407-6 DISH	100-150			
	1144-3 CANDLESTICK	100-150			
	5-8 URN	100-150			
	2-6 VASE	75-100			
	409-12 PIN TRAY	125-175			
	397-14 CONSOLE	125-175			
	398-6 BOWL	175-200			
	4-8 VASE	100-125			
	3-8 VASE	100-125			
	2 CORNUCOPIA	175-225			
	410 SHELL	150-200			
	396-10 DISH	100-125			
	395-9 DISH	100-125			
	6-9 VASE	100-150			
	9-10 VASE	100-150			
	10-12 VASE	150-175			
	398-8 BOWL	200-225			
	7-9 VASE	100-150			
	8-10 VASE	125-175			
	11-15 VASE	250-275			

ROZANE ROYAL 1904

COMPLIMENTS OF THE OHIO HISTORICAL SOCIETY

X	DESCRIPTION	SECONDARY MARKET	PRICE PAID	DATE BOUGHT	CONDITION
	954-21 VASE	1900-2300			
	R27-19 1/2 VASE	1800-2500			
	932-17 VASE	1500-1900			
	865-19 VASE	1300-1700			
	815-20 VASE	2200-2600			
	822-16 VASE	1100-1600			
	933-13 1/2 VASE	1300-1700			
	R11-19 VASE	1900-2500			
	R9-16 1/2 VASE	1100-1500			
	887-16 1/2 VASE	1100-1700			

ROZANE ROYAL 1904

COMPLIMENTS OF THE OHIO HISTORICAL SOCIETY

X	DESCRIPTION	SECONDARY MARKET	PRICE PAID	DATE BOUGHT	CONDITION
	931-14$^{1/2}$ VASE	1600-2000			
	R42-17 VASE	1500-2000			
	R10-20 VASE	2000-2600			
	R32-15$^{1/4}$ VASE	1200-1600			
	861-16 VASE	1800-2200			
	850-24 FLOOR VASE	3000-3500			
	953-30 FLOOR VASE	4000-4500			

ROZANE ROYAL   1904

**COMPLIMENTS OF THE OHIO
HISTORICAL SOCIETY**

X	DESCRIPTION	SECONDARY MARKET	PRICE PAID	DATE BOUGHT	CONDITION
	R5-101/2 VASE	450-550			
	958-111/4 VASE	350-450			
	970-10 VASE	375-475			
	903-91/4 VASE	300-450			
	974-111/2 VASE	400-500			
	R48-91/2 VASE	400-475			
	R3-101/2 VASE	375-475			
	961-101/2 VASE	325-425			
	R8-12 VASE	425-475			
	R33-111/2 VASE	325-425			
	879-101/2 VASE	475-575			
	R46-101/2 VASE	375-475			
	985-10 VASE	1100-1600			
	973-111/2 VASE	550-650			
	867-101/2 VASE	375-475			
	R15-111/2 VASE	550-650			

**COMPLIMENTS OF THE OHIO
HISTORICAL SOCIETY**

X	DESCRIPTION	SECONDARY MARKET	PRICE PAID	DATE BOUGHT	CONDITION
	R50-4 VASE	275-350			
	984-51/2 VASE	325-375			
	990-41/2 VASE	400-425			
	980-51/4 VASE	325-375			
	R1-71/4 VASE	325-425			
	R43-71/2 VASE	352-425			
	R16-71/2 VASE	375-475			
	R22-31/2 VASE	275-325			
	R981-51/2 VASE	325-375			
	R23-51/4 VASE	275-325			
	823-61/2 VASE	250-300			
	987-8 VASE	425-525			
	R35-81/4 VASE	250-300			
	971-9 VASE	325-425			
	R29-14 VASE	1100-1300			
	955-18 VASE	1600-1900			
	987-15 VASE	425-525			
	814-10 VASE	475-525			
	959-7 VASE	250-350			

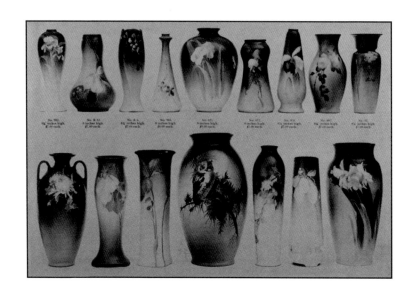

COMPLIMENTS OF THE OHIO HISTORICAL SOCIETY

X	DESCRIPTION	SECONDARY MARKET	PRICE PAID	DATE BOUGHT	CONDITION
	982-81/4 VASE	375-425			
	R12-8 VASE	375-425			
	R6-81/4 VASE	375-425			
	983-8 VASE	350-425			
	821-9 VASE	550-600			
	972-8 VASE	350-450			
	978-81/2 VASE	350-450			
	892-81/4 VASE	300-400			
	R51-81/4 VASE	350-450			
	818-12 VASE	575-675			
	R45-111/2 VASE	400-500			
	R25-121/4 VASE	375-475			
	891-14 VASE	900-1100			
	893-121/2 VASE	700-800			
	R14-111/2 VASE	375-475			
	812-131/4 VASE	800-1000			

ROZANE ROYAL 1904

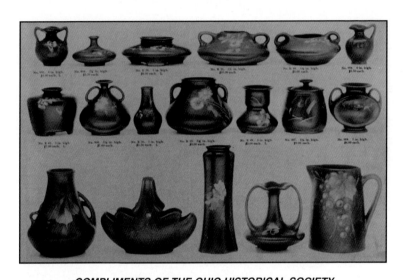

X	DESCRIPTION	SECONDARY MARKET	PRICE PAID	DATE BOUGHT	CONDITION
	995-4 VASE	300-350			
	804-2 1/4 VASE	200-250			
	R38-3 VASE	250-300			
	R21-3 1/4 VASE	250-300			
	R18-3 1/2 VASE	250-300			
	994-4 VASE	300-350			
	R41-5 VASE	325-375			
	908-5 1/2 VASE	325-425			
	R36-5 VASE	275-325			
	R19-5 1/4 VASE	275-325			
	R49-5 VASE	275-325			
	897-5 1/2 TOBACCO JAR	900-1100			
	904-5 VASE	450-550			
	R17-8 1/4 VASE	500-550			
	993-8 VASE	550-650			
	R7-12 VASE	425-475			
	843-7 VASE	275-325			
	864-8 1/2 VASE	1300-2400			

ROZANE ROYAL 1904

X	DESCRIPTION	SECONDARY MARKET	PRICE PAID	DATE BOUGHT	CONDITION
	R26-9¹/⁴ VASE	350-450			
	R37-9¹/² VASE	350-450			
	997-7¹/⁴ VASE	325-425			
	996-8¹/² VASE	325-425			
	R14-8¹/⁴ VASE	375-475			
	928-9¹/² VASE	375-475			
	896-8¹/⁴ VASE	375-475			
	868-9 VASE	375-475			
	R47-9¹/² VASE	375-475			
	962-14 VASE	550-750			
	858-16 EWER	1100-1300			
	949-15 VASE	1100-1500			
	816-15 VASE	900-1300			
	845-16 EWER	800-900			

X	DESCRIPTION	SECONDARY MARKET	PRICE PAID	DATE BOUGHT	CONDITION
	991-3¹/⁴ VASE	275-375			
	911-6¹/² VASE	275-375			
	977-6¹/² VASE	325-375			
	R13-6¹/² VASE	325-425			
	R2-6¹/² VASE	325-425			
	989-5¹/² VASE	325-425			
	979-7¹/⁴ VASE	325-425			
	950-7¹/² VASE	300-350			
	906-8 EWER	325-425			
	889-7 JUG	375-475			
	895-8 EWER	375-475			
	883-6¹/² VASE	550-650			
	900-6 HANDLED JUG	350-450			
	R31-6 VASE	325-400			
	999-7 VASE	325-425			
	988-6¹/² VASE	425-625			
	976-7 VASE	325-425			
	992-5 VASE	325-425			
	R20-6¹/⁴ VASE	375-425			

ROZANE ROYAL   1904

COMPLIMENTS OF THE OHIO HISTORICAL SOCIETY

X	DESCRIPTION	SECONDARY MARKET	PRICE PAID	DATE BOUGHT	CONDITION
	831-10 VASE	650-800			
	R4-9¼ VASE	450-550			
	986-9 VASE	500-600			
	R44-9½ VASE	450-550			
	813-10 VASE	450-550			
	967-10¼ VASE	650-750			
	837-12¼ VASE	600-650			
	898-13 VASE	675-775			
	807-12¼ VASE	550-650			
	968-10¼ VASE	650-750			

COMPLIMENTS OF THE OHIO HISTORICAL SOCIETY

X	DESCRIPTION	SECONDARY MARKET	PRICE PAID	DATE BOUGHT	CONDITION
	956-8½ VASE	350-400			
	969-12 VASE	550-650			
	882-9 PILLOW VASE	3000-4000			
	870-11 EWER	600-700			
	827-9 VASE	700-800			
	R52-11½ VASE	800-900			
	905-10 EWER	600-700			
	845-11½ VASE	800-900			
	R28-10 VASE	600-700			
	R30-11¼ VASE	600-700			

ROZANE ROYAL   1904

COMPLIMENTS OF THE OHIO HISTORICAL SOCIETY

X	DESCRIPTION	SECONDARY MARKET	PRICE PAID	DATE BOUGHT	CONDITION
	R40-61/2 VASE	325-425			
	881-6 VASE	325-425			
	998-61/4 VASE	325-425			
	R39-61/2 VASE	350-450			
	975-6 VASE	275-350			
	886-5 MUG	275-325			
	965-61/2 MUG	300-350			
	884-16 EWER	1000-1150			
	890-121/2 EWER	500-550			
	855-14 EWER	700-800			
	921-11 EWER	600-700			
	966-14 EWER	800-900			
	964-161/2 EWER	900-1100			

COMPLIMENTS OF THE OHIO HISTORICAL SOCIETY

X	DESCRIPTION	SECONDARY MARKET	PRICE PAID	DATE BOUGHT	CONDITION
	836-21 FLOOR VASE	2300-2800			
	832-20 FLOOR VASE	2500-3000			
	863-21 FLOOR VASE	2700-3500			

ROZANE SURPRISE PACKAGE 1905

X	DESCRIPTION	SECONDARY MARKET	PRICE PAID	DATE BOUGHT	CONDITION
	987-8 VASE	500-700			
	823-6 1/2 VASE	300-400			
	R19-5 1/4 VASE	350-450			
	R17-8 3/4 VASE	400-500			
	843-7 VASE	550-650			
	900-6 HANDLED VASE	300-400			
	R44-9 1/2 VASE	400-500			
	R23-10 VASE	500-600			
	867-10 1/2 VASE	400-500			
	814-10 VASE	400-500			
	956-8 1/2 VASE	350-450			
	821-9 VASE	600-700			
	R5-10 1/4 VASE	500-700			
	R15-11 1/2 VASE	500-700			
	921-11 TANKER	550-750			
	830-12 1/2 TANKER	600-700			
	905-10 EWER	500-600			
	807-12 3/4 EWER	500-600			
	893-10 1/2 VASE	500-600			
	R45-11 1/2 VASE	375-475			
	R33-11 1/2 VASE	350-450			
	R31-11 1/2 VASE	400-500			
	974-11 1/2 VASE	400-500			
	R8-12 VASE	500-700			

ROZANE UNTRIMMED 1900

COMPLIMENTS OF THE OHIO HISTORICAL SOCIETY

X	DESCRIPTION	SECONDARY MARKET	PRICE PAID	DATE BOUGHT	CONDITION
	MUG	75-100			
	VASE	100-125			
	VASE	125-150			
	VASE	75-100			
	VASE	100-125			
	VASE	125-150			
	VASE	125-150			
	VASE	125-150			
	VASE	175-225			
	VASE	125-150			
	VASE	125-150			
	VASE	125-150			
	VASE	150-175			
	VASE	125-150			
	VASE	175-225			
	VASE	150-200			
	VASE	150-175			
	VASE	150-175			
	VASE	175-225			
	VASE	175-225			
	VASE	150-175			
	VASE	150-175			
	VASE	200-225			
	VASE	200-225			

ROZANE WOODLAND 1905

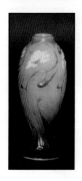   

X	DESCRIPTION	SECONDARY MARKET	PRICE PAID	DATE BOUGHT	CONDITION
	VASE	600-800			
	W-976 VASE	700-850			
	10¾ VASE	900-1000			
	W-999 VASE	800-900			
	W-976 VASE	700-800			
	W-2 VASE	600-700			
	W-6 VASE	800-1000			
	W-997 VASE	900-1000			
	W-978 VASE	800-900			
	W-971 VASE	900-1000			
	W-893 VASE	900-1000			

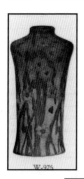   

ROZANE WOODLAND   1905

X	DESCRIPTION	SECONDARY MARKET	PRICE PAID	DATE BOUGHT	CONDITION
	W-961 VASE	900-1000			
	W-969 VASE	700-800			
	W-973 VASE	700-800			
	W-3 VASE	800-900			
	W-15 VASE	900-1000			
	W-974 VASE	900-1100			
	W-955 VASE	1200-1700			
	W-969 VASE	700-800			
	W-933 VASE	1100-1600			
	W-969 VASE	700-800			

  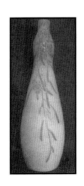

RUSSCO 1934

X	DESCRIPTION	SECONDARY MARKET	PRICE PAID	DATE BOUGHT	CONDITION
	260-12 PLANTER	125-175			
	15-2 FRIG	50-75			
	259-6 BOWL	125-150			
	109-8 VASE	125-150			
	260-6 PLANTER	75-125			
	15-3 FROG	50-75			
	107-8 DOUBLE VASE	100-150			
	697-8 VASE	150-175			
	696-8 VASE	100-150			
	695-8 VASE	100-150			
	694-7 VASE	100-150			
	108-6 URN	125-175			
	109-8 URN	150-200			
	337-10 BASKET	250-300			
	703-15 VASE	200-300			
	702-12 VASE	200-300			
	701-10 VASE	175-200			
	700-10 VASE	175-200			
	698-9 VASE	175-200			
	699-9 VASE	175-200			

COMPLIMENTS OF THE OHIO HISTORICAL SOCIETY

X	DESCRIPTION	SECONDARY MARKET	PRICE PAID	DATE BOUGHT	CONDITION
	375-10 VASE	300-350			
	15-2¹/₂ FROG	50-75			
	185-6 BOWL	150-200			
	15-3¹/₂ FROG	50-75			
	14-4 COMPOTE	100-175			
	1070-3¹/₂ CANDLESTICK	200-250			
	13-4 COVERED URN	200-250			
	376-10 VASE	325-400			
	119-6 BOWL	150-200			
	102-6 FERN DISH	100-125			
	209-10 VASE	250-300			
	1071-4 CANDLESTICK	200-250			
	184-12 COMPOTE	250-300			
	377-11 VASE	375-425			

COMPLIMENTS OF THE OHIO HISTORICAL SOCIETY

X	DESCRIPTION	SECONDARY MARKET	PRICE PAID	DATE BOUGHT	CONDITION
	371-69 VASE	150-200			
	372-6 VASE	150-200			
	1260-8 WALL POCKET	400-500			
	207-6 VASE	100-150			
	186-8 CONSOLE	200-250			
	378-8 VASE	400-450			
	183-10 CONSOLE	175-225			
	379-12 VASE	450-500			
	374-8 VASE	300-350			
	373-8 VASE	300-350			
	222-12 VASE	300-350			

SIGNS

Script

Block

X	DESCRIPTION	SECONDARY MARKET	PRICE PAID	DATE BOUGHT	CONDITION
	SCRIPT	2000-2200			
	BLOCK	1400-1600			
	MODERN	1800-2000			
	LITTLE PRINT	1400-1600			

Modern   Little Print

GEORGE KRAUSE COLLECTION

X	DESCRIPTION	SECONDARY MARKET	PRICE PAID	DATE BOUGHT	CONDITION
	741-4 BOWL	100-150			
	761-4 HANG. BASKET	250-350			
	726-6 PLANTER	75-100			
	708-6 BASKET	150-200			
	730-10 WINDOW BOX	100-175			
	751-3 CANDLESTICK	75-100			
	731-14 WINDOW BOX	150-200			
	757 BRIDGE	100-150			
	727-8 BOWL	100-150			
	756 PLANTER	100-150			
	728-10 WINDOW BOX	125-175			
	742-60 BOWL	300-350			
	729-12 WINDOW BOX	150-200			
	709-8 BASKET	150-175			
	763-8 VASE	400-450			
	710-10 BASKET	200-250			

SILHOUETTE 1950

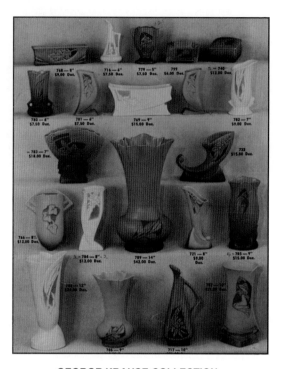

GEORGE KRAUSE COLLECTION

X	DESCRIPTION	SECONDARY MARKET	PRICE PAID	DATE BOUGHT	CONDITION
	768-8 WINDOW BOX	125-150			
	716-6 EWER	100-175			
	779-5 VASE	100-150			
	799 ASHTRAY	175-200			
	740 CIGARETTE BOX	200-250			
	780-6 VASE	100-150			
	781-6 VASE	100-150			
	769-9 CONSOLE	100-150			
	782-7 VASE	100-125			
	783-7 VASE	200-250			
	722 CORNUCOPIA	100-150			
	766-8 WALL POCKET	300-500			
	784-8 VASE	250-350			
	789-14 VASE	450-550			
	721-8 VASE	100-125			
	785-9 VASE	200-300			
	788-12 VASE	175-225			
	786-9 VASE	200-300			
	717-10 EWER	200-300			
	787-10 VASE	400-600			

COMPLIMENTS OF THE OHIO HISTORICAL SOCIETY

X	DESCRIPTION	SECONDARY MARKET	PRICE PAID	DATE BOUGHT	CONDITION
	#3 MATT GREEN	400-500			
	#3 PINK TINTED	400-500			
	#3 BLUE TINTED	400-500			
	#3S YELLOW TINTED	400-500			
	#3S GREEN TINTED	400-500			
	#4 HOLLAND	500-600			
	#4 MATT GREEN	500-600			

COMPLIMENTS OF THE OHIO HISTORICAL SOCIETY

X	DESCRIPTION	SECONDARY MARKET	PRICE PAID	DATE BOUGHT	CONDITION
	4B COAT OF ARMS COMBO. SET	500-700			
	8A (INDIAN) COMBO SET	600-700			
	8B GREEN & GOLD COMBO. SET	400-500			
	9A INDIAN COMBO. SET	700-800			
	10A INDIAN COMBO. SET	500-600			
	10B GREEN & GOLD COMBO. SET	400-500			
	7A INDIAN COMBO. SET	400-500			
	7B GREEN & GOLD COMBO. SET	400-500			
	5B DECOR. ASHTRAY	300-350			
	3A DECOR. ASHTRAY	300-350			
	2 GREEN & GOLD ASHTRAY	125-150			
	4 GREEN & GOLD ASHTRAY	125-150			
	2B COAT OF ARMS TOBACCO JAR	350-450			
	5C DECOR. ASHTRAY	150-175			
	3C DECOR. ASHTRAY	150-175			
	6A DECOR. ASHTRAY	200-300			
	6B GREEN & GOLD ASHTRAY	200-300			
	1B COAT OF ARMS SMOKER SET	800-900			

SNOWBERRY 1947

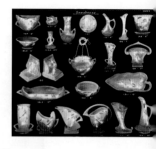

GEORGE KRAUSE COLLECTION

X	DESCRIPTION	SECONDARY MARKET	PRICE PAID	DATE BOUGHT	CONDITION
	1WP-8 WALL POCKET	200-300			
	1CSI-2 CANDLESTICK	100-125			
	1V2-7 VASE	100-150			
	1AT ASHTRAY	100-150			
	1TK-6 EWER	125-175			
	1BV-7 VASE	100-150			
	1PS-5 PLANTER W/DISH	175-200			
	1BL2-6 BOWL	100-150			
	1CS2-41/2 CANDLESTICK	100-150			
	1BE BOOKEND	250-300			
	1HB-5 HANG. BASKET	200-300			
	1V1-7 VASE	100-150			
	1BK-7 BASKET	150-200			
	1BL2-12 BOWL	200-300			
	1BL1-6 BOWL	100-125			
	1BL1-12 BOWL	200-300			
	1V1-8 VASE	150-200			
	1FH-6 FLOWER HOLDER	150-200			
	1FH-7 FLOWER HOLDER	175-225			
	1BK-8 BASKET	175-225			
	1CC-8 CORNUCOPIA	125-175			
	1TK-10 EWER	200-300			

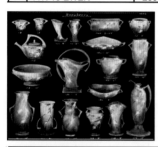

GEORGE KRAUSE COLLECTION

	DESCRIPTION	SECONDARY MARKET	PRICE PAID	DATE BOUGHT	CONDITION
	1S SUGAR	75-100			
	1C CREAMER	75-100			
	1CC-6 CORNUCOPIA	100-175			
	1V-6 VASE	100-150			
	1WX-3X21/2 WINDOW BOX	200-300			
	1J-4 JARDINIERE	125-175			
	1TP TEAPOT	325-425			
	1BL1-10 BOWL	125-175			
	1FB-10 FLOWER BOWL	200-250			
	1BK-12 BASKET	250-300			
	1RB-6 ROSE BOWL	100-150			
	1BL-8 BOWL	100-150			
	1V1-10 VASE	175-225			
	1V1-12 VASE	200-250			
	1V1-9 VASE	150-175			
	1V2-10 VASE	150-175			
	1V2-8 VASE	125-150			
	1V2-9 VASE	150-175			
	1TK-15 EWER	475-550			

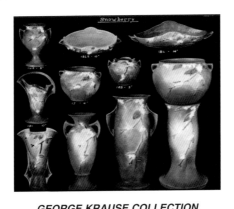

X	DESCRIPTION	GEORGE KRAUSE COLLECTION			
		SECONDARY MARKET	PRICE PAID	DATE BOUGHT	CONDITION
	1UR-8 URN	150-200			
	1BL2-10 BOWL	200-250			
	1BL-14 BOWL	250-350			
	1BK-10 BASKET	225-275			
	1J-6 JARDINIERE	200-250			
	1RB-5 ROSE BOWL	175-200			
	1V2-12 VASE	300-400			
	1V-15 VASE	500-600			
	1V-18 VASE	650-750			
	1JP-8 JARD. & PED.	1400-1600			

1947 Snowberry Ad

SPECIAL   EARLY 1900

COMPLI8MENTS OF THE OHIO HISTORICAL SOCIETY

X	DESCRIPTION	SECONDARY MARKET	PRICE PAID	DATE BOUGHT	CONDITION
	884-16 TANKER	800-1000			
	886-5 MUG	200-250			
	890-121/2 TANKER	600-800			
	886-5 MUG	200-250			
	964-161/2 TANKER	800-1000			
	965-61/2 MUG	250-300			
	966-141/2 TANKER	700-900			
	965-61/2 MUG	250-300			

1940 Ad for The
White Rose Line

SPECIAL EARLY 1900

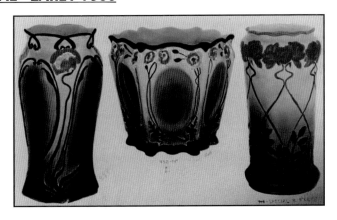

X	DESCRIPTION	SECONDARY MARKET	PRICE PAID	DATE BOUGHT	CONDITION
	718A-9X21 1/2 UMBRELLA	500-600			
	452-14 SAND JAR	500-600			
	719-9X21 1/2 UMBRELLA	500-600			
	429A-26 1/2 JARD. & PED.	1000-1500			
	429B-26 1/2 JARD. & PED.	1000-1500			
	429C-26 1/2 JARD. & PED.	1000-1500			

STORK 1900

X	DESCRIPTION	SECONDARY MARKET	PRICE PAID	DATE BOUGHT	CONDITION
	335-8½ JARDINIERE	150-200			
	408-20 JARD. & PED.	500-700			

PICTURES NOT SHOWN

	DESCRIPTION	SECONDARY MARKET	PRICE PAID	DATE BOUGHT	CONDITION
	355-5½ JARDINIERE	75-100			
	335-6½ JARDINIERE	100-125			
	335-7½ JARDINIERE	125-150			
	335-9½ JARDINIERE	200-250			
	335-10½ JARDINIERE	250-300			
	408-15 JARD.& PED.	350-450			
	408-25 JARD.& PED.	700-800			
	UMBRELLA	400-500			

SUNFLOWER   1930

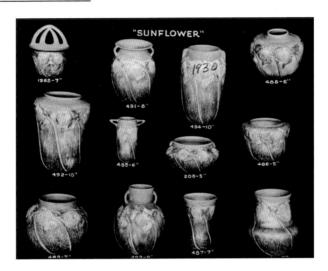

X	DESCRIPTION	SECONDARY MARKET	PRICE PAID	DATE BOUGHT	CONDITION
	1265-7 WALL POCKET	800-1200			
	491-8 VASE	800-1000			
	494-10 VASE	1500-1800			
	488-6 BOWL	600-900			
	492-10 VASE	1100-1300			
	485-6 VASE	500-700			
	208-5 BOWL	400-600			
	486-5 BOWL	400-600			
	489-7 BOWL	900-1200			
	493-9 VASE	900-1200			
	487-7 VASE	500-700			
	490-8 VASE	800-1000			

	619-12 JARDINIERE	2000-3000			
	619-10 JARD. & PED.	7000-12000			
	770-20 UMBRELLA	4000-7000			

SUNFLOWER 1930

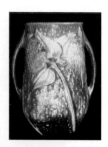
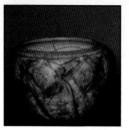

X	DESCRIPTION	SECONDARY MARKET	PRICE PAID	DATE BOUGHT	CONDITION
	1079-4 CANDLESTICK	400-500			
	487-6 VASE	500-700			
	494-5 VASE	400-600			
	4" VASE	300-500			
	51/4" VASE	500-700			
	4X61/2 DISH	500-700			
	566-4 VASE	400-600			
	346-5 HANG. BASKET	1200-1500			
	619-9 JARDINIERE	2000-2500			

SYLVAN 1918

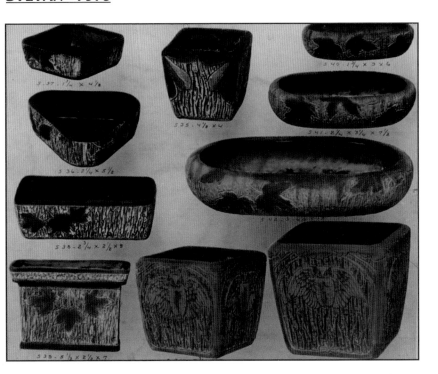

X	DESCRIPTION	SECONDARY MARKET	PRICE PAID	DATE BOUGHT	CONDITION
	537-1³/4X4¹/2 DISH	150-175			
	536-2¹/4X5¹/2 DISH	150-175			
	535-4¹/2X4 PLANTER	200-250			
	540-1³/4X3X6 FERN DISH	150-175			
	541-2¹/4X3X7 FERN DISH	200-250			
	538-2³/4X2¹/2X8 WINDOW BOX	225-275			
	542-3X6¹/2X12 FERN DISH	300-400			
	539-5¹/2X2¹/8X7 PLANTER	350-450			
	534-5³/4X5 PLANTER	275-325			
	533-7X6 PLANTER	450-550			

SYLVAN 1918

X	DESCRIPTION	SECONDARY MARKET	PRICE PAID	DATE BOUGHT	CONDITION
	361-11½X6½ WINDOW BOX	300-350			
	325-7 HANG. BASKET	500-600			
	325-6 HANG. BASKET	500-600			
	325-5 HANG. BASKET	400-500			
	625-4 HANG. BASKET	300-400			
	361-14X8 WIND. BOX	400-500			
	325-10 HANG. BASKET	650-750			
	325-8 HANG. BASKET	600-700			
	361-16½X8½ WINDOW BOX	500-600			
	225-6 BOWL	200-250			
	225-5 BOWL	150-175			
	225-4 BOWL	125-150			
	FLOWER VASE	175-200			

X	DESCRIPTION	SECONDARY MARKET	PRICE PAID	DATE BOUGHT	CONDITION
	568-12X33 JARD. & PED.	3000-4000			

TEA SET 1910

COMPLIMENTS OF THE OHIO HISTORICAL SOCIETY

X	DESCRIPTION	SECONDARY MARKET	PRICE PAID	DATE BOUGHT	CONDITION
	C TULIP SET	400-500			
	D TULIP SET	400-500			
	E TULIP SET	400-500			

	#2 TULIP SET	300-350			
	#5 CERAMIC GREEN S & C	125-150			
	#5 CERAMIC BLUE S & C	125-150			
	#5 CERAMIC GOLD, S & C	125-150			

TEA SET 1910

X	DESCRIPTION	SECONDARY MARKET	PRICE PAID	DATE BOUGHT	CONDITION
	3 LANDSCAPE SET A	350-400			
	3 DUTCH	300-350			
	3 LANDSCAPE SET B	350-400			
	2 DUTCH	300-350			
	3 CERAMIC C	300-350			

TEASEL 1938

GEORGE KRAUSE COLLECTION

X	DESCRIPTION	SECONDARY MARKET	PRICE PAID	DATE BOUGHT	CONDITION
	887-10 VASE	250-350			
	885-8 VASE	150-200			
	883-7 VASE	175-225			
	884-8 VASE	150-200			
	644-4 BOWL	125-150			
	886-9 VASE	225-275			
	342-4 BOWL	100-150			
	36 FROG	125-175			
	1131 CANDLESTICK	200-225			
	343-6 BOWL	175-225			
	349-10 BASKET	350-400			
	882-6 VASE	175-225			
	344-8 CONSOLE	150-200			
	889-15 VASE	275-325			
	881-6 VASE	150-200			
	345-12 CONSOLE	225-275			
	888-12 VASE	275-325			
	890-18 EWER	500-700			

THORNAPPLE 1937

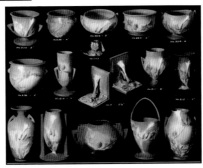

GEORGE KRAUSE COLLECTION

X	DESCRIPTION	SECONDARY MARKET	PRICE PAID	DATE BOUGHT	CONDITION
	809-5 FOOTED BOWL	150-175			
	638-4 JARDINIERE	125-150			
	306-5 BOWL	125-150			
	262-5 BOWL	125-150			
	304-4 FOOTED BOWL	125-150			
	638-5 JARDINIERE	175-200			
	814-7 VASE	175-200			
	1117 CANDLESTICK	200-225			
	3-5½ BOOKENDS	300-350			
	811-6 VASE	175-225			
	815-7 VASE	175-225			
	819-7 VASE	175-225			
	816-8 VASE	200-225			
	305-6 CENTERPIECE	275-375			
	342-10 BASKET	350-375			
	818-8 VASE	200-250			

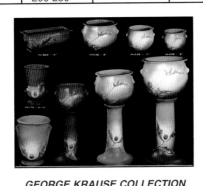

GEORGE KRAUSE COLLECTION

X	DESCRIPTION	SECONDARY MARKET	PRICE PAID	DATE BOUGHT	CONDITION
	382-14 WINDOW BOX	300-350			
	638-9 JARDINIERE	525-550			
	638-7 JARDINIERE	325-350			
	638-6 JARDINIERE	300-325			
	774-8X12 URN	300-375			
	638-8 JARD. & PED.	1200-1400			
	638-10 JARD. & PED.	1400-1600			
	638-12 JARD. & PED.	1600-2000			

THORNAPPLE 1937

GEORGE KRAUSE COLLECTION

X	DESCRIPTION	SECONDARY MARKET	PRICE PAID	DATE BOUGHT	CONDITION
	355 HANG. BASKET	300-400			
	312 CENTERPIECE	325-425			
	808-4 VASE	125-175			
	307-6 CONSOLE	125-150			
	309-8 CONSOLE	175-225			
	313 CENTERPIECE	325-425			
	308-7 CONSOLE	150-200			
	310-10 CONSOLE	225-275			
	311-12 CONSOLE	275-325			
	825-15 EWER	450-500			
	823-12 VASE	325-400			
	824-15 VASE	450-550			

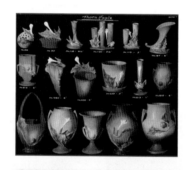

GEORGE KRAUSE COLLECTION

X	DESCRIPTION	SECONDARY MARKET	PRICE PAID	DATE BOUGHT	CONDITION
	29 FROG	200-250			
	30 FROG	200-250			
	1118-4½ BUD VASE	175-225			
	1120-5½ TRIPLE BUD VASE	450-550			
	1119-5 DBL BUD VASE	325-375			
	127-6 CORNUCOPIA	100-150			
	812-6 VASE	125-175			
	1280-8 WALL POCKET	350-450			
	356-4 WALL POCKET	700-800			
	639-5 PLANTER W/DISH	250-300			
	813-7 VASE	150-200			
	810-6 VASE	150-200			
	343-12 BASKET	500-600			
	820-9 VASE	250-300			
	817-8 URN	200-250			
	821-10 VASE	300-350			
	822-10 VASE	275-325			

TOPEO 1934

X	DESCRIPTION	SECONDARY MARKET	PRICE PAID	DATE BOUGHT	CONDITION
	246-2³/⁴ DISH	125-150			
	245-6 BOWL	200-250			
	658-7¹/⁴ VASE	275-350			
	657-6³/⁴ VASE	200-225			
	656-6 VASE	125-175			
	1093-4 CANDLESTICK	300-350			
	659-8 VASE	300-350			
	660-8¹/⁴ VASE	300-350			
	661-9¹/⁴ VASE	300-350			
	662-9 VASE	350-400			
	663-10 VASE	400-450			
	666-15 VASE	800-1000			
	665-14¹/⁴ VASE	600-800			
	664-12¹/⁴ VASE	500-600			
	246-3 FERN DISH	125-150			

Blue Add 25%

TOURIST 1910

X	DESCRIPTION	SECONDARY MARKET	PRICE PAID	DATE BOUGHT	CONDITION
	726-10X23 UMBRELLA	5000-5500			
	226-6 DISH	600-650			
	569-10 JARDINIERE	3000-3500			
	226-5 DISH	550-600			
	#5-9 VASE	3500-4000			
	WINDOW BOX	3000-3500			
	PEDESTAL	3500-4000			

PICTURES NOT SHOWN

X	DESCRIPTION	SECONDARY MARKET	PRICE PAID	DATE BOUGHT	CONDITION
	JARD. & PEDESTAL	8000-10000			
	#909 CUSPIDOR	1000-1500			
	569-7 JARDINIERE	2500-2800			
	226-4 DISH	500-550			
	326-5 HANG. BASKET	1000-1200			
	326-6¹/² HANG. BASKET	1200-1400			
	326-8¹/² HANG. BASKET	1400-1600			
	1209-10X5 WALL POCKET	1000-1200			
	#5-8 VASE	1200-1400			
	#5-12 VASE	5000-5500			

TOURIST 1910

JOHN J. ZOLOMIJ COLLECTION

X	DESCRIPTION	SECONDARY MARKET	PRICE PAID	DATE BOUGHT	CONDITION
	569-12 JARDINIERE	3500-4000			
	569-9 JARDINIERE	3000-3500			
	569-8 JARDINIERE	2750-3750			

JOHN J. ZOLOMIJ COLLECTION

X	DESCRIPTION	SECONDARY MARKET	PRICE PAID	DATE BOUGHT	CONDITION
	8 1/2 X16 WINDOW BOX	3500-4000			
	8X14 WINDOW BOX	3000-3500			
	6 1/2 X11 WINDOW BOX	2250-3250			

X	DESCRIPTION	GEORGE KRAUSE COLLECTION SECONDARY MARKET	PRICE PAID	DATE BOUGHT	CONDITION
	616-10 VASE	200-250			
	A-429-9 VASE	200-225			
	A-332-8 VASE	200-275			
	A-65-6 VASE	125-175			
	614-8 VASE	175-225			
	615-9 VASE	200-250			
	A-435-10 VASE	250-300			
	238-5 BOWL	125-175			
	A-308-7 VASE	150-200			
	A-152-7 FERN DISH	150-200			
	A-152-6 FERN DISH	100-150			
	241-12 CONSOLE	150-200			
	1089-4½ CANDLESTICK	150-175			
	612-7 VASE	125-175			
	A-517-6 VASE	100-175			
	613-8 VASE	150-175			
	A-444-12 VASE	275-325			
	611-6 VASE	150-175			
	A-200-4 VASE	100-150			
	A-425-8 VASE	150-200			

TUSCANY 1924

GEORGE KRAUSE COLLECTION

X	DESCRIPTION	SECONDARY MARKET	PRICE PAID	DATE BOUGHT	CONDITION
	342-6 VASE	200-250			
	341-5 VASE	150-175			
	1254-7 WALL POCKET	300-350			
	344-8 VASE	225-275			
	349-12 VASE	350-400			
	343-7 VASE	200-250			
	1255-8 WALL POCKET	350-400			
	347-10 VASE	250-325			
	345-8 VASE	225-275			
	346-9 VASE	250-300			
	348-10 VASE	300-375			

GEORGE KRAUSE COLLECTION

X	DESCRIPTION	SECONDARY MARKET	PRICE PAID	DATE BOUGHT	CONDITION
	71-6 VASE	150-200			
	1066-3½ CANDLESTICK	100-175			
	1067-4 CANDLESTICK	125-200			
	67-4 COMPOTE	125-175			
	70-5 VASE	150-200			
	173-10 CONSOLE	225-300			
	66-5 FROG	125-175			
	SMALL FROG	75-100			
	LARGE FROG	75-100			
	171-6 COMPOTE	125-175			
	69-5 FROG	150-200			
	172-9 COMPOTE	150-200			
	68-4 VASE	150-200			
	174-12 CONSOLE	200-300			

VASE ASSORTMENT 1903

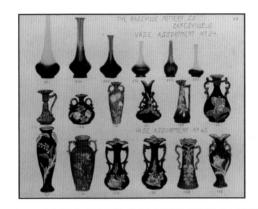

X	DESCRIPTION	SECONDARY MARKET	PRICE PAID	DATE BOUGHT	CONDITION

ASSORTMENT #24

X	DESCRIPTION	SECONDARY MARKET	PRICE PAID	DATE BOUGHT	CONDITION
	201 VASE	325-400			
	200 VASE	275-325			
	203 VASE	225-275			
	206 VASE	200-225			
	204 VASE	175-200			
	205 VASE	150-175			
	202 VASE (BELOW)	200-250			

ASSORTMENT #60

X	DESCRIPTION	SECONDARY MARKET	PRICE PAID	DATE BOUGHT	CONDITION
	111 VASE	150-175			
	104 VASE	150-175			
	112 VASE	175-225			
	101 VASE	175-225			
	108 VASE	200-250			
	106 VASE	275-325			
	103 VASE	275-325			
	110 VASE	275-325			
	105 VASE (GREEN)	200-250			
	105 VASE (BLUE)	200-250			
	108 VASE	250-325			
	102 VASE	200-250			

VELMOSS 1   1916-1919

GEORGE KRAUSE COLLECTION

X	DESCRIPTION	SECONDARY MARKET	PRICE PAID	DATE BOUGHT	CONDITION
	116-6 FERN DISH	125-150			
	116-5 FERN DISH	100-125			
	199-8 VASE	250-300			
	117-6 DISH	125-150			
	193-5 BOWL	125-150			
	196-6 URN	225-275			
	200-8 URN	250-300			
	194-6 VASE	250-300			
	197-8 VASE	250-300			
	1044-8 CANDLESTICK	300-400			
	1226-11 WALL POCKET	450-550			
	1227-12 WALL POCKET	500-600			
	195-6 VASE	250-275			
	205-12 VASE	400-450			
	198-8 VASE	250-300			
	204-10 VASE	350-400			
	202-10 VASE	350-400			
	1045-10 CANDLESTICK	400-500			
	203-10 VASE	350-400			
	201-10 VASE	350-400			

VELMOSS 1   1916-1919

GEORGE KRAUSE COLLECTION

X	DESCRIPTION	SECONDARY MARKET	PRICE PAID	DATE BOUGHT	CONDITION
	335-6 HANG. BASKET	450-500			
	254-6 DISH	200-250			
	115-5 DISH	125-150			
	115-6 DISH	150-175			
	118-6 DISH	175-200			
	118-7 DISH	200-225			
	14-8 FOOTED BOWL	150-200			
	600-5 JARDINIERE	150-200			
	600-7 JARDINIERE	250-275			
	600-6 JARDINIERE	200-250			
	600-8 JARDINIERE	275-300			
	600-9 JARDINIERE	300-325			
	600-10 JARD. & PED.	1200-1600			

VELMOSS II   1935

GEORGE KRAUSE COLLECTION

X	DESCRIPTION	SECONDARY MARKET	PRICE PAID	DATE BOUGHT	CONDITION
	718-8 VASE	250-300			
	115-7 VASE	175-225			
	1100-4 1/2 CANDLESTICK	100-150			
	266-5X8 WINDOW BOX	200-275			
	266-6x12 WIN. BOX	275-325			
	1274-8 URN	200-275			
	717-8 URN	200-275			
	265-6 JARDINIERE	200-250			
	715-7 VASE	150-200			
	714-6 VASE	150-200			
	117-8 DBL. CORNUCOPIA	200-275			
	116-8 DOUBLE VASE	250-300			
	716-7 VASE	175-225			
	264-5 JARDINIERE	175-225			
	721-12 VASE	400-500			
	720-10 VASE	350-400			
	719-9 VASE	300-400			
	119-10 VASE	350-400			
	722-14 VASE	500-600			

VELMOSS (EARLY)

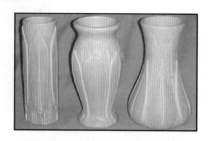

X	DESCRIPTION	GORDEN HOPPE COLLECTION SECONDARY MARKET	PRICE PAID	DATE BOUGHT	CONDITION
	577-7 JARDINIERE	350-450			
	577-8 JARDINIERE	450-550			
	577-9 JARDINIERE	550-650			
	577-10 JARDINIERE	650-750			
	577-12 JARDINIERE	750-850			
	578-7 JARDINIERE	350-450			
	578-8 JARDINIERE	450-550			
	578-9 JARDINIERE	550-650			
	578-10 JARDINIERE	650-750			
	577-10X29 JARD. & PED.	2750-3200			
	577-12X34 JARD. & PED.	3000-3500			
	578-10X28 JARD. & PED.	2750-3200			
	754-10X21 UMBRELLA	2000-3000			
	56-6 BOWL	150-200			
	54-8 BOWL	175-225			
	5-10 BOWL	225-250			
	127-6 VASE	400-450			
	132-8 VASE	500-550			
	125-6 VASE	400-450			
	126-6 VASE	400-450			
	128-6 VASE	400-450			
	129-8 VASE	500-550			
	130-8 VASE	500-550			
	131-8 VASE	500-550			
	134-10 VASE	550-600			
	135-10 VASE	550-600			
	136-10 VASE	550-600			
	140-12 VASE	700-800			
	137-12 VASE	700-800			
	138-12 VASE	700-800			
	139-12 VASE	700-800			
	133-10 VASE	550-600			

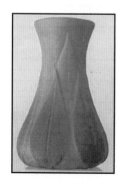

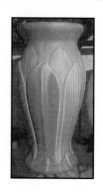

VENETIAN BEFORE 1900

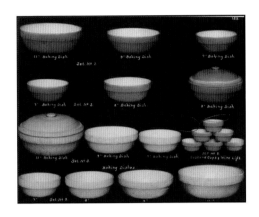

X	DESCRIPTION	SECONDARY MARKET	PRICE PAID	DATE BOUGHT	CONDITION
	11" BAKING DISH	125-150			
	9" BAKING DISH	100-125			
	7" BAKING DISH	75-100			
	7" BAKING DISH	75-100			
	8" BAKING DISH	100-125			
	9" BAKING DISH	125-150			
	11" BAKING DISH	125-150			
	9" BAKING DISH	100-125			
	7" BAKING DISH	75-100			
	7" BAKING DISH	75-100			
	8" BAKING DISH	100-125			
	9" BAKING DISH	100-125			
	11" BAKING DISH	125-150			
	CUSTARD CUPS & WIRE (6PC SET)	200-250			

	WIRE HANDLED BAKING DISH	250-275			

VICTORIAN ART POTTERY 1924-1928

COMPLIMENTS OF THE OHIO HISTORICAL SOCIETY

X	DESCRIPTION	SECONDARY MARKET	PRICE PAID	DATE BOUGHT	CONDITION
	132-4 BOWL	250-300			
	256-6 VASE	275-325			
	257-7 VASE	300-350			
	258-7 VASE	300-350			
	259-7 VASE	300-350			
	261-8 VASE	700-800			
	133-6 BOWL	350-400			
	260-8 VASE	375-425			
	263-10 VASE	600-700			
	262-10 VASE	500-600			
	265-12 VASE	800-900			
	264-91/2 VASE	800-900			

VOLPATO 1918-1921

GEORGE KRAUSE COLLECTION

X	DESCRIPTION	SECONDARY MARKET	PRICE PAID	DATE BOUGHT	CONDITION
	1040-8 CANDLESTICK	350-400			
	3-8 COVERED URN	200-250			
	188-5 URN	100-150			
	98-5 DISH	100-150			
	191-10 VASE	225-275			
	1041-10 CANDLESTICK	350-400			
	97-4 BOWL	100-150			
	12-8 COMPOTE	150-200			
	101-6 DISH	125-175			
	599-6 PLANTER W/DISH	225-275			
	105-14 PIN TRAY	200-250			
	2-51/2 URN	125-175			

GEORGE KRAUSE COLLECTION

X	DESCRIPTION	SECONDARY MARKET	PRICE PAID	DATE BOUGHT	CONDITION
	1042-10 CANDLESTICK	400-500			
	99-5 DISH	100-150			
	189-7 VASE	150-200			
	100-6 DISH	125-175			
	103-8 FERN DISH	150-200			
	1039-8 CANDLESTICK	200-275			
	1043-12 CANDLESTICK	500-600			
	108-6 DISH	150-200			
	104-10 FERN DISH	150-200			
	190-9 VASE	250-300			
	13-10 COMPOTE	200-250			
	192-12 VASE	300-350			

GEORGE KRAUSE COLLECTION

X	DESCRIPTION	SECONDARY MARKET	PRICE PAID	DATE BOUGHT	CONDITION
	206-6 VASE	150-200			
	119-6 COMPOTE	125-175			
	1046-10 CANDLESTICK	300-350			
	208-8 URN	175-225			
	207-6 VASE	125-150			
	1047-12 CANDLESTICK	400-500			
	120-8 BOWL	200-250			
	5-10 URN W/LID	300-350			
	209-10 VASE	200-250			

WATER LILY   1943

GEORGE KRAUSE COLLECTION

X	DESCRIPTION	SECONDARY MARKET	PRICE PAID	DATE BOUGHT	CONDITION
	174-6 VASE	150-200			
	72-6 VASE	150-175			
	10-6 EWER	150-175			
	664-5 PLANTER W/DISH	200-250			
	73-6 VASE	150-175			
	12 BOOKEND	250-350			
	445-6 SHELL	150-200			
	380-8 BASKET	175-225			
	175-8 VASE	200-275			
	663-5 JARDINIERE	150-200			
	76-8 VASE	175-225			
	437-6 BOWL	150-175			
	82-14 VASE	425-475			
	79-9 VASE	175-225			
	12-15 EWER	450-550			
	81-12 VASE	275-375			
	83-15 VASE	450-550			

WATER LILY   1943

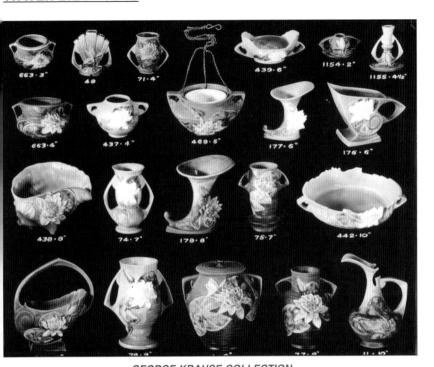

X	DESCRIPTION	SECONDARY MARKET	PRICE PAID	DATE BOUGHT	CONDITION
		GEORGE KRAUSE COLLECTION			
	63-3 JARDINIERE	75-125			
	48 FROG	100-150			
	71-4 VASE	100-150			
	439-6 CONSOLE	100-175			
	1154-2 CANDLESTICK	125-175			
	1155-4 1/2 CANDLESTICK	125-175			
	663-4 JARDINIERE	100-150			
	437-4 BOWL	75-100			
	468-5 HANG. BASKET W/LINER	225-325			
	177-6 CORNUCOPIA	100-150			
	176-6 PLANTER	150-200			
	438-8 SHELL	200-275			
	74-7 VASE	150-200			
	178-8 CORNUCOPIA	175-225			
	75-7 VASE	150-200			
	442-10 CONSOLE	150-200			
	381-10 BASKET	225-325			
	78-9 VASE	175-225			
	1-8 COOKIE JAR	400-500			
	77-8 VASE	175-225			
	11-10 EWER	225-325			

WATER LILY   1943

X	DESCRIPTION	*GEORGE KRAUSE COLLECTION*			
		SECONDARY MARKET	PRICE PAID	DATE BOUGHT	CONDITION
	444-14 CONSOLE	250-350			
	443-12 CONSOLE	200-300			
	441-10 CONSOLE	125-175			
	80-10 VASE	200-250			
	382-12 BASKET	250-350			
	440-8 CONSOLE	125-175			
	84-16 VASE	500-600			
	85-18 VASE	700-800			
	663-8 JARD. & PED.	1000-1500			
	663-10 JARD. & PED.	1500-2000			

1943 AD FOR THE WATER LILY LINE

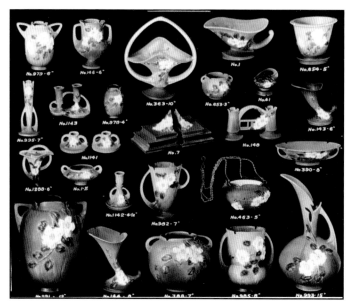

GEORGE KRAUSE COLLECTION

X	DESCRIPTION	SECONDARY MARKET	PRICE PAID	DATE BOUGHT	CONDITION
	979-6 VASE	100-150			
	146-6 VASE	100-150			
	1 CORNUCOPIA	150-200			
	654-5 PLANTER W/DISH	175-225			
	995-7 VASE	200-250			
	1143 DBL. CANDLESTICK	300-400			
	978-4 VASE	100-150			
	363-10 BASKET	275-375			
	653-3 BOWL	100-150			
	41 FROG	125-175			
	1141 CANDLESTICKS	100-200			
	7 BOOKENDS	250-350			
	148 BRIDGE	125-175			
	143-6 CORNUCOPIA	100-150			
	1288-6 WALL POCKET	300-400			
	1-S SUGAR	75-100			
	1142-4 1/2 CANDLESTICK	100-150			
	982-7 VASE	225-300			
	463-5 HANG. BASKET W/LINER	200-250			
	390-8 CONSOLE	100-150			
	991-12 VASE	350-450			
	144-8 CORNUCOPIA	125-150			
	388-7 JARDINIERE	225-300			
	985-8 VASE	225-300			
	993-15 EWER	150-200			

WHITE ROSE   1940

GEORGE KRAUSE COLLECTION

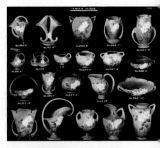

X	DESCRIPTION	SECONDARY MARKET	PRICE PAID	DATE BOUGHT	CONDITION
	1289-8 WALL POCKET	350-450			
	145-8 DBL. CORNUCOPIA	150-200			
	984-8 VASE	200-300			
	983-7 VASE	150-200			
	986-9 VASE	200-300			
	981-6 EWER	100-150			
	1143 DBL. CANDLESTICK	300-400			
	1C CREAMER	75-100			
	653-4 JARDINIERE	100-150			
	387-4 BOWL	125-150			
	389-6 CONSOLE	100-150			
	362-8 BASKET	225-300			
	980-6 VASE	100-150			
	653-5 JARDINIERE	125-175			
	1324 PITCHER	275-375			
	392-10 CONSOLE	175-225			
	987-9 VASE	200-250			
	364-12 BASKET	300-450			
	147-8 URN	100-125			
	990-10 EWER	200-300			
	988-10 VASE	275-375			

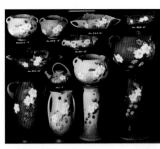

GEORGE KRAUSE COLLECTION

X	DESCRIPTION	SECONDARY MARKET	PRICE PAID	DATE BOUGHT	CONDITION
	653-7 JARDINIERE	275-325			
	653-6 JARDINIERE	250-275			
	393-12 CONSOLE	350-450			
	391-10 CONSOLE	300-400			
	382-9 WINDOW BOX	150-200			
	394-14 CONSOLE	225-325			
	1-T TEAPOT	250-300			
	994-18 VASE	450-550			
	992-15 VASE	400-500			
	653-8 JARD. & PED.	800-1200			
	653-10 JARD. & PED.	1200-1500			

WINCRAFT 1948

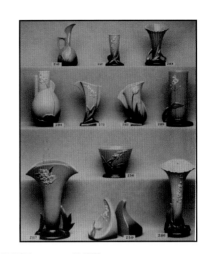

GEORGE KRAUSE COLLECTION

X	DESCRIPTION	SECONDARY MARKET	PRICE PAID	DATE BOUGHT	CONDITION
	216-8 EWER	100-150			
	281-6 VASE	75-100			
	283-8 VASE	100-150			
	284-10 VASE	175-200			
	273-8 VASE	100-150			
	282-8 VASE	125-150			
	285-10 VASE	175-200			
	256-5 PLANTER	100-150			
	287-12 VASE	175-200			
	259-6 BOOKENDS	125-175			
	286-12 VASE	160-200			

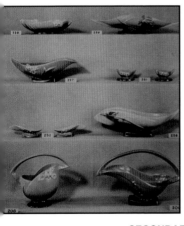

GEORGE KRAUSE COLLECTION

X	DESCRIPTION	SECONDARY MARKET	PRICE PAID	DATE BOUGHT	CONDITION
	226-8 CONSOLE	100-150			
	229-10 CONSOLE	100-150			
	227-10 CONSOLE	100-150			
	251 CANDLESTICKS	75-100			
	252 CANDLESTICKS	100-150			
	228-12 CONSOLE	125-150			
	208-8 BASKET	175-200			
	209-12 BASKET	175-200			

WINCRAFT 1948

GEORGE KRAUSE COLLECTION

X	DESCRIPTION	SECONDARY MARKET	PRICE PAID	DATE BOUGHT	CONDITION
	242 BOWL	125-175			
	210-12 BASKET	200-250			
	274-7 VASE	125-150			
	232 CONSOLE	125-175			
	231-10 CONSOLE	125-175			
	290-10 VASE	350-400			
	218-18 EWER	350-450			
	275-12 VASE	250-350			
	263-14 VASE	275-325			

GEORGE KRAUSE COLLECTION

X	DESCRIPTION	SECONDARY MARKET	PRICE PAID	DATE BOUGHT	CONDITION
	271C CREAMER	75-100			
	271S SUGAR	75-100			
	271T TEAPOT	250-300			
	221-8 CORNUCOPIA	75-100			
	272-6 VASE	100-150			
	268-12 WINDOW BOX	200-250			
	288-15 VASE	350-450			
	241-6 VASE	125-150			
	289-18 VASE	425-500			

WINCRAFT 1948

GEORGE KRAUSE COLLECTION

X	DESCRIPTION	SECONDARY MARKET	PRICE PAID	DATE BOUGHT	CONDITION
	250S SUGAR	75-100			
	250C CREAMER	75-100			
	250P COFFEE POT	250-350			
	217-6 EWER	75-150			
	257-6 PLANTER	125-150			
	230 PIN TRAY	125-175			
	261 HANG. BASKET	200-250			
	266-4 WALL POCKET	225-325			
	233 COMPOTE	125-175			
	267-5 BOWL	150-200			
	222-8 CORNUCOPIA	100-150			
	240B CIGARETTE BOX	50-75			
	240T ASHTRAY	50-75			
	253 CANDLESTICKS	250-300			

WINDSOR

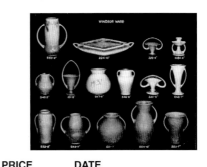

COMPLIMENTS OF THE OHIO HISTORICAL SOCIETY

X	DESCRIPTION	SECONDARY MARKET	PRICE PAID	DATE BOUGHT	CONDITION
	553-9 VASE	700-900			
	224-10 CONSOLE	400-500			
	329-4 BASKET	500-600			
	1084-4 CANDLESTICK	400-500			
	545-5 VASE	400-500			
	331-8 BASKET	700-900			
	547-6 VASE	600-700			
	546-6 VASE	600-700			
	330-5 BASKET	700-800			
	548-7 VASE	600-700			
	552-8 VASE	700-800			
	549-7 VASE	600-700			
	551-7 VASE	600-700			
	554-10 VASE	800-900			
	550-7 VASE	700-800			

WISTERIA   1937

GEORGE KRAUSE COLLECTION

X	DESCRIPTION	SECONDARY MARKET	PRICE PAID	DATE BOUGHT	CONDITION
	632-5 JARDINIERE	400-600			
	242-4 BOWL	400-550			
	630-6 VASE	450-600			
	631-6 VASE	500-700			
	629-4 VASE	400-500			
	1091-4 CANDLESTICK	500-700			
	634-7 VASE	700-900			
	636-8 VASE	700-900			
	637-6 1/2 VASE	600-800			
	635-8 VASE	600-800			
	243-5X9 WINDOW BOX	400-550			
	644-12 VASE	1200-1500			
	638-9 VASE	775-975			
	633-8 VASE	550-750			
	639-10 VASE	700-900			
	641-15 VASE	1500-2500			

	632-24 1/2 JARDINIERE & PEDESTAL	5000-7500			

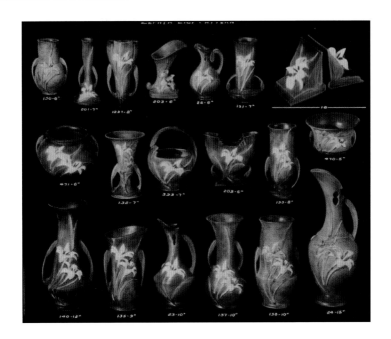

COMPLIMENTS OF THE OHIO HISTORICAL SOCIETY

X	DESCRIPTION	SECONDARY MARKET	PRICE PAID	DATE BOUGHT	CONDITION
	130-6 VASE	75-150			
	201-7 VASE	125-175			
	1297-8 WALL POCKET	200-300			
	203-6 CORNUCOPIA	100-150			
	22-6 EWER	150-200			
	131-7 VASE	100-150			
	16 BOOKEND	225-275			
	471-6 JARDINIERE	175-225			
	132-7 VASE	125-150			
	393-7 BASKET	175-225			
	205-6 VASE	175-225			
	133-8 VASE	150-200			
	470-5 PLANTER	100-175			
	140-12 VASE	200-250			
	135-9 VASE	200-250			
	23-10 EWER	225-275			
	137-10 VASE	200-250			
	138-10 VASE	250-300			
	24-15 EWER	400-450			

ZEPHYR LILY 1946

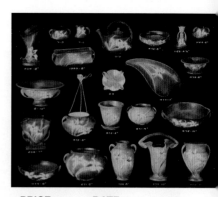

COMPLIMENTS OF THE OHIO
HISTORICAL SOCIETY

X	DESCRIPTION	SECONDARY MARKET	PRICE PAID	DATE BOUGHT	CONDITION
	204-8 CORNUCOPIA	150-200			
	7S SUGAR	75-100			
	7C CREAMER	75-100			
	7T TEAPOT	300-350			
	1393-8 WINDOW BOX	200-250			
	472-6 FERN DISH	250-300			
	1163-4½ CANDLESTICK	175-225			
	1162-2 CANDLESTICK	100-150			
	8-10 COMPOTE	200-250			
	29 ASHTRAY	125-175			
	477-12 PIN TRAY	175-225			
	473-6 COMPOTE	100-150			
	206-7 TRIPLE VASE	175-225			
	472-5 HANG. BASKET W/LINER	250-300			
	672-5 PLANTER W/DISH	175-225			
	671-4 JARDINIERE	100-150			
	134-8 VASE	175-225			
	396-10 BASKET	275-375			
	202-8 VASE	125-175			

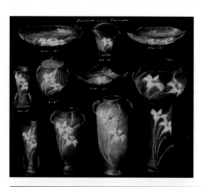

COMPLIMENTS OF THE OHIO
HISTORICAL SOCIETY

	479-14 CONSOLE	200-300			
	394-8 BASKET	200-275			
	478-12 CONSOLE	150-200			
	136-9 VASE	175-225			
	5-8 COOKIE JAR	450-550			
	475-10 CONSOLE	150-200			
	139-12 VASE	275-325			
	141-15 VASE	500-700			
	142-18 VASE	700-800			
	671-8 JARD. & PED.	900-1500			

WALL POCKETS (PICTURES NOT SHOWN PRIOR)

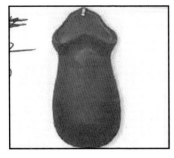 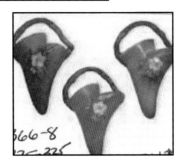

JIM JOHNSON COLLECTION

JIM JOHNSON COLLECTION

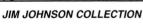

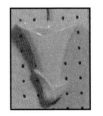

JIM JOHNSON COLLECTION

X	DESCRIPTION	SECONDARY MARKET	PRICE PAID	DATE BOUGHT	CONDITION
	1211-12 ANIQUE MATT GREEN	350-450			
	366-8 APPLE BLOSSOM	275-325			
	AZURINE-ORCHID-TURQUOISE	500-600			
	82B BURMESE (MALE)	200-300			
	72B BURMESE (FEMALE)	275-375			
	1013-5 CAPRI	150-175			

WALL POCKETS (PICTURES NOT SHOWN PRIOR)

 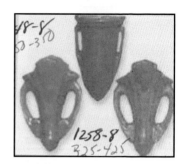

JIM JOHNSON COLLECTION

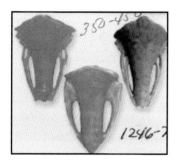 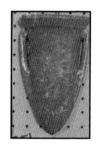

JIM JOHNSON COLLECTION

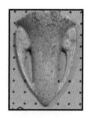 

X	DESCRIPTION	SECONDARY MARKET	PRICE PAID	DATE BOUGHT	CONDITION
	1246-7 CARNELLIAN I	400-500			
	1248-8 CARNELLIAN I	250-350			
	1258-8 CARNELLIAN I	325-425			
	1247-8 CARNELLIAN I	350-450			
	1246-7 CARNELLIAN I	350-450			
	1847-8 CARNELLIAN II	600-700			
	1246-7 CARNELLIAN II	400-600			
	1252-8 CARNELLIAN II	450-500			

WALL POCKETS (PICTURES NOT SHOWN PRIOR)

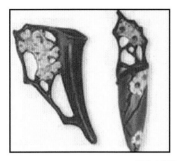 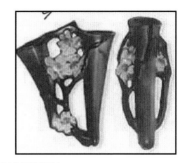

JIM JOHNSON COLLECTION

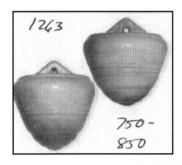 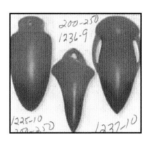

JIM JOHNSON COLLECTION

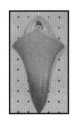 

X	DESCRIPTION	SECONDARY MARKET	PRICE PAID	DATE BOUGHT	CONDITION
	10" DOGWOOD II	400-500			
	1217-15 DOGWOOD II	650-750			
	9" DOGWOOD II	325-375			
	10" DOGWOOD II	400-450			
	1263 EARLAM	750-850			
	1225-10 FLORANE	200-250			
	1236-9 FLORANE	175-225			
	1237-10 FLORANE	175-225			
	1236-9 FLORANE	200-250			
	1237-10 FLORANE	175-225			

WALL POCKETS (PICTURES NOT SHOWN PRIOR)

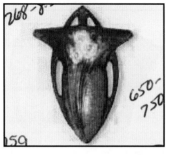
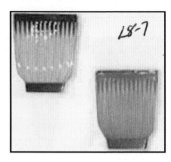

JIM JOHNSON COLLECTION

JIM JOHNSON COLLECTION

JIM JOHNSON COLLECTION

X	DESCRIPTION	SECONDARY MARKET	PRICE PAID	DATE BOUGHT	CONDITION
	1268-8 1/2 JONQUIL	650-750			
	L8-7 LOTUS	300-400			
	L8-7 LOTUS	300-400			
	MATT GREEN	225-275			
	1206-5 MATT GREEN	150-175			
	MATT GREEN	175-225			
	1204-10 MATT GREEN	250-300			
	MATT GREEN	300-350			
	15" MATT GREEN	400-450			

WALL POCKETS (PICTURES NOT SHOWN PRIOR)

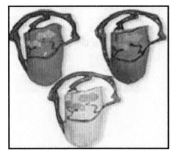
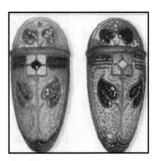

JIM JOHNSON COLLECTION

JIM JOHNSON COLLECTION

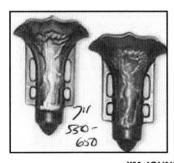
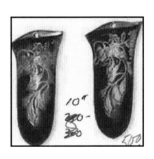

JIM JOHNSON COLLECTION

X	DESCRIPTION	SECONDARY MARKET	PRICE PAID	DATE BOUGHT	CONDITION
	566-8 MING TREE	275-325			
	1224-10 MOSTIQUE	550-650			
	ROSECRAFT BLENDED	300-400			
	1240-8 ROSECRAFT HEXAGON (BLUE)	500-600			
	7" ROSECRAFT PANEL NUDE	550-650			
	10" ROSECRAFT PANEL PUMPKINS	500-600			

WALL POCKETS (PICTURES NOT SHOWN PRIOR)

JIM JOHNSON COLLECTION

JIM JOHNSON COLLECTION

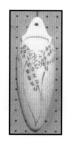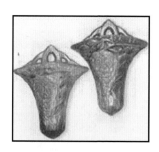

JIM JOHNSON COLLECTION

X	DESCRIPTION	SECONDARY MARKET	PRICE PAID	DATE BOUGHT	CONDITION
	9" ROSECRAFT PANEL DAISIES	500-600			
	9" ROSECRAFT PANEL VINTAGE	400-500			
	9" ROSECRAFT PANEL VINTAGE	400-500			
	73/4" ROZANE LINE	275-350			
	1260-8 SAVONA	300-400			
	11" VELMOSS SCROLL	450-550			
	1271-81/2 WISTERIA (BLUE)	1500-1800			
	1271-81/2 WISTERIA (BROWN)	1200-1500			

WALL POCKETS (PICTURES NOT SHOWN PRIOR)

GORDON HOPPE COLLECTION

X	DESCRIPTION	SECONDARY MARKET	PRICE PAID	DATE BOUGHT	CONDITION
	IVORY TINT BALL	450-550			
	MATT GREEN BALL	450-550			

WALL SCONCES (NOT SHOWN PRIOR)

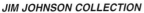

JIM JOHNSON COLLECTION

X	DESCRIPTION	SECONDARY MARKET	PRICE PAID	DATE BOUGHT	CONDITION
	LIGHT SCONCE MADE FOR THE ROGGE HOTEL	1000-1500			
	17" CHLORON	1200-1400			

ASSORTED JARDINIERES EARLY 1900s

X	DESCRIPTION	SECONDARY MARKET	PRICE PAID	DATE BOUGHT	CONDITION
	446-8 G JARDINIERE	350-450			
	446-8 R JARDINIERE	350-450			
	446-8 Y JARDINIERE	350-450			
	446-9 G JARDINIERE	400-500			
	446-9 R JARDINIERE	400-500			
	446-9 Y JARDINIERE	400-500			
	446-10 G JARDINIERE	450-550			
	446-10 R JARDINIERE	450-550			
	446-10 Y JARDINIERE	450-550			
	446-12 G JARDINIERE	500-600			
	446-12 R JARDINIERE	500-600			
	446-12 Y JARDINIERE	500-600			
	444-8 R JARDINIERE	350-450			
	444-8 Y JARDINIERE	350-450			
	444-8 G JARDINIERE	350-450			
	444-9 R JARDINIERE	400-500			
	444-9 Y JARDINIERE	400-500			
	444-9 G JARDINIERE	400-500			
	444-10 R JARDINIERE	450-550			
	444-10 Y JARDINIERE	450-550			
	444-10 G JARDINIERE	450-550			
	444-12 R JARDINIERE	500-600			
	444-12 Y JARDINIERE	500-600			
	444-12 G JARDINIERE	500-600			

ASSORTED JARDINIERES   EARLY 1900s

COMPLIMENTS OF THE OHIO HISTORICAL SOCIETY

X	DESCRIPTION	SECONDARY MARKET	PRICE PAID	DATE BOUGHT	CONDITION
	447-8R JARDINIERE	300-400			
	447-8G JARDINIERE	300-400			
	447-8Y JARDINIERE	300-400			
	447-9R JARDINIERE	350-450			
	447-9G JARDINIERE	350-450			
	447-9Y JARDINIERE	350-450			
	447-10R JARDINIERE	400-500			
	447-10G JARDINIERE	400-500			
	447-10Y JARDINIERE	400-500			
	447-12R JARDINIERE	450-550			
	447-12G JARDINIERE	450-550			
	447-12Y JARDINIERE	450-550			
	445-8Y JARDINIERE	300-400			
	445-8R JARDINIERE	300-400			
	445-8G JARDINIERE	300-400			
	445-9Y JARDINIERE	350-450			
	445-9R JARDINIERE	350-450			
	445-9G JARDINIERE	350-450			
	445-10Y JARDINIERE	400-500			
	445-10R JARDINIERE	400-500			
	445-10G JARDINIERE	400-500			
	445-12Y JARDINIERE	450-550			
	445-12R JARDINIERE	450-550			
	445-12G JARDINIERE	450-550			

ASSORTED JARDINIERES   EARLY 1900s

COMPLIMENTS OF THE OHIO HISTORICAL SOCIETY

X	DESCRIPTION	SECONDARY MARKET	PRICE PAID	DATE BOUGHT	CONDITION
	446-7 JARDINIERE	300-350			
	446-8 JARDINIERE	350-400			
	446-9 JARDINIERE	400-450			
	446-10 JARDINIERE	450-500			
	446-12 JARDINIERE	550-600			
	451-7 JARDINIERE	300-350			
	451-8 JARDINIERE	350-400			
	451-9 JARDINIERE	400-450			
	451-10 JARDINIERE	450-500			
	451-12 JARDINIERE	550-600			
	448-7 JARDINIERE	300-350			
	448-8 JARDINIERE	350-400			
	448-9 JARDINIERE	400-450			
	448-10 JARDINIERE	450-500			
	448-12 JARDINIERE	550-600			
	450-7 JARDINIERE	300-350			
	450-8 JARDINIERE	350-400			
	450-9 JARDINIERE	400-450			
	450-10 JARDINIERE	450-500			
	450-12 JARDINIERE	550-600			
	447-7 JARDINIERE	300-350			
	447-8 JARDINIERE	350-400			
	447-9 JARDINIERE	400-450			
	447-10 JARDINIERE	450-500			
	447-12 JARDINIERE	550-600			
	448-7 JARDINIERE	300-350			
	448-8 JARDINIERE	350-400			
	448-9 JARDINIERE	400-450			
	448-10 JARDINIERE	450-500			
	448-12 JARDINIERE	550-600			

ASSORTED JARDINIERES   EARLY 1900s

COMPLIMENTS OF THE OHIO HISTORICAL SOCIETY

X	DESCRIPTION	SECONDARY MARKET	PRICE PAID	DATE BOUGHT	CONDITION
	454-4 JARDINIERE	75-100			
	533-4 JARDINIERE	75-100			
	537-4 JARDINIERE	75-100			
	533-3 JARDINIERE	75-100			
	454-4 JARDINIERE	75-100			
	537-5 JARDINIERE	100-125			
	454-5 JARDINIERE	100-125			
	537-5 JARDINIERE	100-125			
	473-6 JARDINIERE	125-150			
	533-5 JARDINIERE	100-125			
	419-6 JARDINIERE	125-150			
	533-5 JARDINIERE	100-125			
	454-5 JARDINIERE	100-125			
	537-4 JARDINIERE	75-100			
	454-6 JARDINIERE	125-150			
	547-7 JARDINIERE	150-175			
	533-6 JARDINIERE	125-150			
	537-7 JARDINIERE	150-175			
	479-8 JARDINIERE	175-200			
	547-7 JARDINIERE	150-175			
	533-7 JARDINIERE	150-175			
	419-8 JARDINIERE	175-200			
	537-8 JARDINIERE	175-200			
	479-8 JARDINIERE	175-200			

ASSORTED JARDINIERES   EARLY 1900s

X	DESCRIPTION	SECONDARY MARKET	PRICE PAID	DATE BOUGHT	CONDITION
	410-A JARDINIERE	275-325			
	410-B JARDINIERE	275-325			
	410-C JARDINIERE	275-325			
	410-D JARDINIERE	275-325			
	419-A JARDINIERE	275-325			
	419-B JARDINIERE	275-325			
	419-C JARDINIERE	275-325			
	419-D JARDINIERE	275-325			

X	DESCRIPTION	SECONDARY MARKET	PRICE PAID	DATE BOUGHT	CONDITION
	411-A JARDINIERE	300-350			
	411-B JARDINIERE	300-350			
	411-C JARDINIERE	300-350			
	411-D JARDINIERE	300-350			
	411-E JARDINIERE	300-350			
	411-F JARDINIERE	300-350			

ASSORTED JARDINIERES   EARLY 1900s

COMPLIMENTS OF THE OHIO HISTORICAL SOCIETY

X	DESCRIPTION	SECONDARY MARKET	PRICE PAID	DATE BOUGHT	CONDITION
	407-A JARDINIERE	275-325			
	407-B JARDINIERE	275-325			
	407-C JARDINIERE	275-325			
	405-A JARDINIERE	275-325			
	405-B JARDINIERE	275-325			
	405-C JARDINIERE	275-325			
	405-D JARDINIERE	275-325			
	405-E JARDINIERE	275-325			
	405-F JARDINIERE	275-325			

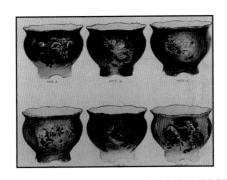

COMPLIMENTS OF THE OHIO HISTORICAL SOCIETY

X	DESCRIPTION	SECONDARY MARKET	PRICE PAID	DATE BOUGHT	CONDITION
	409-A JARDINIERE	350-450			
	409-B JARDINIERE	350-450			
	409-C JARDINIERE	350-450			
	409-D JARDINIERE	350-450			
	409-E JARDINIERE	350-450			
	409-F JARDINIERE	350-450			

ASSORTED JARDINIERES   EARLY 1900s

COMPLIMENTS OF THE OHIO HISTORICAL SOCIETY

X	DESCRIPTION	SECONDARY MARKET	PRICE PAID	DATE BOUGHT	CONDITION
	1421-6 JARDINIERE	100-125			
	1421-7 JARDINIERE	125-150			
	1421-8 JARDINIERE	150-175			
	1421-9 JARDINIERE	175-200			
	1419-9 JARDINIERE	175-200			
	1419-8 JARDINIERE	150-175			
	1419-7 JARDINIERE	125-150			
	1419-6 JARDINIERE	100-125			
	1427-6 JARDINIERE	100-125			
	1427-7 JARDINIERE	125-150			
	1427-8 JARDINIERE	150-175			
	1427-9 JARDINIERE	175-200			

	403-A JARDINIERE	200-250			
	403-B JARDINIERE	200-250			
	403-C JARDINIERE	200-250			
	422-A JARDINIERE	200-250			
	422-B JARDINIERE	200-250			
	422-C JARDINIERE	200-250			

UMBRELLA STANDS   EARLY 1900s

X	DESCRIPTION	SECONDARY MARKET	PRICE PAID	DATE BOUGHT	CONDITION
	713-A-23 UMBRELLA	2400-2800			
	715-B-23 UMBRELLA	2400-2800			
	725-A-23½ UMBRELLA	2000-2500			
	725-A-23½ UMBRELLA	2000-2500			

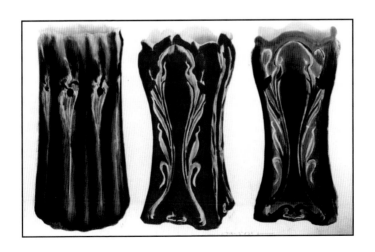

	716-8X23 UMBRELLA	1500-2500			
	713-9X23 RED UMBRELLA	2000-2500			
	713-9X23 BLUE UMBRELLA	2000-2500			

UMBRELLA STANDS   EARLY 1900s

X	DESCRIPTION	SECONDARY MARKET	PRICE PAID	DATE BOUGHT	CONDITION
	711-8¹/₂X11X26Y UMBRELLA	4000-5000			
	711-8¹/₂X11X26R	4000-5000			
	717-10X24G UMBRELLA	3500-4500			
	717-10X24 Y	3500-4500			

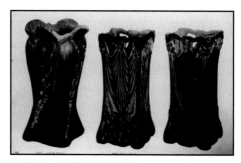

X	DESCRIPTION	SECONDARY MARKET	PRICE PAID	DATE BOUGHT	CONDITION
	717-10X23¹/₂ UMBRELLA	3500-4500			
	717-9¹/₂X22¹/₂ Y UMBRELLA	3000-4000			
	717-9¹/₂X22¹/₂ B UMBRELLA	3000-4000			

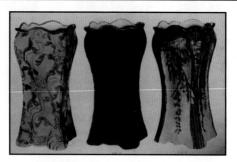

X	DESCRIPTION	SECONDARY MARKET	PRICE PAID	DATE BOUGHT	CONDITION
	756-9X23G UMBRELLA	3000-4000			
	756-9X23R UMBRELLA	3000-4000			
	756-9X23Y UMBRELLA	3000-4000			

707-9½X23 UMBRELLA	2000-2500			
707-9½X23 UMBRELLA	2000-2500			
720-9½X22½ UMBRELLA	2000-2500			

X	DESCRIPTION	SECONDARY MARKET	PRICE PAID	DATE BOUGHT	CONDITION
	710-12½X22Y UMBRELLA	1500-1750			
	710-10½X22G UMBRELLA	1500-1750			
	709-11X23 UMBRELLA	1500-1750			

UMBRELLA STANDS   EARLY 1900s

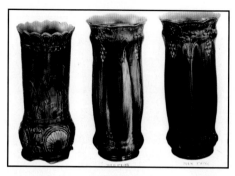

705-8X18 UMBRELLA	1250-1500			
708A-8X19¹/² UMBRELLA	1200-1400			
708B-8X19¹/² UMBRELLA	1250-1500			

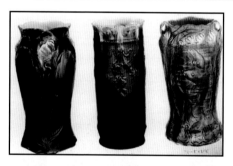

X	DESCRIPTION	SECONDARY MARKET	PRICE PAID	DATE BOUGHT	CONDITION
	718-9X21 UMBRELLA	1250-1750			
	703-9X22 UMBRELLA	1250-1500			
	721-8X21 UMBRELLA	1250-1500			

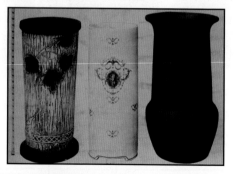

750-21 SYLVAN	1500-1800			
723-21 ROSALIE	2000-2500			
740-22 MATT GREEN	1000-1200			

UMBRELLA STANDS   EARLY 1900s

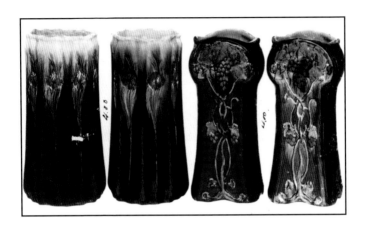

716-8 1/2 X23 UMBRELLA	1250-1500			
716-8 1/2 X23 UMBRELLA	1250-1500			
714-8 1/2 X23 1/4 UMBRELLA	2000-2500			
714-8 1/2 X23 1/4 UMBRELLA	2000-2500			

729A UMBRELLA	1000-1250			
729B UMBRELLA	1000-1250			
727A UMBRELLA	1000-1250			
727B UMBRELLA	1000-1250			

UMBRELLA STANDS   EARLY 1900s

X	DESCRIPTION	SECONDARY MARKET	PRICE PAID	DATE BOUGHT	CONDITION
	741-10½X20 IMPERIAL	2000-2500			
	770-10X20 SUNFLOWER	4000-5000			
	753-10X21 DONATELLO	2000-2500			
	763-8½X20 FLORENTINE I	1500-2000			

ASSORTED JARDINIERES/JARDINIERES & PEDESTALS EARLY 1900s

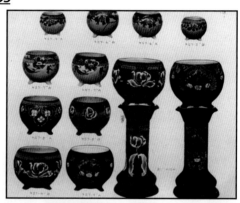

X	DESCRIPTION	SECONDARY MARKET	PRICE PAID	DATE BOUGHT	CONDITION
	457-5A JARDINIERE	125-150			
	457-6B JARDINIERE	150-175			
	457-6A JARDINIERE	150-175			
	457-5B JARDINIERE	125-150			
	457-7B JARDINIERE	175-200			
	457-7A JARDINIERE	175-200			
	457-8A JARDINIERE	200-250			
	457-8B JARDINIERE	200-250			
	457-9B JARDINIERE	250-300			
	457-9A JARDINIERE	250-350			
	457-10BX31 JARD. & PED.	3000-4000			
	457-10AX31 JARD. & PED.	3000-4000			

ASSORTED JARDINIERES/JARDINIERES & PEDESTALS
EARLY 1900s

X	DESCRIPTION	SECONDARY MARKET	PRICE PAID	DATE BOUGHT	CONDITION
	405-10 JARDINIERE	200-250			
	422-9 JARDINIERE	200-250			
	411-8 JARDINIERE	150-200			
	419-7 JARDINIERE	150-200			
	429-10 JARD. & PED.	800-1000			
	1203-10 JARD. & PED.	500-700			
	427-9 JARD. & PED.	500-700			
	421-9 JARD. & PED.	500-700			

X	DESCRIPTION	SECONDARY MARKET	PRICE PAID	DATE BOUGHT	CONDITION
	442-14X30 JARD. & PED.	1400-1800			
	442-12X28 JARD. & PED.	1200-1600			
	442-71/2 JARDINIERE	175-225			
	442-81/2 JARDINIERE	200-250			
	442-91/2 JARDINIERE	225-275			
	442-101/2 JARDINIERE	250-300			

ASSORTED JARDINIERES/JARDINIERES & PEDESTALS
EARLY 1900s

442-7 JARDINIERE	175-200			
442-8 JARDINIERE	200-225			
442-9 JARDINIERE	225-250			
442-10 JARDINIERE	250-275			
442-10 JARD. & PED.	1000-1200			
442-12 JARD. & PED.	1200-1400			

X	DESCRIPTION	SECONDARY MARKET	PRICE PAID	DATE BOUGHT	CONDITION
	420-6X13½	500-700			
	420-7X15	500-700			
	407-13	400-600			
	406-13	400-600			

405-13X34	1500-1700			
414-14X33	1200-1500			
414-14X33	1200-1500			

ASSORTED JARDINIERES/JARDINIERES & PEDESTALS
EARLY 1900s

X	DESCRIPTION	SECONDARY MARKET	PRICE PAID	DATE BOUGHT	CONDITION
	411-37	2500-3500			
	411-22	1500-2000			
	410-22	1500-2000			
	403-55	2500-3500			

	414-12X27	1000-1200			
	414-14X33	1200-1500			
	439-13X34	1250-1750			

ASSORTED JARDINIERES & PEDESTALS   EARLY 1900s

X	DESCRIPTION	SECONDARY MARKET	PRICE PAID	DATE BOUGHT	CONDITION
	440-15X12X45	3000-3500			
	440-15X12X45	3000-3500			

	477-6X12	500-750			
	475-6X141/2	700-800			
	477-7X17	900-1000			
	475-7X181/4	900-1000			

X	DESCRIPTION	SECONDARY MARKET	PRICE PAID	DATE BOUGHT	CONDITION
	475-9X25$3/4$	1000-1250			
	475-9X25$3/4$	1000-1250			
	479-8X24$1/2$	1000-1250			

	486-11X26	1000-1500			
	421-10X25	1000-1500			
	427-9X22	750-1000			

ASSORTED JARDINIERES & PEDESTALS   EARLY 1900s

X	DESCRIPTION	SECONDARY MARKET	PRICE PAID	DATE BOUGHT	CONDITION
	410-38	2500-3000			
	410-22	2000-2500			
	411-38	2500-3000			
	411-22	2000-2500			

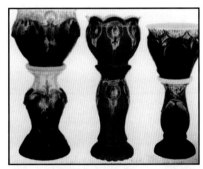

	405-15x34	1200-1500			
	423-12x32	1400-1600			
	432-18x29	1400-1600			

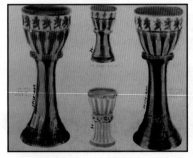

X	DESCRIPTION	SECONDARY MARKET	PRICE PAID	DATE BOUGHT	CONDITION
	495-10x30	2000-2500			
	495-6x12	750-1000			
	495-6x12	750-1000			
	495-10x30	2000-2500			

ASSORTED JARDINIERES & PEDESTALS   EARLY 1900s

1427-22R	750-1000			
1427-22G	750-1000			
1427-22P	750-1000			
1427-22B	750-1000			

X	DESCRIPTION	SECONDARY MARKET	PRICE PAID	DATE BOUGHT	CONDITION
	508A-10X34 BLENDED	1000-1500			
	508B-10X34 YELLOW TINT	1000-1500			
	508C-10X34 MATT GREEN	1000-1500			
	508D-10X34 GREEN TINT	1000-1500			

X	DESCRIPTION	SECONDARY MARKET	PRICE PAID	DATE BOUGHT	CONDITION
	475-10X30 LANDSCAPE	2000-3000			
	475-10X30 PINECONE	3500-4500			
	475-10X30 IRIS	2000-3000			

ASSORTED JARDINIERES & PEDESTALS   EARLY 1900s

X	DESCRIPTION	SECONDARY MARKET	PRICE PAID	DATE BOUGHT	CONDITION
	534A-10X30 BLENDED	1500-2000			
	534B-10X30 PERSIAN	1500-2000			
	534C-10X30 MATT GREEN	1500-2000			

X	DESCRIPTION	SECONDARY MARKET	PRICE PAID	DATE BOUGHT	CONDITION
	410-12X38	2000-3000			
	441-9X11X38	3500-4500			

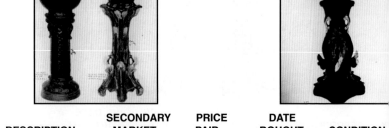

X	DESCRIPTION	SECONDARY MARKET	PRICE PAID	DATE BOUGHT	CONDITION
	433-13-39	3000-4000			
	440-15X12X45	4000-5000			
	425-15X44	3000-4000			

416-28	1000-1500			
422-29	1500-2000			

X	DESCRIPTION	SECONDARY MARKET	PRICE PAID	DATE BOUGHT	CONDITION
	457A-12X38	3000-4000			
	457B-12X38	3000-4000			

439-13X34	1250-1750			
438-14X32$^{1/2}$	1250-1750			

ASSORTED SAND JARS

X	DESCRIPTION	SECONDARY MARKET	PRICE PAID	DATE BOUGHT	CONDITION
	764-11X14 FLORENTINE	500-600			
	769-11½X14 IMPERIAL	600-700			
	768-12X14 NORMANY	650-750			

FLORENTINE SAND JAR

WROUGHT IRON BASES   EARLY 1900s

X	DESCRIPTION	SECONDARY MARKET	PRICE PAID	DATE BOUGHT	CONDITION
	740-38½	100-150			
	150-38½	125-150			
	160-38½	100-150			

ASSORTED PLATES

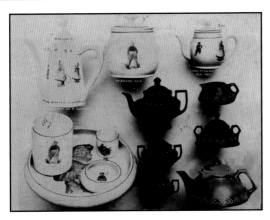

X	DESCRIPTION	SECONDARY MARKET	PRICE PAID	DATE BOUGHT	CONDITION
	DUTCH #4 TEAPOT	300-400			
	DUTCH TOBACCO JAR	300-400			
	DUTCH INDIV. TEAPOT	200-300			
	DUTCH SMOKER SET	400-500			
	BLUE TEA SET (SET#1)	500-600			
	BLUE TEA SET (SET#2)	500-600			

X	DESCRIPTION	SECONDARY MARKET	PRICE PAID	DATE BOUGHT	CONDITION
	FLORANE II 52-12	150-175			
	FLORANE II 51-10	125-150			
	FLORANE II 50-8	100-125			
	FLORENTINE SAND JAR #299	500-600			
	FLORENTINE UMBRELLA #298	800-1000			
	FLORENTINE SAND JAR #297	600-700			

EXPERIMENTALS

X	DESCRIPTION	SECONDARY MARKET	PRICE PAID	DATE BOUGHT	CONDITION
	MOCK ORANGE MOLD 911-10 W/GOLD	350-450			
	8" VASE	750-1000			
	8 1/2" BLUE VASE	500-750			
	107-8" VASE W/ BOTH SIDES DIFF. COLORS	500-750			
	8" VASE #92	750-1000			
	BROWN VASE	2000-3000			
	BLUE VASE	1500-2000			
	BLUE VASE	2000-3000			

EXPERIMENTALS

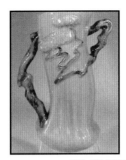
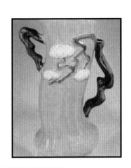

JIM JOHNSON COLLECTION

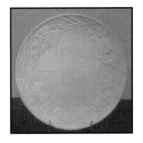

X	DESCRIPTION	SECONDARY MARKET	PRICE PAID	DATE BOUGHT	CONDITION
	9" BLUE FLORAL VASE	2000-3000			
	852-8 MING VASE W/ DIFF. COLOR SIDES	450-550			
	BLACKBERRY PLATE (FINISHED)	750-1000			
	9" FLORAL VASE	2000-3000			
	BLACKBERRY PLATE (UNFINISHED)	750-1000			
	VASE	750-1000			
	VASE	1000-1250			
	VASE	750-1000			

EXPERIMENTALS

X	DESCRIPTION	SECONDARY MARKET	PRICE PAID	DATE BOUGHT	CONDITION
	10" VASE	2200-2500			
	9" VASE	2000-3000			
	LAMP	2000-3000			

REPRODUCTIONS: APPLE BLOSSOM

THIS SECTION IS TO SHOW THE ROSEVILLE REPRODUCTION MADE. SHOWING THE PICTURE WITH THE NUMBER LISTED ON IT PLUS SHOWING THE ACTUAL MOLD NUMBER.

FAKE

MOLD 305-8

REPRODUCTIONS: BITTERSWEET

LISTED 756-12
MOLD 829-12

MOLD 866-7

LISTED 754-4 1/2
MOLD 857-4

LISTED 749-8

MOLD 809-8

MOLD 842-7

MOLD 805-8

LISTED 757   MOLD 858

LISTED 753-11 1/2   MOLD 827-8

LISTED 752-10 1/2
MOLD 828-10

LISTED 389-8
MOLD 828-10

LISTED 755-3
MOLD 851-3

REPRODUCTIONS: BITTERSWEET

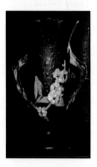

MOLD 885-10

LISTED 760-15
MOLD 888-16

MOLD 881-6

LISTED 758-7
MOLD 874-7

LISTED 761-8
MOLD 884-8

REPRODUCTIONS: BLACKBERRY

MOLD 570-5

MOLD 572-6

MOLD 576-8

MOLD 573-6

MOLD 574-6

MOLD 568-4

MOLD 623-6

REPRODUCTIONS: BLACKBERRY

MOLD 1086-4 1/2

LISTED 769-8   MOLD 575-8

MOLD 569-5   MOLD 577-10   MOLD 578-12   LISTED 229-12   MOLD 228-10

JARDINIERE & PEDESTAL 623-10

REPRODUCTIONS: BLEEDING HEART

MOLD 1287-8

REPRODUCTIONS: CLEMATIS

MOLD 1159-4 1/2

MOLD 454-6

REPRODUCTIONS: DAHLROSE

MOLD 343-6

REPRODUCTIONS: DONATELLO

JARDINIERE

REPRODUCTIONS: EXPERIMENTALS

 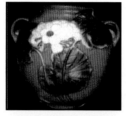 

REPRODUCTIONS: FOXGLOVE

MOLD 51-10   MOLD 375-12

MOLD 1292-8

  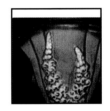

MOLD 52-12   MOLD 47-8

MOLD 420-10

MOLD 58-14

REPRODUCTIONS: FREESIA

 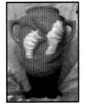  

MOLD 1296-8   MOLD 121-8

REPRODUCTIONS: FREESIA

MOLD 669-4

MOLD 464-6

MOLD 124-9

MOLD 463-5

MOLD 123-9

MOLD 125-10

MOLD 1296-8

REPRODUCTIONS: FUCHSIA

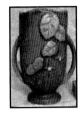  

MOLD 886-8

MOLD 891-6   MOLD 893-6

MOLD 1133-5

MOLD 1132-2

8" WALL
POCKET

 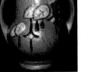 

MOLD 898-8   MOLD 351-10

REPRODUCTIONS: FUTURA

MOLD 399-12

MOLD 197-6

REPRODUCTIONS: IRIS

MOLD 361-8

 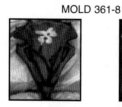 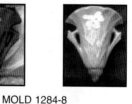 

MOLD 1284-8

MOLD 922-8   MOLD 917-6

 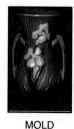

MOLD 358-6   MOLD 928-12

MOLD 920-7

REPRODUCTIONS: IRIS

MOLD 924-9

REPRODUCTIONS: JONQUIL

MOLD 542-5½   MOLD 94-5½

MOLD 324-8   MOLD WALL POCKET

MOLD 328-9

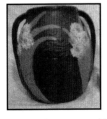  

LISTED 663-8   MOLD 527-7

REPRODUCTIONS: JONQUIL

MOLD 529-8

 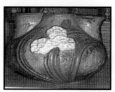 

MOLD 93-4½

 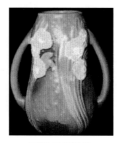 

MOLD 528-8

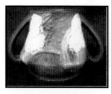 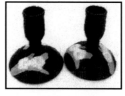 

MOLD 523-3   MOLD 1082-4   MOLD 96-7

MOLD 531-12   MOLD 219-8X6X3½

REPRODUCTIONS: JONQUIL

4" POT

MOLD 539-4

MOLD 538-4

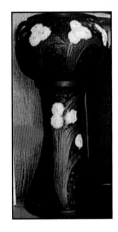

LISTED 539-4
MOLD 621-10

REPRODUCTIONS: LAUREL

MOLD 673-8

REPRODUCTIONS: LUFFA

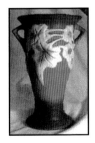

MOLD 691-12

MOLD 685-7

REPRODUCTIONS: LUFFA

MOLD 686-7

MOLD 1272-8

LISTED 815-4
MOLD 631-4

REPRODUCTIONS: MAGNOLIA

   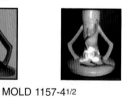

MOLD 91-8   MOLD 1157-4½

  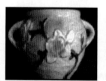 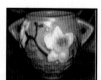

MOLD 665-3

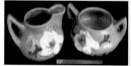  

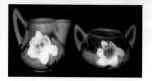

MOLD 4-S & C

REPRODUCTIONS: MAGNOLIA

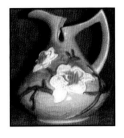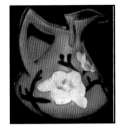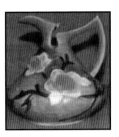

MOLD 14-10

WATER CAN

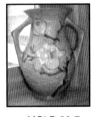

MOLD 90-7   MOLD 180-6

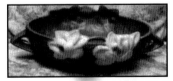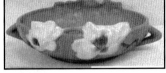

MOLD 448-8

MOLD 389-8

REPRODUCTIONS: MAGNOLIA

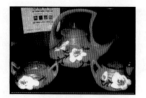 

#4 TEAPOT

MOLD 2-8

MOLD 88-6   SMALL VASE   MOLD 1156-2$^{1/2}$

REPRODUCTIONS: MISCELLANEOUS

 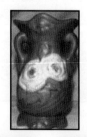 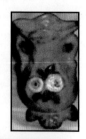

 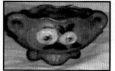

REPRODUCTIONS: MONTACELLO

MOLD 555-4   MOLD 556-5   WALL POCKET

REPRODUCTIONS: PANEL

7" WALL POCKET

REPRODUCTIONS: PEONY

MOLD 428-6

MOLD 1293-8

REPRODUCTIONS: PINECONE

MOLD 748-6

MOLD 353-11

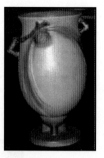
MOLD 840-7

MOLD 124-5

MOLD 850-14

MOLD 842-8

MOLD 848-8

MOLD 490-8

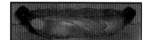

MOLD 261-6

REPRODUCTIONS: ROSEVILLE SIGN

REPRODUCTIONS: SNOWBERRY

MOLD IV2-7

REPRODUCTIONS: SNOWBERRY

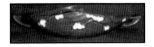 

MOLD 1BL-10

REPRODUCTIONS: VELMOSS

MOLD 266-5X8

REPRODUCTIONS: WATER LILY

MOLD 74-7

REPRODUCTIONS: WHITE ROSE

MOLD 387-4

MOLD 987-9

REPRODUCTIONS: WHITE ROSE

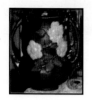

MOLD 985-8

REPRODUCTIONS: WOODLAND

10" VASE   PITCHER   8" VASE

REPRODUCTIONS: ZEPHYR LILY

MOLD 24-15   MOLD 23-10

   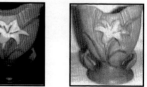

MOLD 204-8   MOLD 205-6

REPRODUCTIONS: ZEPHYR LILY

MOLD 135-9   MOLD 202-8

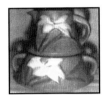  

MOLD 7-C AND 7-S

MOLD 136-9   MOLD 133-8

MOLD 139-12   MOLD 140-12   MOLD 671-8